CAMBRIDGE STUDIES IN ECONOMIC HISTORY

PUBLISHED WITH THE AID OF THE ELLEN MCARTHUR FUND

GENERAL EDITOR
M. M. POSTAN
Professor of Economic History in the University of Cambridge

British Trade and
The Opening of China 1800-42

BUSINESS MEN

By Ch'en Tzu-ang (A.D. 656-98)

Business men boast of their skill and cunning
But in philosophy they are like little children.
Bragging to each other of successful depredations
They neglect to consider the ultimate fate of the body.
What should they know of the Master of Dark Truth
Who saw the wide world in a jade cup:
By illumined conception got clear of heaven and earth:
On the chariot of mutation entered the gate of immutability?

———

'In this age of civilisation we are unwilling to see anything that can detract from that distinguished character which in former times gained to the Merchants the title of "Princes" and to traffickers that of the "Honourable of the Earth".'

James Matheson in *The Canton Register*, 19 April, 1828.

'POLITICAL ECONOMY. A wish has been expressed in a respectable quarter to have the elements of the science translated into Chinese; and to this end the latest editions of Dr Adam Smith's work on the Wealth of Nations, Malthus, McCulloch and Mill's Principles, have been consulted. The impossibility of making such subjects understood to a cursory native reader is self-evident. The illustration of the great principles of Political Economy, applicable to the errors and abuses which may exist in China, would require a special book written for this purpose. We should be glad to see such an essay . . .'

Notice printed in *The Canton Register*, May, 1831, offering a prize of £50 for such an effort.

British Trade and
The Opening of China 1800-42

BY

MICHAEL GREENBERG

Formerly Fellow of Trinity College, Cambridge

CAMBRIDGE
AT THE UNIVERSITY PRESS
1951
REPRINTED
1969

CAMBRIDGE UNIVERSITY PRESS
Cambridge, New York, Melbourne, Madrid, Cape Town, Singapore, São Paulo

Cambridge University Press
The Edinburgh Building, Cambridge CB2 8RU, UK

Published in the United States of America by Cambridge University Press, New York

www.cambridge.org
Information on this title: www.cambridge.org/9780521077743

© Cambridge University Press 1951

First published 1951
Reprinted 1969
This digitally printed version 2008

A catalogue record for this publication is available from the British Library

ISBN 978-0-521-07774-3 hardback
ISBN 978-0-521-07916-7 paperback

CONTENTS

MONEY, WEIGHTS AND ABBREVIATIONS

1. *Money*

The basic circulating coin in foreign commerce at Canton during this period was the Spanish dollar, with an intrinsic value of 4s. 2d. and an exchange value ranging from 3s. 11d. to 5s. The tael was a hypothetical coin of pure silver used only in the East India Company's accounts and in all cotton transactions. The equivalents generally used were:

1 tael = 10 mace = $1·388 = 6s. 8d.
$1 = 10·72 taels = 5s. = 2·5 current rupees.
1 lac = 100,000.

2. *Weights*

1 Picul = 133⅓ lb. = 100 catties = 1,600 taels weight.
The tael was a Chinese ounce weight as well as a unit of money.

3. *Abbreviations*

L.B. = Letter Book.
I.L.B., E.L.B., P.L.B., C.L.B., = India/Europe/Private/Coastal Letter Book.
W.J. = William Jardine.
J.M. = James Matheson.
R.T. = Robert Taylor.
M. & Co. = Magniac & Co.
Y. & Co. = Yrissari & Co.
J.M. & Co. = Jardine Matheson & Co.
C.I.C. = Canton Insurance Company.
B.P.P. = British Parliamentary Papers.
S.C.H. of C./H. of L. =Select Committee of House of Commons/ Lords.
E.I.C. = East India Company.
C. of D. =Court of Directors.
F.Rs. = Factory Records of East India Company.

Chronicles = *Chronicles of the East India Company trading to China, 1635-1834,* by H. B. Morse.

Proc.M.Ch. = Proceedings of Manchester Chamber of Commerce.

Corresp. = Correspondence relating to China, 1840 (Blue Book).

C.Reg. = *Canton Register.*

Ch.Rep. = *Chinese Repository.*

'The Company'—is sometimes used to indicate the East India Company; 'the firm' refers to the variously styled Beale, Magniac, Jardine, Matheson concern. See Appendix II.

AUTHOR'S PREFACE

This study gives an account of the activities of the British merchants in China in the crucial years before the Treaty of Nanking
(1842), which transformed the relations between the Celestial
Empire and the Western 'barbarians' and placed them upon a
footing that was to last for a hundred years. An historical epoch
which is only now drawing to its end was inaugurated by the
decisive pressures of an expanding British economy in the early
19th century.

A century ago, the West invaded China with commodities,
guns, ideas. The *economic* conquest of China by the European
invaders passed through three broad stages. First, the balance of
trade changed in favour of the foreigners, the flow of silver
reversing its direction from about 1826. In the second phase,
British manufactures began to pour into China, so that the
country which had for centuries been famous for its textiles was
by the 1870s taking in Lancashire cotton goods to the extent of
one-third of its entire imports. Thirdly, the inflow of foreign
manufactures was followed by that of foreign capital, bringing with
it railways, cotton mills and similar undertakings requiring a
capital accumulation which China lacked. It is mainly with the
first period of this development that we are concerned in this
volume.

This period has been studied, hitherto, almost wholly from the
standpoint of the diplomatic historian; which is here especially
inadequate, both because—apart from three abortive embassies—
there were then no direct governmental relations, and because
what in fact brought British subjects into daily contact with
Chinese was avowedly commerce. This commerce, 'the China
trade', has indeed been much written upon, its picturesque
character appealing to the *litterateur* as much as its acquisitive

possibilities attracted the *entrepreneur*. The mass of contemporary Blue Books and statistical compilations on the subject, which reflects its importance, yields much quantitative information about the trade. But the operations of the traders are concealed rather than illumined in the evidence collected by the many Commissioners and Parliamentary Committees which reported thereon.

More revealing are the *Chronicles of the East India Company trading to China, 1635-1834*, set forth in five volumes by Morse. This work is an abstract of documentary and statistical information, and as such is more of a source book than a finished study of British Trade with China. Moreover, analysis of the China trade from the side of the East India Company is misleading in our period for two reasons: first, because the business practice of the Company differed strongly in its content, mechanisms and animating spirit from that of the private British merchants at Canton; and secondly, because the emergence of the latter was clearly the determinant of the decisive events of the 1830s. Our meagre knowledge of these private merchants, gleaned from travellers' tales and odd memoirs, could only be supplemented by information derived from economic documents, the records of the actual firms concerned. The discovery in a Hongkong *godown* of the old papers of Jardine Matheson & Co., the only firm of 'pre-treaty days' to survive, makes possible the following account.

These papers, displaying as they do the nature of 'Agency business', throw light on the second aspect of our theme—the China trade as part of the expansion of the British economy overseas. The creation of a world market was an integral part of Britain's industrial development in the 19th century. Concentration by historians of the industrial revolution on internal changes in technology and organisation has tended to blur the fact that the export merchant was as significant a figure in the development of large-scale, power-driven industry as the manufacturer. True, the Eastern trade was only one field of export, and not the largest at that. Its importance, from this point of view, lay not in the absolute volume of British manufactures it could absorb, but in its taking the surplus output necessary to keep the new machines running when the home market sagged. Hence the constant pressure of the British manufacturers to open the gates of China, despite the paradox which has puzzled some recent writers that China was a relatively small market.

The scope of this study is obviously determined by the character of the sources of information available. The main source used is the Jardine Matheson collection of manuscripts; though, of course, the evidence drawn from it is fitted with that derived from other sources new and old, the Minutes of the Manchester Chamber of Commerce, Blue Books, pamphlets, and newspapers, etc., which are listed in the bibliography. But one limiting factor is that all these sources are English, or at least European. The foreign merchants at Canton were in China, not of it; but few could speak even a smattering of the language. It is, therefore, impossible from their writings to answer certain historical questions about the precise economic and social impact of a technically superior 'western' economic invasion upon a semi-feudal 'Asiatic economy'.

The value of the Jardine Matheson papers lies elsewhere. They shed an intimate light, from the inside as it were, on the operations of the foreign merchants in China. They display the inner workings. Since the outcome of business transactions depended upon a regular supply of exact knowledge, the correspondence of the firm is a mine of accurate information on everything that concerned the foreign traders during the period. The problem of Jardine Matheson & Co.'s being a 'representative' firm does not really arise. The magnitude of their trade, as James Matheson wrote in 1832, rendered the firm 'a general focus or medium for the business of the port' (of Canton). They were easily the largest of the handful of British firms established in China. Though the bulk of their letters are concerned with routine matters, yet in the aggregate their content is by no means narrow. They make possible a treatment of the China trade which avoids being a mere commentary on the ebb and flow of exports and imports, and which goes beyond the fetish of commodities, because it places in the foreground the actual people brought into relation with one another by the process of exchange. Unfortunately, the early account books are frequently defaced or eaten away by termites. On the other hand the letters provide very full statements of the nature of the business conducted; which is after all the heart of the matter, even if it does make some of the following pages rather technical.

It is now over twelve years since the late Sir John Clapham first told me of the existence of the Jardine Matheson papers in a cellar at the Cambridge University Library. It was under his direction that I carried out the original research. In the laborious task of sorting out the then unclassified mass of archive material I was helped by Dr B. F. Atkinson, Under-Librarian at the University Library. My first draft was already completed in the summer of 1939 before war compelled to less academic pursuits. Subsequent revision has been slight. For clarification of some problems in Chinese history I am indebted to Dr Chi Chao-ting, a former colleague at the Institute of Pacific Relations, and to Professor John K. Fairbank of Harvard University. Over many years I have benefited from the rare knowledge of my friend Victor Kiernan, a former Fellow of Trinity. I wish also to thank the General Editor, Professor Postan, for reading the typescript and offering points of criticism. Sir John Pratt also read the typescript and made several valuable suggestions. My last acknowledgment is to Trinity College, Cambridge, which, by nurturing me as Scholar, Research Student, and Fellow, made this research possible.

CAMBRIDGE   M.G.

August 1948

Chapter I

THE OLD CHINA TRADE[1]

What brought East and West into contact in modern times
was commerce. But it was the occidental who came out to seek
the riches of Cathay, and not the other way. The dominant fact
for nearly three hundred years of their commercial intercourse, *initial*
from the 16th to the 19th century, was that the westerner desired *trade*
the goods of the East and was able to offer little merchandise in *balance*
return. Until the epoch of machine production, when technical *favours*
supremacy enabled the West to fashion the whole world into a *China*
single economy, it was the East which was the more advanced in
most of the industrial arts. During the early 18th century British
textile manufacturers fought successfully to secure Parliamentary
protection against the East India Company's imports of calicoes,
wrought silks, muslins and other fabrics, with which they were
not yet able to compete. There were a whole series of protective
Acts passed in the reigns of William III, Anne, and George I
against the imports of Eastern fabrics, and culminating in the
prohibition of certain categories, especially calicoes.[2] As late as
the 1830s, the market intelligence sent out by Jardine Matheson
& Co., Canton, to their correspondents spoke of the superiority
of the Chinese native 'nankeen' cotton cloth over Manchester
cotton goods in point of quality and cost.[3]

The colourful commerce between the Red and Yellow Seas,
which existed long before the European ventured eastwards,

[1] The epithet 'Old' applied to the China trade is used throughout to signify
the condition of affairs 'before Treaty days', i.e. pre-1842.

[2] For a full list of protected piece goods see Bal Krishna, *Commercial Relations
between India and England*, p. 326.

[3] See also the market reports in *Chinese Repository*, February 1834, for the
same opinion.

defies statistical measurement; but in the aggregate it must have been enormous. The China junks alone annually carried to and from the marts of the Eastern Archipelago and India huge quantities of raw silk and stuffs, porcelain, tutenag, rhubarb, camphor, shells, sandalwood, tin, ivory, spices and jewels, etc. The volume of this trade astonished early Western travellers, who brought back tales of the fabulous wealth of the Orient, highly attractive to the land-hungry younger sons of Spanish and Portuguese grandees and the equally adventurous tradesmen of the maritime countries.[1] No one went East to 'open up' markets for European products.

British trade 'between the Cape of Good Hope and the Straits of Magellan' was for over three hundred years the legal monopoly of the East India Company. That unique institution, in the East successively Factor, *Diwan* and *Raj*, at home so closely bound up for generations with the fortunes of the leading families that Edmund Burke could declare 'to say the Company was in a state of distress was neither more nor less their saying the Country was in a state of distress',[2] was nurtured on pepper and sustained its ripe years on tea. It was conceived when in 1599 a group of London merchants met to form an association to trade with the Indies, because the Dutch had raised the price of pepper from 3*s.* to 8*s.* 6*d.* per pound.[3] The Company proceeded to traffic in a variety of goods, spices for preserving and flavouring the meat of the many, silks and ornaments demanded by the increasing sophistication of the few. But when in the 18th century the Company was deprived, in the interests of the home manufacturers, of the opportunity of profiting from the imports of Indian textiles,

[1] On its foundation the English East India Company resolved not to employ 'gentlemen'—Bruce, *Annals* I.

[2] In 1785, quoted Pritchard, *Crucial Years of Early Anglo-Chinese Relations*, p. 213. One of the first political tasks of the rising class of industrial manufacturers was to challenge this identification of 'Country' and 'Company'. See Chapter VII below.

[3] For the early trade of the Company, cf. Bruce, *op. cit.* I; Foster, *England's Quest for Eastern Trade*, passim; D. Macpherson, *European Commerce with India* p. 72 ff.; Bal Krishna, *op. cit.*

it turned its whole commercial attention to the import of China tea.

Tea was the only available article which could be forced into universal consumption without competing against home manu-facture. In 1664 2 lb. and 2 oz. of tea were imported into England; in 1783 the quantity sold at the Company's sales was 5,857,882 lbs. Then in the following year was passed the Commutation Act which reduced the duties on tea from over 100% to 12½%.[1] In 1785 over 15 million pounds of tea were sold, and in the last years of the Company's monopoly the amount it exported from China averaged about 30 million pounds.[2] Imports of 'luxury goods' from China—porcelain, lacquered cabinets, silks, etc.—con-tinued and even increased with the cult for 'chinoiserie' which the Age of Reason and rococo sometimes affected. But the Honour-able Company tended by the end of the 18th century to leave this trade to the 'privilege tonnage' of its captains and officers, and concentrate on tea. In the last few years of its monopoly its sole export from China was tea.[3] Tea had become so much the national drink that the Company was required by Act of Parlia-ment to keep a year's supply always in stock. The revenue which tea brought into the British Exchequer averaged, in the last years of the monopoly, £3,300,000 per annum.[4] Tea from China provided about one-tenth of the total revenue of England and the whole profit of the East India Company.

The amounts of profit which tea brought to the Company are more difficult to ascertain because of the curious mode in which

[1] These tea figures are compiled from W. Milburn, *Oriental Commerce* II, 531; Pritchard, *op. cit.*, p. 150; and tables appended to *S.C.H. of C.* 1830.

[2] Before the Commutation Act of 1784 it was said that three-quarters of the tea consumed in England was smuggled. The effect of this Act was, therefore, to check smuggling as well as to increase consumption.

[3] *S.C.H. of C.* 1830, 1746, 4297. The following figures from Appendix A(2) of the *S.C.H. of L.* 1830 are illustrative: 1811-19, total E.I.C. imports into England from China—£72,168,541. Total E.I.C. imports of tea from China—£70,426,244.

[4] 'Privilege' trade for the same years came to about another £9 million, of which teas accounted for just under £5 million—*S.C.H. of C.* 1830, Q.5605.

its accounts were drawn up, but the estimates of various witnesses before the Select Committee of the House of Commons in 1830 ranged between £1,000,000 and £1,500,000 a year.[1] Even before its India trade monopoly was abandoned, in 1813, the Company was directing all its commercial energies to the China tea trade. T. C. Melville, the Company's Auditor-General, pointed out to the Select Committee of the House of Commons that all the Company's commercial accounts were formulated as costs in terms of tea 'investment'. In its last years the Company exported nothing but tea. Tea had become the *raison d'être* of the Company's commerce.[2]

Tea could be procured only from China. In the 1820s the Company began experimenting with tea cultivation in its own Indian territories. Shrubs were brought from China and transplanted in the Himalayas. But it was many years before Indian tea challenged China.

As the English thirst for tea increased, however, China developed no reciprocal appetite. The essence of the situation was that China had not sought for contacts with the Europeans, but possessed goods which had attracted them. When, in 1793, Lord Macartney was sent out as Ambassador to China with samples of British manufactures,[3] he received from the Emperor Chien Lung the oft-quoted reply: 'Strange and costly objects do not interest me. As your Ambassador can see for himself we possess all things. I set no value on strange objects and ingenious[4], and have no use for your country's manufactures.' This declaration was

---

[1] *Loc. cit.* 1006. The higher figure is given by the American, Bates, who would be tempted to put it high—see his evidence, 3237 ff.

[2] *Ibid.* Q.4297. See statistics appended *loc. cit.*

[3] He took out with him a small assortment of articles from the principal manufacturing towns in England, including Birmingham hardware from Mathew Boulton, cottons from Manchester, and other samples from Sheffield, Leeds, Exeter, Norwich, Coventry, Gloucestershire and Wiltshire (cloth), Paisley, and Frome. Pritchard, *op. cit.* 2, 296-7.

[4] This alludes to 'singsongs', for which see next Chapter.

not inspired by 'arrogance' or 'anti-commercialism',[1] as the puzzled
and frustrated foreign merchants believed, but reflected the basic
self-sufficiency of China's agrarian economy, huge internal trade
and urban handicrafts; which latter sufficed for the production of
such manufactures as were beyond the resources of rural domestic
industry or peasant needs.[2] Sir Robert Hart wrote a century
later: 'Chinese have the best food in the world, rice; the best
drink, tea; and the best clothing, cotton, silk, fur. Possessing
these staples and their innumerable native adjuncts, they do not
need to buy a penny's worth elsewhere'.[3] This lack of effective
demand on the part of China brought with it the fundamental
problem of the Old China Trade, its one-sided balance.

The problem, as it presented itself concretely, was how to
provide the wherewithal at Canton to buy the teas, and to a
lesser extent silks, and other 'China goods' demanded in England.[4]
In view of China's indifference to European staples, its products
could only be bought by gold and silver, bullion and coin.
A China that lacked adequate media of exchange (the copper
'cash' being useless for large-scale transactions and the 'sycee'
silver shoes too unwieldly) developed a capacity for absorbing
dollars, silver dollars minted in Old and New Spain. The early
Spanish and Portuguese traders were able to use the plunder of
the Americas, in so far as they retained it, to pay in part for China
goods. Periodic Portuguese piracy in the Eastern Seas added to

[1] See Chapter III for a discussion of contemporary English opinion as to the
motives of the restrictive Canton commercial system.
[2] China's self-sufficiency and the extent of its modification by foreign trade is
discussed in Chapter III.
[3] Hart, *These from the land of Sinim* As director of the Chinese Customs he
was in a position to know.
[4] In this section I am largely indebted to Morse's suggestive article on the
'Provisions of Funds for the East India Company's trade at Canton during the
18th century'—*Transactions Royal Asiatic Society*, 1922. But Morse, as usual,
regards the question from the Company's angle only, and moreover, confines
himself to the 18th century.

the 'stock' available for Macao.[1] The English East India Company found itself from the beginning faced with the necessity of taking out large quantities of bullion and coin to finance its Eastern trade. During the first twenty-three years of its activity, 1601-24, it exported to the East £753,336 of treasure (mainly Spanish dollars) and only £351,236 of goods.[2] A century later this was still the proportion of treasure to goods. In the fifty seasons after the amalgamation of the Old and New East India Companies, 1710-59, the exports from England to the East consisted of £26,833,614 in treasure and only £9,248,306 in goods.[3]

Turning to the China trade proper, we find that the first English venture to Canton, Captain Weddell's celebrated expedition of 1637, sold no English goods at all, but disposed of 80,000 'pieces of eight'.[4] The first China ships of the East India Company sold very little in the way of English goods. Morse gives the cargoes of one or two of the early ships to China.[5] Thus in 1699 the 'stock' of the *Macclesfield* belonging to the new 'English Company' consisted of £26,611 in silver and £5,475 in goods, chiefly woollens, one quarter of which was left unsold;[6] and in 1751 four ships left England for China with £119,000 worth of silver and only £10,842 in goods.

Now, as is well known, this continuous export of treasure from England excited the critics of the East India Company's monopoly. Contemporary bullionist theories furnished them with a

(margin note: Problem)

---

[1] The Portuguese traded in China at Macao, not Canton. See Chapter III below. On the early Portuguese trade, see Chang T'ien-tse, *Sino-Portuguese Trade, 1514-1644* (1934).

[2] Bal Krishna, *op. cit.*, Appendix A, p. 182. The author has compiled figures showing the proportion of money and goods exported by the Company to the East, from 1658-82, 1698-1710. The proportion is generally about 3 to 1, and in some years much higher. Pp. 296-7.

[3] Morse, *Chronicles of the East India Company*, I, 8.

[4] *Ibid.*

[5] Morse: *Transactions R.A.S. loc. cit.*

[6] Until 1775 the accounts of each ship were usually treated as a separate enterprise. *Chronicles*, II, 3.

[handwritten margin notes: "Bullionist throws — mercantilism. Calls to export more 'goods' rather when ..."]

powerful argument. To render its monopolist position less vulnerable, the Company was not content with the verbal arguments of its defenders such as Thomas Mun,[1] but undertook to take at least one-tenth of its stock in goods, 'the growth, produce or manufacture of the Kingdom'. In the majority of seasons during the first two-thirds of the 18th century, it did not exceed this 'tenth' of British goods, which was embodied in the statutory requirement. Morse gives instances in which the proportion of silver was as high as 98% of the cargo.[2]

England's commerce had been built up on the sale of wool, and later woollen cloths, to European markets. It was the principal commodity the country had to offer before the spectacular rise of cotton. Woollen goods, broadcloths, longells, camlets, together with some lead and occasionally Cornish copper or tin, comprised the chief items of 'British Goods' sent to China by the Company. But even when the entire 'stock'[3] of English goods was sold, it was generally either at a loss, or in such a way that the loss was concealed by a process of barter for China goods. This process was known as 'trucking'; the English woollens, etc., were sold at prices on which the prices of tea and silk depended.[4] In 1820 it was estimated that the net loss on English products sold at Canton in the preceding 23 years amounted to £1,688,103.[5] Moreover, British goods were also a source of loss to the Chinese merchants, who only took them because the Company insisted,

[1] The author of *England's treasure by foreign Trade.*
[2] *Loc. cit.*
[3] 'Stock' and 'investment' have a slightly technical meaning in connection with the Old China Trade, which was directed at obtaining China goods, for which end the selling of British manufactures was only a means. 'Stock' was the total of the resources brought out to Canton to be 'invested' in the return cargoes. The term 'tea investment' implies no fixed allocation of capital; but it expresses well the basic fact that imports into Canton were regarded solely as resources to finance exports.
[4] The Chinese merchants were known to give as high a premium as 35% on goods trucked for teas. *S.C.H. of C.* 1830, 2764.
[5] *S.C.H. of L.* 1820.

as a condition of its tea purchases.[1] The main reason why the Chinese Hong merchants were so friendly with the Americans was that a very high proportion of their imports consisted of silver dollars, Spanish, Mexican, South American.[2] A native of Manchester who settled in Philadelphia, whence he travelled to China, declared that the Chinese merchants 'prefer what they call in their own language a *rich* cargo', i.e. one comprised of treasure.[3]

Finally, towards the end of the 18th century, at a time when, mainly as a consequence of Pitt's Commutation Act, the volume of tea shipments was expanding rapidly, the East India Company found increasing difficulty in obtaining enough specie to send to Canton. In 1779 Spain entered the American War of Independence; the market for Spanish dollars was closed and from 1779 to 1785 not a dollar was sent from England to China. Even after the resumption of shipments of treasure, the investment of tea increased more rapidly than the flow of silver. With a strictly limited market for English goods at Canton,[4] even when sold at a loss, and an increasingly uncertain supply of silver from Europe, the gap between British imports to and exports from China became alarming. Thus, from 1792 to 1807 the Company's shipments to England from Canton were worth £27,157,006, whereas the English exports to Canton came to only £16,602,338.[5]

[1] See evidence of J. F. Davis, of the Company's Canton Establishment, that British goods were the worst mode of paying for tea. *S.C.H. of C.* 1830, 5079, Q.408. This loss was one of the reasons why the Chinese Hong merchants frequently became insolvent. See Chapter III below.

[2] Statistics of the American trade are given in the Appendix.

[3] Richard Milne, evidence, *S.C.H. of C.* 1830.

[4] The imports of woollens do show a considerable increase from 1788, and on occasion even a small profit. But the tea export increased even more rapidly. *Cf.* Pritchard, Tables, Appendix 4.

[5] Milburn II, 475. In 1765-66 the Company's exports were 202% greater than merchandise imports. In 1785-86 they were greater by 328%. Pritchard, 143. In 1811-28 East India Company exports from China to England were £72,680,541. Merchandise exports to China from England were £13,244,702. Tables in *S.C.H. of L.* 1830.

In any case the reliance on treasure was, though bullionist theories were no longer so prevalent, still an unsatisfactory way of trading, a *pis aller*. How to provide *commodities* which would be acceptable to the Chinese and which would pay for the teas, and even perhaps themselves bring a profit—this was the problem.

The solution was finally found in India. It was discovered that while the Chinese had little taste for British goods, they were eager to accept the produce of British India, particularly raw cotton and opium, though China itself produced the one and prohibited the other. The resources of India could be used to finance the China investment. That this was being realised in the last decades of the 18th century is shown by the declaration in the instructions to the first British mission to China, the abortive Cathcart Embassy of 1787, that the prosperity of India 'would be promoted by procuring a secure vent for (its) products and manufactures in the extensive Empire of China, at the same time that the produce of such sales would furnish resources for the Investment (teas, etc.) to Europe'.[1]

Such a development was made feasible by the growth of British political power in India during the period; especially by the assumption of the *diwani*, the revenues in kind, which gave the Company a large measure of control over the resources of Bengal in particular. It was able to raise directly considerable revenues in kind by means of monopolies in the articles of saltpetre and opium. It had indirect control over the production of cotton cloth, since it made advance payments to the native weavers, which kept them perpetually in its debt—'a form of serfdom' a recent writer designates it.[2] Part of these goods, quantities of which the

---

[1] Quoted Pritchard, *op. cit.* p. 232.

[2] Parkinson, *op. cit.* Chapter 3. Actually, Bombay *raw* cotton which formed a large proportion of the cotton exports to China was not a Company monopoly, and was shipped to the extent of over £1 million a year, by private merchants; though an opponent of the Company alleged that, even in Bombay, half the cotton crop was often appropriated as land tax. *S.C.H. of C.*, 1830, 3488.

Company was able to dispose of yearly, was sent to Europe; but an increasingly large volume went to Canton.[1]

The effect of this can be seen in the changing balance of the China trade. After 1804 very little or no silver had to be sent from Europe to China by the Company. On the contrary, the rapid increase of Indian imports into Canton soon reversed the flow of treasure. In the three years from 1806-9 some $7 million of silver bullion and coin was shipped *from* China *to* India, to make up the balance of payments[2]; from 1818 to 1833 fully one-fifth of the total exports *from* China was treasure.[3] By 1817 non-European merchandise brought to Canton totalled over $10 million compared with 3½ million of British goods; in 1825 the figures were just over $17½ million and $3½ million respectively; in 1833, $20 million and $3½ million.[4] The volume of British goods maintained its level; it was the trade between India and China which revolutionised the balance at Canton.

The trade between India, the Eastern Archipelago and China was known from the end of the 17th century until the advent of steam in the middle of the 19th as 'the Country Trade'.[5] The origin of the term is obscure; applied at first to the coastal trade of India and nearby ports, it came to refer especially to Eastern trade from India, whether carried on by natives or Europeans. To this Country Trade the East India Company looked, as a means of providing funds at Canton for the all-important tea investment. The vital role played by this Country commerce within the China trade as a whole had important economic and political repercussions. For the Honourable Company, after a few spasmodic attempts during the early and middle 18th century to engage in

---

[1] Statistics are to be found in Morse, *Chronicles*, passim.
[2] *Chronicles*, III, 56, 80, 100, 102.
[3] Morse, *International Relations*, I.
[4] *Chronicles*, III, 328; IV, 118, 369.
[5] W. H. Coates, preface.

the Country Trade itself,[1] decided to leave it to private merchants in India, both natives and English residents, who were to conduct it under licence from the Company. Here was a chink in the wall of monopoly. While, therefore, Chinese imports from India increased very rapidly from the close of the 18th century, those shipped on the Company's account actually declined for a time. In 1783 nearly one quarter of a million taels were realised at Canton for the *Company's* Indian products; but this figure was never again reached until well into the next century. In some years, as in 1798, there were no Indian goods at all taken to China on Company's account.[2] The Country Trade became increasingly a private trade.[3]

A further characteristic of the Country Trade which fitted it for its role within the China trade was the fact that China took from India large quantities of commodities of relatively high value, cotton, opium, etc., while in return she sent to India, apart from raw silk, goods of low value, such as sugar and tutenag and small quantities of a variety of 'fancy goods' whose aggregate value was little. Milburn calculated that in the early years of the 19th century the surplus of Indian exports to Canton over imports from China averaged about £1 million per annum.[4] It was this surplus which made the Country Trade complementary to that of the Company; and this complementary character of the two components of the Chinese trade made possible the large-scale banking procedure at Canton, whereby the resources of India were utilised to finance the purchase of China tea for England.

The Company, as we saw, did not itself send large enough quantities of Indian produce to provide its Canton Treasury with adequate funds for the tea investment. Instead, it experimented

---

[1] Examples can be found in Morse's article, *loc. cit.*
[2] Pritchard, *op. cit.*, gives tables in his Appendix III.
[3] See Appendix I, Table A.
[4] *Op. cit.* II, 483.

with a number of financial devices to draw into its service the proceeds of the India produce brought to China by private Country merchants. Thus, in 1778 the Government of Fort St. George, India, advanced 483,544 Sicca rupees to a Mr Thomas Fergusson, private Country merchant, who undertook to pay the equivalent in Spanish dollars into the Company's Treasury at Canton, at a fixed rate of exchange, out of the proceeds of his Indian cotton sales to the Chinese.[1] Similar arrangements were made with other private merchants. Likewise, certificates for moneys payable in London at 90 or 365 days sight were guaranteed to the Company's captains and officers in the proceeds of their 'privilege' trade if paid in to the Canton Treasury.[2] The captain of an Indiaman was usually allowed 56 tons free of charge, later 99 tons, and the other officers 47 tons between them. (This space was often eagerly sought by private Country merchants at Canton for £20-£40 per ton.)

Another device was the practice of granting 'transfers in the treasury' at Canton, whereby the private creditors of a Chinese merchant to whom they had sold Indian goods would be paid by the Company to the extent of its indebtedness to them for tea purchases.[3] But the main method was for the Company's Treasury at Canton to accept specie from Country merchants which their Indian produce yielded, in return for Bills on the Court of Directors in London, or on the Government of Bengal (rarely Bombay). These Bills were eagerly sought by the Country merchants, whose imports from India far exceeded their exports from China, as a means of remittance of their funds to England or India. The private merchants were not allowed to send teas, etc., to England, and they had difficulty in securing profitable return cargoes from China. Country ships often returned from Canton to India in ballast, carrying the Company's China Bills, which could easily be marketed in Calcutta.[4]

---

[1] Morse, *loc. cit.*   [2] *Ibid.*   [3] *Chronicles*, II, 143.
[4] *S.C.H. of L.* 1830, p. 288, and see Chapter IV below.

This banking mechanism provided by the Company at Canton was advantageous to both parties. It provided the Company with a method of financing its China investments, and the Country merchants with a channel for returning the profits of Indian cotton and opium. The problem of the Old China Trade seemed solved.

We are now in a position to analyse the general balance of the China trade as a whole, as it had fully developed in the last decades before the end of the Company's Charter in 1834. From 1817 onwards, full quantitative details of each season's trade can be set forth from the data given in the *Chronicles*. The year ending June 30th, 1828, may be taken as a 'sample' because it has the advantage of having had a detailed statement of its transactions placed before the Select Committee of the House of Commons of 1830, by an ex-president of the Company's establishment at Canton.[1] The total of British *imports* at Canton came to $20,364,600; of which $4,518,957 was on account of the Company and $15,364,600 on private account, the latter including a small unspecified pro-portion of the 'privilege' cargoes brought in Company's ships. Of the Company's imports, almost half was Western produce ($2,189,237 of which $1,764,217 were accounted for by woollens) while almost the whole of its Eastern goods ($2,329,720) consisted of Indian raw cotton. Of the private imports under 2% came from Europe, while of the $15,590,136 of Eastern products, raw cotton accounted for $3,480,083 and opium for $11,243,496 (the next item being sandalwood at a mere $125,504). No silver was brought to Canton throughout the season. The *exports* from Canton on British account came to a total of $18,136,052, of which just over half was on private account. Of the Company's exports of $8,479,285 all but a fraction of 1% ($9,000 worth) consisted of tea. But of $9,656,767 exported on private account, $6,094,646 was sent in silver, the next largest item being raw

[1] Charles Marjoribanks, *S.C.H. of C.* 1830, 635.

silk at $1,145,220.[1] The remittances through the Honourable
Company's Canton Treasury were as follows — Bills on the
Court of Directors, London, $7,820; on the Bengal settlement,
$2,417,560; captains' certificates,[2] $447,143; making a total of
$2,942,904. That these figures are typical in their ratios may
be confirmed by analysing the balances for other years of this
period from the data given in the *Chronicles* (Vol. III, IV
passim).

A number of important points about the Old China Trade in
its last phase emerge: (*a*) Western products paid for about a
quarter of the Company's tea investment; (*b*) the Company's
total imports were equal to about half of its tea investments;
(*c*) the private trade was practically all 'Country Trade'; (*d*) its
India exports were now predominantly composed of opium,
though raw cotton was still a substantial item, greater than the
Company's quantity of the article;[3] (*e*) the proceeds of opium
sales alone were enough to pay for more than the whole tea
investment of the Company; (*f*) but since only a portion of
this was taken by the Company's Treasury for that purpose, a
very large quantity of silver had to be shipped to India in return
for Bills of Exchange on private account as remittance to the
exporters of the opium.

Such was the anatomy, if not the physiology, of the Old China
Trade in its ripe age. Its proper functioning was important
not only for its own sake but because of its role in India's
balance of payments with Britain. T. C. Melville, the Company's
Auditor-General, declared in 1830, 'I am prepared to say that India

[1] In several of these items I follow Morse's figures (*Chronicles*, IV, 158-9) as
being likely to be based on more material than was available to Marjoribanks at
the time. But the differences are unimportant.

[2] The certificates were largely bought up by private Canton merchants from
the captains. See *I.L.B.*, 1827.

[3] On the reasons why, and the manner in which, opium out-distanced cotton
as the principle article of the Country Trade after 1823, see Chapter IV
below.

does entirely depend upon the profits of the China trade'. To understand this far-reaching and responsible pronouncement, it is necessary to follow Melville's intricate elaboration of the rather complicated connections between the East India Company's territorial and commercial accounts.[1] In substance the position was as follows. Almost £4 million had to be transferred annually, from India to Great Britain, during this period, in one way or the other; £3 million of this sum represented Government remittances, the obligatory 'home charges' of the Company, and the other million the accumulation of private British fortunes, official and mercantile, pensions, etc., seeking return to England. The Company was compelled to make the China trade the channel of remittance from India to London. This was partly because a considerable proportion of the Company's surplus territorial revenue was obtained in kind, in such goods as could be sold profitably only in Canton; partly because by remitting through China via the Country Trade, the Company was able to gain a large advantage from its control over the rate of exchange of its Bills.[2] The surplus of *Indian* revenues were thus sent home in teas from China, a procedure made possible by the development of the Country Trade from India to China. The private Country merchants were, indeed, mere licensees of the Company; but the latter had to depend on them not only to redress the balance of trade at Canton, but to convey its own funds to England.

From about 1817 the Country Trade provided three-quarters of the total British imports at Canton, a proportion which it maintained, except for two years, till the end of the Company's monopoly. In 1833 it was declared in a debate at East India

[1] *S.C.H. of C.*, Q.4338, 5706 and Chapters V and VIII below.
[2] Melville, *S.C.H. of C.*, Q.5706. The Company's control of the rate of exchange between China, India and England was one of the major grievances of the private merchants in the struggle for the abolition of the Company's Charter in 1830. See *S.C.H. of C.*, 5238, and Chapter VII below.

House that the trade between India and China was three times the value of that of England and China.[1]

There is a further point in the triangular web between England, India, and China which Melville does not develop. After the opening of the India trade to private British merchants in 1813, India, for centuries an exporter of textiles, became inundated with Manchester cotton goods to such an extent that the rupee, previously valued at 2s. 6d., fell to 2s. and under in a few years. For the Lancashire exporter, the most profitable mode of remittance from India was via China. Calcutta led to Canton.

The Country Trade had become the keystone of the whole structure.

The foregoing introductory analysis of the Old China Trade has been concerned not to describe its organisation or development but to bring out its peculiar nature. The expanding British market for the products of China (more especially tea), without a reciprocal demand for British goods on the side of the Chinese, posed a problem whose solution was found in the Country Trade. The significance of the Country Trade as the dominant factor in the Old China Trade, one which indeed was finally to transform it, clearly emerges. Its importance lay in its increasing magnitude, in its vital role as the indispensable means of providing funds at Canton for the tea investment and furnishing a channel of remittance from India to England; but above all in the fact that it was a private trade. For the private merchants trading with Canton were the dynamic element in the Eastern Commerce. Whereas the Company was content to maintain its lucrative tea monopoly at a steady level, the private Country merchants were 'free traders', eager to develop trade to unprecedented proportions, prepared to

[1] $32 million compared with $11 million, cf. J. Phipps, *A Practical Treatise on the China Trade*. Phipps gives an interesting estimate (p. 272) of the entire foreign trade of China, including the junk trade, as being worth $70-$80 million per annum. There are, however, too many unknown factors to warrant any such estimate in the period.

overcome all obstacles. The following pages will trace the rise of these Country merchants, the nature of their business, their relations with the Company and their part in the struggles to end its monopoly, culminating in their efforts to break down the Great Wall of Chinese resistance to foreign penetration.

Chapter II

THE HONOURABLE COMPANY
AND THE PRIVATE ENGLISH

A community of British merchants in China could only emerge in opposition to the most powerful commercial unit of the time, the Honourable East India Company. Until 1834 'the sole exclusive right of trading, trafficking and using the business of merchandize into or from the dominions of the Emperor of China' was, as far as British subjects were concerned, legally vested in the Company. Even after 1813, when the India trade was practically thrown open to private British merchants, the Company jealously guarded its monopoly of the China trade. It was the policy of the Court of Directors, who managed the affairs of the Company from London, to safeguard this monopoly by preventing any 'free merchant' from taking up his residence in China. Only its own agents, the Supercargoes at its Canton 'Factory', that is, its establishment of 'factors' or agents, were to remain in China.

A Supercargo, in the 18th century, was an officer aboard a merchant ship whose duty it was to superintend the cargo and commercial transactions of the voyage. But the term came to be used, rather loosely, of an agent who managed a merchant's business in a foreign country. The shift in the connotation of the word expressed the changing function of the agent. From 1770 the Company's Supercargoes were no longer ordered to return in the ships in which they were specifically interested, but to form themselves into a single body which should remain in China from year to year.[1] There were generally about twelve Supercargoes, and it became the practice for the three or four senior members to

[1] *Chronicles*, II, 2.

form a President and Select Committee—ironically called 'the Select' by the private merchants—which acted as the governing body for the affairs of the Company in China, subject to the orders of the Court of Directors in London.

Now these Supercargoes, in addition to their main duty of managing the Company's affairs, were at first allowed to engage in private trade on their own account. This mode of remunerating the Company's servants by permitting them to trade privately was then a principle of what would today be called business management: it can be seen at work, during this period, in the Company's administration of India, and in the 'privilege tonnage' allowed free to the commanders and officers of the Company's marine. The China Supercargoes were not, however, to trade in goods shipped on the Company's vessels, but to act as agents for private merchants in India—in fact the Country traders. It appears from an appeal made in 1786 by a Supercargo named Lane, who asked permission to continue in private trade because his promotion to the Select Committee was but temporary, that only the junior Supercargoes were allowed to trade on their own account. In 1787 two junior Supercargoes, Messrs Lance and Fitzhugh, asked to go to Manila to supply the Spaniards there with India goods on private account; and we hear of Messrs Lane, Lance and Fitzhugh founding a private co-partnership to handle agency business.[1] The proceeds of these transactions were paid into the Company's Treasury at Canton in return for Bills on London, or else loaned to the Chinese merchants at high interest. The extent of this private business of the Supercargoes is not known precisely, but that it must have been large is shown by the fact that in 1777 Mr W. H. Pigou, a Supercargo, paid into the Treasury a sum of 235,539 taels on private account.[2]

But the Country merchants in India, whose business was rapidly increasing, were not content to entrust their consignments of goods and silver to China to the Supercargoes of the East India

---

[1] *Chronicles*, II, 124. [2] *Ibid.* II, 26.

Company. The Country ships, built and registered in India, generally carried their own Supercargoes, often Parsees, who were of course not allowed to remain in China beyond the departure of the last ships of each season. From the efforts of these men to stay on at Canton or Macao under various pretexts there emerged in the 1770s the first group of 'private English' in China.

By this time the Country Trade was already beginning to play its important role of financing the Company's 'investment' at Canton. In 1775 over $500,000 was paid into the Company's Treasury from the proceeds of the Country Trade. The Select Committee was therefore eager to encourage these private ships sailing from India under licence of the Company, even if it meant occasionally relaxing the prohibition against their 'free' Supercargoes staying awhile in China. As early as 1764 we find the name of a private merchant, one George Smith, among that select and jealous band of Englishmen resident in China.[1] He had been given permission to stay on for two years to wind up his private affairs, but, in defiance of repeated orders to depart, remained until 1780. During the 1770s the names of several individuals, not of the Company's service, were recorded as resident at Canton.

These men appeared under the following circumstances. In 1771 the Supercargoes had secured the dissolution of the Cohong[2] by bribing the senior Hong merchant Puankequa with 100,000 taels. This weakened the bargaining power of the Hong merchants, the feebler of whom were soon unable to meet their financial obligations. The result was an influx of Country merchants, who in an attempt to collect their debts refused to leave China in accordance with the Company's orders. In the season 1773-4 the Company issued few Bills on London on account of its financial difficulties in Europe. The Country traders, unable to remit their funds to England and attracted by the oriental rates of interest offered by hard-pressed Chinese merchants, lent them extensive

[1] *Chronicles*, II, 4, 5.
[2] On the Cohong system, see Chapter III below.

sums of money. By 1777 only four of the eleven Hong merchants were solvent. About $3,000,000 was claimed from the Chinese as owed on account of private Country merchants; of this sum the original debt for goods sold on credit and money lent was no more than $1,079,000—the rest represented the accumulation of compound interest, sometimes at the rate of 20% per annum.[1]

Nevertheless these private merchants boldly appealed to the British Government to approach the Court of Pekin to obtain redress.[2] They argued that these debts represented fortunes accumulated in India, sent to China to be remitted home in Company's Bills, in the absence of which they had been forced to lend to the Chinese merchants, which procedure had been of advantage to the Company. In 1779, at the instance of these private creditors in India, Admiral Vernon sent a frigate to Canton to demand from the Viceroy of the Son of Heaven that 'justice be done to His Majesty's oppressed subjects in China'.[3]

This appeal to the British Government to intervene at Pekin and this early instance of 'gunboat diplomacy' at the instigation of these 'private English' annoyed the Select Committee. It had other reasons to be irritated by their activities. For one thing, they brought the Company into disfavour with the Chinese customs officials, because many of the Country ships, having paid in the proceeds of their import cargoes to the Company's Treasury, departed for India in ballast, thus diminishing the duties payable to the Chinese.[4] Secondly, these private agents of 'China ventures' were a turbulent lot who gave a good deal of trouble. There was the case of one Abraham Leslie, who forcibly occupied the premises of a Hong merchant (Coqua) with armed Lascars. Equally disturbing were the semi-piratical activities of Captain

---

[1] *Chronicles*, II, 43–6. Messrs Hutton & Gordon were the biggest creditors with claims for $1,176,000.

[2] See 'Macartney Documents', quoted Pritchard, p. 203.

[3] *Chronicles*, II, 47–9.

[4] *Chronicles*, II, 62. Chinese duties were payable on both imports and exports.

MacClary of the Country ship *Dadabhoy* of Bengal.[1] For 'irregularities' on the part of private British merchants the Chinese held the Company responsible.

The vigilant Court of Directors in London determined to enforce its powers. In 1780 it sent strict orders to the Select Committee to expel from China all British subjects who were not attached to the Factory. In 1786 it secured the passage of an Act of Parliament confirming in the Select Committee full powers of control over licensed 'Country merchants' voyaging to China.[2] As a result, whereas in 1780 seven 'private English' were recorded as resident in China, there was only one in 1783. The Company had succeeded in scotching these first crude attempts of unruly persons outside its service to gain a footing in the Celestial Empire.

The one 'free' merchant left after the expulsion of Smith and the others was John Henry Cox. He was in China on a different basis from the others, as a dealer in English 'singsongs', a peculiar trade which we shall examine in a moment. 'Squire Cox' is important because he points to the future, and the co-partnership which he founded in 1782 with Daniel Beale was the beginning of the firm which developed, with change of partners' names but continuity of business, into Jardine Matheson & Co.[3] Cox came to Canton 'for the benefit of his health', according to Morse,[4] though in fact he had been given permission by the Court of Directors in London to stay in China for three years to sell 'singsongs'.[5]

The latter was the not inapt pidgin-English term for the clocks, watches and fantastically-shaped mechanical toys (such as 'snuff boxes concealing a jewelled bird which sang when the

[1] *Chronicles*, II, 63-6.   [2] 26. Geo. III, *c.*57.
[3] A fragment of Cox's invoice book of 1782 survives in the J.M. archives. On Cox, see *Factory Records, China* (96), 1.1.1790; (101), 2.11.1791, and *Chronicles*, II, passim.
[4] *Chronicles*, II, 142.   [5] *Factory Records, China* (77), 30.9.1783.

lid was opened') which were then manufactured in Birmingham and elsewhere for the oriental market.[1] These automata had the advantage of being one of the few articles which the West could produce before the age of machinery of interest to the East. They amused the Mandarins in Canton and Pekin,[2] and were given by the Hong merchants as obligatory New Year presents to the Government officials. The chief suppliers were John Cox, of Shoe Lane, London, and Francis Magniac, of Clerkenwell. On the death of the former, his son John Henry Cox was allowed to go to China in 1782 to sell off the remainder of his stock. But since many of the Chinese merchants were insolvent, Cox was obliged to take payment in goods. He thus found himself trading at Canton in competition with the Company. Moreover, instead of confining himself to this business of 'singsongs', he began to act as Canton agent for the 'privilege' trade of the Honourable Company's officers and for private British Country merchants in India. Soon he launched out into the Country Trade on his own account, bought two Bengal-built ships, *Supply* and *Enterprise*, which he freighted with cotton and opium from Calcutta.[3] Finally, being a man of initiative, he turned his attention to another channel of commerce, which the Company had neglected, the new Pacific fur trade.

In 1779 Captain Cook's flotilla, anchoring at Whampoa, the seaport of Canton, had found that sea-otter skins sold high in China ($120 per piece). In 1783 the Russians had sent Alaskan furs to Pekin. Two years later Cox, seeking to broaden out the basis of his position in China beyond the precarious support derived from uncertain 'singsongs' and surreptitious Country

---

[1] See J. Cox,: *A descriptive inventory of several exquisite and magnificent pieces of mechanism and jewellery*, 1773.

[2] *S.C.H. of C.* 1830, 4536. Apparently, the Chinese always wore watches in pairs, on the quaint grounds that when one went to sleep the other would still be awake. Certainly the invoices among the J.M. papers always mark watches as sold in pairs. There were at this time no Chinese watches.

[3] *Factory Records, China* (70), 6.4.1782; (86), 6.9.1787 and 2.11.1787.

agency, fitted out a small brig, the *Hanna*, with a cargo of iron bars to barter with the North American Redskins for furs. The venture was a financial success, but in order to exploit this new field—articles for which the Chinese would pay well were but rare—more capital was needed. In 1785, therefore, Cox and his Calcutta constituents founded the Bengal Fur Society, which sent several expeditions to 'Nootka' on the 'North-West Coast' (of America) to procure furs for Canton.[1] It thus seemed possible that the private British merchants would develop the China trade in a trans-Pacific direction. But during the Napoleonic Wars the fur trade to Canton passed into the hands of the Americans, bringing the Yankees to the Pacific coast and a fortune to John Jacob Astor.[2]

A less spectacular but more important development than trans-Pacific adventures in skins was Cox's success in enlarging his business as agent for the India merchants—important because it was at the expense of the private trade of the Company's Super-cargoes. In 1787 the Governor-General at Fort William, Bengal, wrote to the Select Committee at Canton that leading private merchants in India had complained to him 'of the obstructions that they have met with in their mercantile adventures at Canton ... they have ventured to assert that some of the Supercargoes have engaged in private trade, which they partly carry on under the name of Mr Cox, a free merchant, and in many instances make use of their influence to force private traders to buy and sell their opium and other commodities upon disadvantageous terms'.[3]

---

[1] Capt. J. Meares has left accounts of these voyages, which were not always successful. In 1789 two ships belonging to Cox's syndicate were seized at Nootka by the Spanish Government of Mexico. These ships were actually flying the Portuguese flag, because Cox found he could save $2,000 per ship if it anchored at Macao and the skins transferred to the next Country ship bound up-river for Whampoa, thus anticipating the practice of his successors forty years later, who used the same technique, except that the islands of Lintin and Hongkong were found more convenient than Macao. See below, Chapter III.

[2] K. W. Porter, *J. J. Astor*, Vol. I, Chapters 7-9; Vol. II, Chapters 13-16.

[3] E.I.C. *Factory Records, China* (82), 2.4.1788.

Thereupon they patronised Cox. 'The Select', taking the alarm, forced Cox to leave China, just as they had got rid of his predecessors. Legally, no private British could stay on.

But now a stratagem was devised to force the legal barrier. In 1779 a Scotsman named John Reid, whose service in the Bengal Marine had brought to his notice the possibilities of the China trade, had arrived at Canton with His Imperial Austrian Majesty's commission as Consul and head of the Imperial Factory. When presented with Austrian naturalisation papers, the Supercargoes decided it would be 'improper to give him any molestation'.[1] The Imperial Austrian Company went bankrupt eight years later and John Reid left China. But the device had worked politically if not financially; it was soon to be taken up by almost every 'private English' merchant.

In 1787 Daniel Beale, who had a share with Reid in the *Imperial Eagle*, which in 1780 sailed from Ostend to the North-West coast of America under Austrian colours, arrived in China armed with a commission as Consul for the King of Prussia. The firm of Cox & Beale was founded to take over the business of Cox and Reid. When therefore Cox was expelled by the Select Committee, the House remained, as Beale was protected by Prussian papers. Cox went back to Europe and, obtaining a commission in the Swedish navy, fitted out an armed brig, ostensibly to attack the Russian settlement at Alaska (the Russians and Swedes being then at war). Instead he cruised the Indian and Pacific Oceans in search of seal skins, which he brought to Whampoa in September 1791. When the Select Committee refused him permission to land, he hoisted Prussian (not Swedish!) colours. He died in the same year and was 'succeeded' by Thomas Beale, who had come out to join his brother, as Secretary to the Prussian Consul!

The Court of Directors of the Honourable East India Company were in a dilemma. They could not but be alarmed at this growth of a British firm at Canton masquerading under Prussian colours.

[1] *Chronicles*, II, 85.

On the other hand the Country Trade was becoming so vital to the Company that it had to be supported. In 1787, the year in which Daniel Beale came out, it supplied 53% of the funds needed for the Canton 'investment'; and in the same year the Governor-General of Bengal, Lord Cornwallis, wrote to the Select Committee that 'if any impediment was placed on its persecution, the consequence to the Company . . . is too obvious to need a comment, the loss of revenue to our settlements by the non-export of their commodities, the loss of supplies to China by the amount of such export being withheld from you, for it is not to be expected that the Indian Company can be enabled to furnish annually supplies in specie equal to your wants, nor can there be any other mode of furnishing your Treasury than by commodities of India being sold in China, but this trade cannot be carried on under a competition with the Company's agents there'.[1] As a way out of this dilemma the Select Committee decided, on the instructions of the Court in 1782, to provide its own machinery for carrying on the Agency business, by creating an official House of Agency for transacting private Country business on commission. Two junior members of the Factory, Messrs Drummond and Sparkes, were to manage it; one half of the profits were to be divided between them, and the other half among the rest of the Factory; the rates of commission were to be 3% on sales and purchases, 2% on bullion and remittances.[2]

This experiment of a Company's House of Agency was a complete failure. It was disliked by the other Supercargoes because it deprived them of their individual commission. It was resisted by the shippers of Country produce in India, who formed a combination to circumvent it, consigning their Country ships to the Beales. The Secret and Superintending Committee of the Supercargoes protested to the Court of Directors—'we thought it our duty in our public letters to Bengal and Bombay to touch on the danger as well as the impropriety of British subjects under your

[1] *Chronicles*, II, 141.   [2] *Ibid.* 196-7.

prosecution consigning to Foreign houses, particularly as a British House was established at Canton, competent to the business and under your sanction'. The protest was of no avail; in 1797 the commission earned was a mere $1,160. In 1796, when Messrs Drummond and Sparkes resigned from the management of the House of Agency, Messrs Parry and Williams were persuaded to undertake it only with difficulty. Within a short time the Company's House of Agency was abolished and the members of the Factory allowed to trade privately again.[1]

The failure of the House of Agency meant prosperity for Cox & Beale, a prosperity which soon attracted other private merchants to Canton. During the middle 'nineties two more Scotsmen, Robert Hamilton and David Reid, came out to form an agency partnership. The former was unprovided with foreign papers, and therefore never able to reside the whole year round in China. Reid informed the Committee that he held a commission as Captain of Infantry in His Danish Majesty's service 'and it is in consequence of orders from that court that I am now here'.[2] They were joined by one Alexander Shank, 'a free mariner' who, being without papers from a European state, was obliged to 'make the best way out . . . by short annual absences' from China, mostly in Malacca.[3] These newcomers apparently joined forces with Thomas Beale, who became Prussian Consul in 1797 when Daniel Beale left for England.

Daniel Beale's Prussian papers were almost inherited by the firm which became Jardine Matheson & Co. When Thomas Beale became Prussian Consul, Charles Magniac, who came out to China in 1801, acted as Prussian Vice-Consul, and his brother Hollingworth came out in 1811 as Secretary to the Prussian Consulate! James Matheson took out Danish papers, W. S. Davidson was a Portuguese subject, and Thomas Dent held a commission as Sardinian Consul. Robert Berry had Swedish

---

[1] On the House of Agency, see *Chronicles*, II, 196, 206, 285, etc.
[2] *Chronicles*, II, 206,   [3] *L.B.* 31.8.1806.

protection, Alexander Robertson, Sicilian. The partners of Ilberry Fearon & Co. were Hanoverian Consul and Vice-Consul. In 1794 one Dickerson claimed to be a representative of the almost extinguished Court of Poland; while in the same year another British-born merchant infuriated 'the Select' by informing them that he 'at present resided in China in the capacity of Vice-Consul for the Supreme Republic of Genoa'.[1]

The Jardine Matheson ledgers have survived from 1799, when the firm was Hamilton & Reid, in which Beale and Shank were also partners. In that year Hamilton died and in the following Reid went home. His place was filled by Charles Magniac, son of the Francis Magniac whose London 'singsong' establishment the elder Beale had joined on returning from China. (The further business history of the firm will be traced, with the aid of its surviving letter book and ledgers, in a later chapter.)

In this way, by the opening of the 19th century, one private 'Prussian' house was firmly established in China. The attempt of the Company to drive them out of the Country Trade by means of an official House of Agency had failed. But there was still commercial competition in this limited, though rapidly increasing, agency business from the junior Supercargoes dealing on their own account. Glimpses of these 'speculations by gentlemen of the Factory' appear in the early letter books of Beale & Magniac.

In 1807 one of the younger Baring Brothers, George, who was then a junior Supercargo at Canton, established a house of agency under the style of Baring & Co., which with the adhesion of two other Supercargoes became Baring, Moloney & Robarts.[2] This private firm was, like that of Lane, Lance & Fitzhugh in the

---

[1] Cf. the evidence of Davidson before the *S.C.H. of L.* 1830. A copy of Matheson's oath of allegiance to His Danish Majesty is preserved in the J.M. archives.

[2] These Barings were presumably related to Francis Baring, whose Chairmanship of the Court of Directors of the E.I.C. in 1793 may have contributed to his London House becoming interested in the China trade. But its connection with the Supercargoes is not clear.

1780s, within the orbit of the Company's Factory. When in 1799 the Chinese authorities definitely prohibited the import of opium, which had first been forbidden in 1729 but was now rapidly becoming a most important element in the Country Trade, the Court of Directors was faced with the necessity of deciding its attitude to the disposal of its Indian opium in China.[1] In 1809 it decided to prohibit its servants from acting as agents for the sale of opium. Mr Baring protested that his acting as agent for the proprietors of opium did not interfere with his duty to the Company; that the merchants of Bengal would otherwise consign their opium to the disreputable Portuguese. The Select Committee discussed the matter: 'Mr Pattle was of the opinion that this connection with the opium trade threw discredit on the Company, which could not dissever itself from the actions of its own servants; and declaring that Baring & Co. had coerced a Hong merchant, Manhop, into engaging in an opium transaction in which he was a heavy loser, he warned the Court that such an action was a real danger to the Company's interest. Mr Robarts ... declared his opinion that it was a great convenience to private traders that the Company's Supercargoes should act as their agents; that it had been found that the consignment of cotton to native, Parsee, or Moorish agents had been injurious to the trade of Canton; that opium should be consigned only to English agents over whose doings the Company could exercise absolute control; and that the Portuguese would welcome any change which would drive to Macao that part of the trade which now went to Canton'. The last word was had by Mr Branston, who was 'convinced that the Company's interests are suffering and have long suffered from private agencies and that the privilege should be abolished'.[2] Messrs Baring, Moloney & Robarts were forbidden to deal further in opium agency.

They did not, however, discard their firm, but invited W. S.

[1] The Company's opium policy is discussed in Chapter V.
[2] *Chronicles*, III, 79-80.

Davidson, who had visited China in 1807, to come out and join their establishment as manager of the opium department. Davidson, a native of Scotland, came out in 1811 as a naturalised Portuguese subject,[1] to enter the Baring firm on the basis of the commission on opium going to himself, and that of all other articles to his partners.[2] When the Court of Directors went further and in 1813, after 'capriciously changing its regulations two or three times', finally prohibited its Supercargoes from acting as India agents in *any* commodity, Davidson succeeded to the whole business, which became Davidson & Co., and later Dent & Co. Thus was established the second private British firm in China, and the great rival of Jardine Matheson & Co. until its failure in the 1860s. The success of these two houses attracted others; but the two pioneer firms dominated the private trade during our period, controlling some two-thirds of the whole. By 1831 there were five British firms and a dozen unattached individuals resident in China, besides the Parsees.

The Company had been forced to abandon the Canton agency of the Country Trade to thinly-camouflaged 'private English'. When in 1815 the Court of Directors made a last attempt to revive its House of Agency, none of the Supercargoes were willing to undertake it.[3] For the last twenty years of the Factory's existence, its members accepted as neighbours an increasing number of these 'free merchants'. That the two groups were able to live side by side was due above all to the fact that, except for the one article of Indian cotton imports, their business was not competitive but complementary. The private merchants were in practice confined to the Country Trade. Their trade on European account was negligible. 'Singsongs' soon lost their novelty: an attempt made by Alexander Shank in 1802 to carry on a 'Drug

---

[1] He maintained that he was a Portuguese subject in China only and not in England. *S.C.H. of L.* 1830, p. 453-4.
[2] Evidence before *S.C.H. of C.* 1830, Q.2500-2515.
[3] *Chronicles*, III, 231.

Concern', shipping rhubarb, etc., to London, failed through lack of lawful shipping.[1] They did extend their reach all over the Eastern seas in ventures to Manila and Java and the islands; and the Select Committee were persuaded to let them ship tea to Botany Bay, though not to the Cape, under licence from the Company. But their 'two grand staples' were articles of India produce, raw cotton and opium, whose increased import into China was very convenient to the Company, since the proceeds were paid into its Treasury in return for its Bills on India or London.[2] Until the last years of the Company's rule, this financial interdependence of the two groups of British merchants in China was the basic reason for their co-existence.

Personal relations were often close. Both groups, the Company's Supercargoes and the private merchants, were exiles in a distant land, and, even if undesired, social intercourse would have been impossible to escape. In later years, members of the Select Committee, on returning to England, often left their private financial arrangements in the hands of Magniac & Co., who furnished them with letters of credit and introductions to their numerous correspondents throughout the world. Not indeed that the relations of the two groups were ever altogether harmonious. An ever-present source of friction, which reflected their relative strength, was the degree to which the Select Committee could enforce its legal control of the Country ships which they licensed. In 1814, when 'the Select' took a stand against the Chinese, it stopped all British trade at Canton, including that of the protesting Country merchants.[3] Whereupon the merchants of Bombay complained against being forced to partake in this embargo, and wrote to the Lords Commissioners for India that 'for the successful prosecution of this trade [from Bombay] it is indispensably necessary that those concerned in it should not be subject to such interference or impediment as is calculated not

---

[1] See Chapter IV below.   [2] See Chapters I, VI.
[3] *S.C.H. of C.* 1830, Q.282-3.

only to diminish its advantage, but which in its exercise brings inevitable ruin upon the individuals engaged in it'.[1] The private merchants, having forced the opening of the India trade in 1813, were restive under the restrictions still imposed on the China trade. The Court of Directors retaliated by stiffening their 'licensing' regulations to Country ships and urging the Select Committee to enforce their statutory control over the 'private English' who remained in China. In 1816 the Committee attempted to deport a Mr Edward Watts, who claimed to be a naturalised Austrian, but who had been a partner in two Madras houses which had failed and subsequently was dismissed by Palmer & Co., the great Calcutta firm, for financial malpractice.[2] But even in this case the agents of the Company were powerless. After this rebuff the policy of the Court of Directors was to interfere as little as possible with the Country traders, but not to support them actively. In 1822 the Bombay house of Forbes & Co. asked the Select Committee to handle a consignment of their cotton, but met with refusal. In the same year the native, i.e. Parsee and Hindu, merchants of Bombay in vain petitioned the Select Committee to help them collect their debts from the Hong merchants. 'The Select' wrote to the Court of Directors: 'it would rather be our duty to protect the Chinese from the over-reaching abilities and craftiness of the Parsees'.[3] The Parsees were, of course, British subjects, but the age of Palmerston and Don Pacifico was not quite yet.

In the last decade of the Company's charter, the tables were gradually turned. The private merchants, increasingly strong in numbers at Canton and in influence in London, began boldly to criticise the policy of the Select Committee and flout its authority.[4] In 1825 James Innes scorned the protection of foreign papers. To the usual question enquiring under what authority he continued to stay in China, he replied that 'if the Gentlemen entrusted with

¹ *Chronicles*, III, 233.   ² *Ibid.* 254.
³ *Ibid.* IV, 55.   ⁴ See Chapter VII below.

the power *for the time* here, consider the non-residence of any British subject here necessary for the public good, they will enforce that non-residence against about 200 Parsees and 40 born Englishmen[1] equally as against me, and however I may suffer, I shall yield ready obedience to such authority and suffer in silence; but as it has been reported to several of the Directors that I came out here clandestinely and secretly, I feel very much gratified in having so direct an opportunity given me of contradicting this in the most decided manner'. The Committee capitulated, and some time afterwards wrote home 'we cannot but express our conviction that the residence of respectable individuals, British subjects, in China, is more desirable as far as the interests of the Honourable Company are concerned, than that of Foreigners over whom we have no control and into whose hands the conduct of the very important Trade in Opium and other branches of the commerce of India will necessarily fall, if British subjects are prohibited from forming commercial establishments for that purpose in Canton.'[2] In the last years of the monopoly, private merchants of 'great respectability' were allowed to reside without foreign diplomatic cover.[3]

It was, however, the later development of the opium trade which more than anything else placed the private merchants beyond the reach of the Company's Supercargo. The enormously augmented opium shipments were, after 1821, not smuggled into Canton river at all but disposed of at the 'outer anchorages'. Opium clippers from India would call at Lintin or run up the Eastern Coast of China without coming within observation range of the Factory. Chinese Governmental logic might hold the English 'Chief' responsible for the numerous affrays in which his country-

---

[1] A somewhat rhetorical estimate of the actual number of British residents, which was then under half that number.

[2] *Chronicles*, IV, 163-4. James Innes was evidently a man of spirit. In 1833 he was so annoyed at the Chinese Customs Commissioner, the *Hoppo*, that he deliberately set fire to his house. Truly a 'barbarian'!

[3] *S.C.H. of C.* 1830, Q.278.

men and their opium ships' crews were involved; but in fact the 'outside' locale of the opium trade, which had become by far the most extensive branch of the Country Trade, made the legal control of the Select Committee impossible to enforce. In 1833 the last Select Committee of the Canton Factory, angered by more than usually violent and provocative proceedings on the part of the commanders of two of Jardine Matheson's opium ships, the *Sylph* and the *Hercules*, suspended their licence. Their action in this 'grand contest', as William Jardine enthusiastically called it, was but a dying gesture.[1] 'They [the S.C.] have committed many other foolish acts this season for which they are laughed at by all, despised by many. So much for the expiring efforts of the Select.'

The conflict had deeper roots. Under cover of a legal subterfuge there had grown up at Canton a small but peculiarly compact merchant community of free traders, whose economic basis was the Country Trade with India. It therefore had standing behind it the great East India Agency Houses. These were a number of old and powerful firms of considerable standing in the City of London, with branch houses in India. They had originated in the late 18th century, when private merchants, following in the wake of British arms in India, had been allowed by the Company to carry on local trade. From small beginnings they had developed a composite trading, financial and shipping business with up-country connections, especially in Bengal, where they concentrated on indigo manufacture. This latter was perhaps the main pillar of their prosperity, as it was the cause of their partial collapse in 1829-33.[2] At the height of the indigo boom, in 1828, it was estimated that these Calcutta agency houses controlled some 12 lacs of acres of indigo plantations and nearly 300 indigo factories, giving subsistence to 500,000 native families whose annual produce was valued at £2-3 million above the £1¼

[1] *P.L.B.* of W.J. 2.10.33.   [2] See Chapter VI below.

million which it cost to keep them.[1] Indigo was, of course, not the sole component of the business developed by these agency houses; among the Bombay firms raw cotton was more important; opium later became their main preoccupation. The early history of these concerns is little known and perhaps never will be in any detail; but something will be said of their commercial and credit relations with the Canton houses in the chapter on the working of the Agency System.[2] Here the point to be stressed is the significance of this handful of East Indian concerns in the growth of the Canton trade.

Actually, the official East India Register lists no less than 29 'East India Agency Houses' as existing in 1803, 20 in 1811, 24 in 1818, 27 ten years later—to take four dates at random.[3] These figures are misleading since but few of these were the 'great houses'. Many were mere camp-followers of the British forces in the East—outfitters' establishments, passengers' agents, purveyors and the like. Others were small-fry in the commercial world, retired officers of the Company's marine, generally operating from the Jerusalem Coffee House, striving to turn their maritime connections into regular mercantile houses. The mortality among these minor firms was very high, but there was a core of some half dozen of old staple houses which, despite bewildering changes of names consequent on changes of partners and amalgamations, persisted—some for nearly half a century.

The two leading ones were the 'Fairlie' and 'Palmer' Houses. The former was founded by William Fairlie and John Fergusson, who came out to Calcutta in the 1780s. David Reid was a partner in the 'nineties before settling at Canton. This Calcutta firm, known successively as Fairlie Fergusson & Co., Fairlie Gilmore & Co., Fergusson Clark & Co., was closely associated with our Canton firm the Beale-Magniac, Jardine Matheson concern, right until its

---

[1] Evidence of Alexander & Co., quoted Phipps' *Indigo*.
[2] See Chapter VI.
[3] *E.I. Register*, India List, 1803.

failure in 1833. There was the same intimate relation with the London house, established at 9 Broad Street Buildings for forty years, originally as David Scott & Co., which became Fairlie Bonham & Co. on old William Fairlie's going home in 1812, and in 1832 Fairlie, Clark, Innes & Co. Its partners were men of influence. David Scott and Henry Bonham were M.P.s. The former was for a while a Director of the E.I.C., the latter a director of the E.I. Dock Company. The House of Palmer, which was founded by John Palmer, who also came out to Calcutta in the 1780s, was the close associate of the rival Canton firm, Dents. Their London house was even more long-lived than that of 'our Broad Street friends', being variously known as Palmer & Horsley, Palmer Mackillop & Co. of Throgmorton Street, Old Jewry and other addresses. At a later period, after 1834, Palmer Mackillop & Co. were one of the small group of powerful acceptance houses which competed with Barings for the financing of the American and China trades.[1] (A prominent member of the Palmer family was Horsley Palmer, Governor of the Bank of England in 1830, whose opinions on credit policy contributed to shape the Bank Charter Act of 1833.) Another old-established East India House was that known under the names of a list of successive partners, but with one single address —the Bruce, Bazett, Farquhar, Crawford, Colvin firm of 71 Old Broad Street, whose Bombay firm Bruce Fawcett & Co. (from 1815 Remington Crawford & Co.) was the main Bombay correspondent of Jardine Matheson's throughout our period. The rival Forbes House of Bombay and Mansion Court Place, London, engaged a similar relation with Dents. From 1815, for twenty years, Thomas Weeding, the first business associate of William Jardine, carried on Eastern trade from Old South Sea House. Other leading firms were: Rickards Mackintosh & Co., in whose Calcutta firm young James Matheson served his apprenticeship and which supported his first Canton establishment; Yrissari

[1] See Chapter VI below.

Matheson & Co., 1821-7;[1] Fletcher Alexander & Co., whose Calcutta firm owned 56 indigo factories in which £2 million was invested, before the crash; Gregson, Melville and Knight, who in the 1830s took a leading part in financing the silk trade from China. These were some of the great East India Houses.

What is important in this context is that this powerful interest was thrown behind the private merchants of Canton. The operative fact was that the China trade was essential to the India merchants as a means of profitable remittance to London. The Canton firms were largely outgrowths of these India houses, frequently stemming directly from them in personnel and capital, and being continuously associated with them in business transactions. It will be recalled that it was the action of the two Bengal firms in preferring to transact their Canton business through their own agents, Cox & Beale, which had defeated the East India Company's project of an official House of Agency and so made possible the existence of resident 'private English' in China. It was the powerful backing of the great East India Houses which enabled the Canton community to flourish and attain independence in its struggle against the Honourable Company's rule.

A second element of strength possessed by the private trade is to be found in the closely-knit character of its entrepreneurial personnel. It is a remarkable characteristic of the expansion of Britain's Eastern trade that it was largely developed by family and clan groups.[2] The reader will have noticed the preponderance of Scottish names among the partners of the great East India Houses. The lesser 'private English' engaged in the Country Trade were equally North British.[3] Of course there were some

---

[1] Mackintosh & Co. were 'our valued Calcutta friends under whose auspices our firm has been established'.—Y. & Co., 4.9.1822.

[2] These special family connections incidentally provide a clue to the prevailing type of organisation of the Eastern trade—the Agency System—see Chapter VI below.

[3] To select at random some of the smaller firms who dealt with J.M. during the period—A. Adamson, J. Leckie, Ritchie Stewart & Co., Burns MacVicar & Co.

who were not Scottish. But it was not unimportant that in this period the Eastern trade was so largely developed by Scotsmen, with family connections in every port east of the Cape, not to speak of relatives in the neighbourhood of Lombard Street. However deeply in contemporary Scottish society the remoter causes of this efflux are to be sought, its effects on the development of the China trade were evident. The 'free' branch of that trade was in the hands of a remarkable group of men, of modest birth but comparatively good education—some, like James Matheson, being graduates of Edinburgh University and similar academies[1]—all shrewd and conspicuously able, seeking a distant outlet for talents for which English church and society then had little use.

Moreover, even in the case of the Sassenachs entering the China trade, the ties of kinship were a cohesive force. Partners of one Canton firm during the period include two Beale and three Magniac brothers; two nephews of William Jardine and two of James Matheson became partners. When, in 1842, the articles of co-partnership of Jardine Matheson & Co. were redrawn, it was provided that the management of the concern should be vested in the immediate relatives of William Jardine and James Matheson. When James Matheson was setting up a third nephew, Hugh, as a Calcutta agent, he enthusiastically approved a connection with Charles Lyall, who had one brother in a London East India House and another in a Bombay firm. 'I consider them a thriving and united family'.[2] The family, acting as a unit of commercial enterprise, was valued as a source of strength.[3]

of Bombay, James Scott & Co., D. MacIntyre & Co. of Calcutta, Tulloch Brodie & Co. of Bombay, A. L. Johnstone of Singapore, etc., etc.

[1] A. Mackenzie, *History of the Mathesons*. About this period the Scottish Universities provided an education admittedly superior to anything south of the Border.

[2] *P.L.B.*, J.M., 4.11.1831.

[3] Kinship was not of itself sufficient to ensure a partnership. There was the case of young Francis Hollingworth, a cousin of the senior partner, 'Holly'

Another such source was the manner in which these entrepreneurs were recruited and trained. There were two fairly well defined routes for young aspirants to merchant prince-ship—one might almost say two royal roads from Scotland to Canton—the counting-house and the quarter-deck. Some, like James Matheson, were apprenticed in a commercial house in London and Calcutta; others, like William Jardine or his nephew Andrew Johnstone, served as surgeons or other officers in the Company's Indiamen.[1] In either case the future China merchant acquired a first-hand knowledge of Oriental peoples and ports, cargoes and commissions, and invaluable connections with others engaged in trade with the East.

The private merchant community which emerged in the early 19th century at Canton is to be seen as part of a wider social group, of remarkable strength and ability, well-fitted to wage battle against the Honourable but dotard East India Company.

In a book of *Hints on the China Trade* published in 1832 by a prominent official of the Company and quoted by the *Canton Register*, the organ of the 'free merchants' in China,[2] which had been founded by James Matheson in 1827 and was the first English newspaper to be printed in China, the following opinion was expressed: 'The free trade and the trade of the Company now move in different spheres, and except for some articles of import

Magniac, who was 'willing, well-disposed and desirous of making himself useful' at Canton. But 'Bell's *Life of London* was oftener in his hands than the books', and so William Jardine, who abhorred idleness, sent him home with a gratuity of £10,000. Hunter has a story of Jardine having no chairs in his office, to discourage loquacious callers.

[1] Matheson, after leaving Edinburgh University, spent two years in a London Agency House, and then entered the counting-house of his uncle's firm in Calcutta, Mackintosh & Co. Jardine was assistant surgeon on H.C.S. *Brunswick*, and surgeon on the *Glatton* and *Windham*, in which capacity he was entitled to 7 tons of 'privilege tonnage'; which both whetted his appetite and provided the capital for starting in the China trade. Johnstone was surgeon on the *Buckinghamshire* for many years while carrying on private trade with Canton.

[2] 5.12.1833. *The Canton Register and Price Current* was its full title.

from India to China, there does not appear any room for competition between them ... But the growth of a body of free adventurers under the wing of an exclusive commerce is not unlikely to lead to consequences of the first moment: and the division of British residents at Canton into two commercial classes so differently constituted and characterised cannot but add to the embarrassments incident to the relations between the British and the natives. The free traders appear to cherish high notions of their claims and privileges. Under their auspices a free press is already maintained at Canton;[1] and should they continue to increase, their importance will rise also. They will regard themselves as the true depositories of the principles of British commerce, and the feeling of submission which they now manifest towards the Company may gradually be expected to give place to one of rivalry if not of hostility'. This diagnosis of the situation in the last years of the Company's rule was, except for the word 'gradually', an accurate analysis.

[1] In the Indian Presidencies the free merchants had to fight hard against the Company to attain a 'free press' of their own. This censorship was the subject of an attack in one of the earliest issues of *The Canton Register*.

Chapter III

THE CANTON COMMERCIAL SYSTEM

When the private British merchants came to Canton they found themselves obliged to fit into the existing Chinese system of arrangements, commercial, fiscal and quasi-political. This system, which had become definitively crystallised and legalized by 1760 and which lasted with only one break until 1842, was highly peculiar. It therefore impressed travellers like Toogood Downing, who, along with such garrulous Old China Hands as Hunter, have given us detailed descriptions of the old, 'pre-treaty days' regime.[1] Moreover, this system so profoundly conditioned the 'old' trade and so obviously constituted that which the Treaty of Nanking sought to change that every writer on 'the opening of China' has had perforce to deal with it, however summarily. But these accounts have been distorted, even when elaborately drawn up as by Morse, because they have been based principally on the practice of the East India Company, whose position in and attitude to the Canton System differed in a number of ways from that taken up by the private merchants. Supplementary material for a more rounded picture, as well as a fresh angle of vision, is provided by the records of the 'free merchants'.

The Canton System was not the outcome of treaty or diplomatic restrictions, but arose entirely from a unilateral Chinese policy towards foreign trade and traders. The latter found that policy, the policy of the 'closed door' as it were, extremely irritating. They strove to explain this perplexing denial of the axiomatic benefits which exchange of 'goods' brought, by the

[1] C. Toogood Downing, *The Fan-qui in China, 1836-7.* 3 vols. W. C. Hunter, *The Fan-Kwai at Canton before Treaty days (1825-1844), Bits of Old China.*

perversity of the Chinese 'character'; thus founding a tradition of explanation in terms of jejune generalisations about oriental psychology, which has impaired most Western attempts at causal analysis of China's development. James Matheson begins his pamphlet by attributing the obnoxious restrictive policy of the Chinese to their 'marvellous degree of imbecility and avarice, conceit and obstinacy'.[1] The 'Letters to the Editor' columns of the earliest British newspapers in Canton are full of such sentiments as the following two propositions over the signature of 'Senex': 'The Chinese know no law except their own, no power beyond the precincts of their dominion. They will ever consider themselves the most superior nation in the world until convinced by some other argument than reason that this perhaps is not the case'.[2] Many modern Western writers on this period continue to attribute the Chinese 'sense of superiority and exclusiveness' to this 'isolation' from the European world.[3] Modern Chinese writers[4] have countered by pointing out that the early (16th and 17th century) policy of the Chinese Government to foreigners was generally one of tolerance and hospitality. In 1685 an Imperial edict opened all Chinese ports to foreign merchants, and it is significant that the first charter of the Canton Colony (i.e. as late as 1720) begins 'Foreigners and Chinese are members of one family . . . and must be on an equal footing'.[5]

Recent trends in international economic relations suggest that even in the West rigid control of foreign trade is the norm and 'free trade' a historical category. But the Parliamentary Committees of 1830 which examined the China trade were much agitated concerning 'the disposition of the Chinese as regards foreign trade'. In their evidence, the representatives of the East India Company thought the Chinese were 'decidedly anti-

[1] J. Matheson, *Present Position and Future Prospects of the China Trade*, 1836.
[2] *Canton Miscellany*, No. 2, 1831.   [3] See Eames, Morse, Eitel, etc.
[4] E.g. see Chang-Su, *China's Foreign Trade*, 1919.
[5] *Chronicles*, I, 164.

commercial', while the private merchants denied that the Chinese people were anti-commercial but only the Chinese Government.[1] The truth was that, however unflattering to the British merchants, foreign trade mattered very little indeed in the Chinese economy. Hart's dictum on China's self-sufficiency has already been cited. Writing of a much later period when the foreign trade had multiplied itself several times, the experts who drew up the Decennial Reports of the Chinese Maritime Customs (1922) declared that 'had the entire foreign trade of China suddenly ceased in 1877, the economic life of the country would have been affected but little'.[2] China's predominantly agrarian economy, in which 'forty centuries of farmers' supplied the bulk of their daily wants themselves and an urban small-scale manufacture of luxury goods provided for the consumption of the wealthy classes, extended over a sub-continent knit together by a huge internal commerce. On the whole, the Company's servants had understood this in a general way, though even their best Sinologist, J. F. Davis, admitted he knew little of the internal condition of China.[3] Marjoribanks, a former President of the Select Committee of Supercargoes at Canton, who had lived there for 17 years, declared that the 'Chinese were as independent as any Government in the world, of foreign trade'; and Davis concurred.[4] But the private merchants argued otherwise. Matheson thought China offered 'a vast field' for foreign trade. William Jardine was impressed by the fact that the stoppage of foreign commerce in 1829 affected many Chinese. He wrote to his Bombay agents: 'Much distress prevails in Canton, and the tea merchants with the silk weavers are becoming very discontented'.[5] It is true that by

---

[1] *S.C.H.* of *C.* 1830. See especially the evidence of Marjoribanks and Davis, lately of the Canton Factory, and of Crawford, Richards, Maxwell, etc.—private merchants.
[2] Quoted in Hubbard, *Eastern Industrialisation and its Effect on the West*, 1935.
[3] *S.C.H.* of *C.* 1830, 449.
[4] *S.C.H.* of *C.* 1830, see evidence of Marjoribanks and Davis, especially Q.275.
[5] W.J. to Remington & Co., Bombay, *I.L.B.* 5.11.29.

1830 certain groups, especially the tea cultivators in Fukien, the silk producers in the Nanking district and the craftsmen of Canton, together with their middlemen, had come to depend on foreign trade. And the question of the degree of China's dependence on foreign trade was already being raised in 1830 with the view to a British naval force exercising a blockade in the China seas. But the relative insignificance of that trade in the whole economy of China, and the fear that any large and abrupt expansion might disturb the internal equilibrium of a traditionalist order, constituted to the end the economic premises of the Manchu's restrictive policy.

When, in the early 18th century, the Chinese authorities found themselves faced with an ever-increasing number of Europeans, come from the ends of the earth to solicit the blessings of the Celestial Empire, the problem as it presented itself to them was not how to stimulate exports or imports. Unlike contemporary England, they had to contend with no rising and ambitious mercantile class striving for control of state policy. Their problem was to devise a system which would both bring in revenue to the receptive Imperial coffers and at the same time keep these uncouth alien *barbaroi* under control. The conduct of the latter was certainly calculated to turn hospitality into 'exclusiveness'. Marjoribanks, who was more unprejudiced than most Old China Hands, admitted 'the early part of our trade with China shows the commerce very ill-conducted and displays the English character to little advantage. The Portuguese, Spaniards, Dutch and English first appeared on the coasts of China as a race of men eagerly desirous of wealth, but careless of the means by which it was obtained. The Chinese were at all times their masters in the art of fraud and deception; but it cannot surprise that a people wisely estimating the advantages of peace as the first of blessings which can be bestowed upon a nation, should have regarded the early adventurers with the contempt and indifference they deserved'.[1]

<hr>

[1] *S.C.H. of C.* 1830, Q.704.

Much more alarming than the periodic violence of drunken English sailors at Canton was the spectacle of European expansion in Asia. The Spaniards had early on massacred forty thousand Chinese in the Philippines. British territorial acquisitions in India during the 18th century were not unknown to the Chinese. The war with Nepal, nominally a feudatory of China, brought the armed power of Britain to the backyard of the Middle Kingdom.[1] The Select Committees of both Houses of Parliament were worried as to the effect of the Indian and Burmese wars upon the Chinese treatment of the British at Canton. Davis stated that it caused the Chinese to hold the English in 'especial distrust'. As early as 1717 the Emperor Kang Hi had warned: 'There is cause for apprehension lest in centuries or millenniums to come China may be endangered by collision with the nations of the West'.[2]

The easy assumptions of the Europeans as to China's 'isolation' from the outside world merely reflected their ignorance of the whole rhythm of Chinese history.[3] For centuries China had been subjected to periodic pressure from the north; barbarian invasion was a permanent threat, to meet which the Great Wall had been built. The Westerners who came in ships were 'sea-barbarians'; their way of life was even more alien and disturbing to Chinese civilisation than that of the northern barbarians. A Great Wall had to be erected against the invaders who came by sea. In view of the notorious naval weakness of the Manchus,[4] underground internal opposition within the Empire, and the lack of an adequate legal system[5] to deal with aliens (who, in the words of the notice

[1] *Ibid.* 529-31.

[2] Quoted in Tsun's Memorial to the Emperor in 1835, cited in J. Slade, *Narrative*, Appendix V, p. 23.

[3] See Owen Lattimore, *Inner Asian Frontiers of China.*

[4] It had been demonstrated in the 17th century in the troubles with Koxinga in Formosa.

[5] Under the Chinese principle of devolution of responsibility each community of foreigners was expected to manage its own affairs under a Headman of their own choosing who was held to be responsible for compelling his nationals to conform to the Chinese laws.

posted up annually in the foreign Factories at Canton, found it 'very difficult to understand the proprieties of the Celestial Empire'), a 'restrictive' policy seemed imperative. Political considerations reinforced economic in urging that the door be closed; possibly not altogether as in Japan,[1] but within the bounds of the elaborately regulated Canton 'security' system.

The Canton System was gradually shaped by a process of trial and error over half a century, though it was more particularly legalised within the five years 1755-60. The several stages of its early development, the various Imperial and local decrees, the efforts of the Company's Supercargoes to resist the imposition of the system, have been chronologically set forth in the standard works of Morse and others. But these deal inadequately with certain aspects of the system as it worked in its full development, from its revival in the 1780s to its abolition by the Treaty of Nanking. Over half a century of the working of any institution would need more than a chapter for full analysis. The following is therefore confined to a consideration of some salient features which are brought out by a reading of the J.M. papers.

The system had two aspects: the confinement of foreign trade to Canton, and the detailed arrangements, of which the Cohong was but the central institution, at that place. Canton was chosen by the Chinese as being situated in the extreme south-eastern corner of the Empire, in a province which was geographically cut off from the rest of the Empire. There were two exceptions to the rule that foreign traders must resort only to Canton. Macao, a small peninsula at the entrance of the Canton River estuary, had been since 1557 a Portuguese settlement.[2] Its status was not clear;

---

[1] Even the Japanese allowed the Dutch to send two ships a year to Nagasaki. When Jardines wanted Japan copper they had to send to Batavia and buy it from the Dutch there.

[2] Cf. Morse, *International Relations*, I (iii) 1-6. It was apparently granted as a reward for Portuguese assistance in suppressing pirates. The Portuguese did not assert full sovereignty over Macao until the middle of the 19th century. The

as far as trade was concerned there were both Portuguese and Chinese duties to be paid. The Portuguese were not allowed to trade elsewhere, nor were any other foreigners legally permitted by the Chinese to trade at Macao.[1] The British used it mainly for residential and social purposes, escaping thither from Canton during the slack season, April to September, which indeed they were compelled to do by Chinese regulation. Any British private trade at Macao had to be handled by Portuguese agents.[2] The Portuguese were never very friendly to the British, especially after 1808, when Macao was occupied by Admiral Drury, allegedly to anticipate the French. Commercially, its main importance in the British trade was in connection with the disposal of opium. In the 1820s a very interesting fiscal war developed between the Portuguese and British opium interests, which will be examined more fully in Chapter VI. Towards the close of the pre-treaty régime Macao had almost completely decayed as a commercial centre; it was finally killed by the development of Hongkong.

Amoy, a much more substantial port giving access to the tea-growing province of Fukien, was open to Spanish trade only. But the right was merely nominal, because Chinese junks could transport goods to and from the Philippines much more cheaply than could the Spaniards. The latter had practically given up the trade; only one Spanish ship put in at Amoy between 1810 and 1830.[3] James Matheson, who laid the foundations of his fortune as junior partner in a Spanish firm, Yrissari & Co., sent a ship, the *San Sebastian*, Captain J. Mackie, to Amoy in 1823 under Spanish colours. But since her cargo was mainly contraband

Portuguese Governor had to pay an annual rent to the Chinese and there was a resident Mandarin. See also Cordier, III, 132.

[1] See letter to *Canton Register* by 'Macaista', 24.3.1833.

[2] The agent at Macao of Jardine Matheson & Co. was for many years a certain B. Barretto, who received a commission. But they had extensive dealings with other Portuguese at Macao, especially Payva & Company.

[3] *S.C.H. of C.* 1830, 170, 389. Another witness said the Spaniards had given up the Amoy trade since 1800. (455).

opium she could hardly expect to avail herself of the legal facilities given to Spaniards at that port. Actually, when the ship left Amoy after four days' stay, 'a deputation of mandarins followed us seven miles out of the port to entreat our return'.[1] Matheson, with an eye on new markets, seriously considered 'instituting a speculation from Manila to Amoy', but the project fell through, chiefly because of his preoccupation with opium. There had been one earlier attempt by 'private English' to trade with Amoy. In November 1806 Beale and Magniac chartered the *Anna Felix*, presumably under the Spanish flag, to take a cargo of Indian raw cotton to Amoy on joint account with a Chinchew merchant living at Canton, 'who gave expectations of it being a very profitable concern, under management of a relative of his' at Amoy. The price anticipated was considerably higher than that prevailing at Canton; but there were difficulties at Amoy, where the Mandarin wanted a huge fee, and the ship returned without making a sale.[2]

A much more important inroad into the foreign trade monopoly at Canton than either Macao or Amoy could ever offer was made by the development of a contraband trade on a huge scale at the 'outer anchorages' after 1821. In that year the Chinese governmental authorities succeeded in driving the opium trade from Whampoa. The private merchants, led by James Matheson, proceeded to remove their opium vessels to the island of Lintin, which together with other 'outside' anchorages such as Camsingmoon and, later, Hongkong remained the centre for opium distribution until the advent of Commissioner Lin in 1839. Removed from proximity to the Canton officials this illicit trade developed enormously, multiplying itself more than five times in little over a decade. This trade, and also the illicit trade up the East Coast of China (which developed a little later but was dependent upon

---

[1] *L.B.* of Y. & Co. 2.9.1823.
[2] See two more letters to Fairlie Gilmore & Co., Calcutta, dated 20.10.1806 and 11.11.1806, and marked 'private and secret'. They are attached to the *L.B.* 1804–6.

supplies from the receiving ships stationed permanently at Lintin) were outside the Canton System.

Moreover, it was not only opium which was smuggled at Lintin. There were a whole number of other articles upon which the Chinese placed restrictions. Thus, the export of silver bullion (sycee), which was vital to the Country Trade,[1] was in most years not permitted. In the early days the private merchants had to smuggle it from Canton under great risk. In 1810, for example, the private merchants had had to resort to smuggling sycee 'in Laskars' turbands (sic) and clothes'.[2] After 1821 the Chinese would, for a consideration, deliver it aboard the Lintin ships with facility. Again, the export of metals from China was prohibited. A partial exception was tutenag, a kind of Chinese zinc, which was very valuable as one of the few China goods suitable for remittance to India (until the competition of spelter from Europe ruined the market), and which was permitted to be exported, but only in inadequate quantities. In 1810 Beale and Magniac wrote: 'The tutenag has been got on board luckily without detection. We are not supposed to know anything about it: as it is on board however, we hope it will make a good remittance'.[3] But with the advent of the Lintin ships, these transactions were less hazardous and more extensive. One more instance—saltpetre. This article could be imported and sold in China only to the Government Salt Hong at Canton. But the salt merchants naturally paid a lower price than could be fetched in the open market. The private merchants would, therefore, frequently retail it to smugglers, often in quite small quantities, from one of the ships permanently stationed at Lintin.[4] Finally there are numerous instances in the

[1] See Chapter IV; and cf. William Jardine to Jamsetjee Jeejeebhoy, *P.L.B.* 4.2.1837. 'Without sycee or gold as remittances to India we should never be able to get on'.
[2] *E.L.B.* 10.1.1811. The sycee 'must all be smuggled under no small danger of detection and seizure'.
[3] *E.L.B.* 11.3.1810. To F. Cowasjee, Bombay.
[4] *I.L.B.* 13.3.1828, and passim.

J.M. papers of ordinary, legal articles of export and import being smuggled via Lintin to avoid the duties payable at Canton.

It is thus evident that a very large proportion of the British trade had, after 1821, been removed from the orbit of the Canton System; how large can be seen from the fact that, in the last decade before 1842, opium alone constituted about two-thirds of the value of all British imports into China.[1] *The Canton Register* gave a list of 38 Country ships which came to China in 1832 and went no farther up-river than Lintin.[2] In addition there were several 'hulks', such as the *Hercules*, which remained anchored at Lintin year after year. The servants of the East India Company refused themselves to partake in this violation of Chinese law; although in 1832 they sent the *Lord Amherst* to open up markets along the East Coast. And when on one occasion the Select Committee participated in the smuggling of sycee by receiving a large amount from Jardines they were censured by the Court of Directors the following year.[3] But the private merchants, it is clear, had, long before new ports were forced open by Treaty in 1842, nullified in a large measure the Chinese restriction of foreign trade to Canton.

To turn now to the second aspect of the 'old' system, the regulations concerning the conduct of foreign trade at Canton itself, and in particular the celebrated Cohong. 'That perfect and wonderful organisation' as Hunter called it,[4] has naturally evoked considerable discussion. It has been likened to the medieval

---

[1] Thus in 1832, a typical 'sample' year, out of $18¼ million imported into Canton on private account, $12,185,000 represented opium. The Company's import was $4 million, none of which, of course, was opium. *Chronicles*, IV, 339: see statistical appendices.

[2] *Canton Register*, 11.2.1834. This figure included several famous opium clippers, the *Red Rover*, *Water Witch*, *Sylph*, *Falcon* and others which made the journey from India two or even three times in the season.

[3] *I.L.B.* 7.11.1832.

[4] *Fan-Kwai at Canton*, p. 153.

European merchant gild,[1] and alternatively to the later Regulated Companies.[2] But though similar in some ways to both, the Cohong was fundamentally different. It was not the outcome of a rising commercial class fighting for trade privileges. Membership of the Cohong was regarded as a burden not a privilege. Merchants were induced by the Chinese Government to join often with the greatest difficulty.[3] Bankruptcies were very frequent, and the survivors were eager to retire from the Cohong as soon as they decently could.

Thus, old Puankequa, who had been Hong merchant since 1788 and Senior since 1796, tried with difficulty to retire in 1808. Old Mowqua tried in the same year and again in 1810. Howqua tried in 1810 and in 1826, and again in 1832, but went on until his death in 1843.[4] The original Howqua who founded the Hong carried on by his relative the great Howqua (who afterwards became the Senior Hong Merchant), rather than become a Hong Merchant, absconded for some time; 'as a punishment for which he is compelled to be a salt merchant which will probably ruin him very shortly'. Toogood Downing tells a story of a fat jovial ex-compradore, named Ahming, who in 1836 was induced to become a Hong merchant and 'soon withered away'.

Nor was the Cohong strictly a monopolist company, a kind of opposite number to the East India Company, as so many writers have implied. Its organisation was very loose indeed.[5] It had no joint stock: each merchant traded on his own account for his own Hong or firm,[6] on his own capital, for his own profits. It rarely

---

[1] By Morse, in his well known essay on *The Gilds of China;* he elaborates the parallel with the 'staple', whose merchants were used as a revenue device by the Crown.

[2] Pritchard, *Crucial Years*, p. 140.

[3] *Chronicles*, II, 82, Vol. III, Ch. 6.

[4] *Ibid.* III, 38, 110, 135; IV, 132, etc.

[5] 'Cohong' is the pidgin-English corruption of the Chinese for foreign *associated* merchants. Cf. Latourette, Chapter 1.

[6] A list of the last merchants of the Cohong prior to its abolition in 1842 is given in the Appendix. This gives the familiar pidgin name by which the merchants

C

(never in its dealings with the foreign private merchants) followed a policy of corporate bargaining; though an Imperial decree of 1780 had directed that it do so. In the season 1813-4 the Chinese Government attempted to remodel the institution by empowering the two or three senior Hong merchants to control the business of the whole, fixing prices, etc. But this measure the Supercargoes successfully resisted by stopping the British trade. In the J.M. ledgers the various Hongs have quite separate accounts with different folio numbers. On occasion, one Hong would take advantage of the temporary embarrassments of another.[1] Jardine wrote: 'The Hong merchants cannot trust each other in any combination'.[2] In their business dealings with the foreigners their corporate character was evident only in one respect. If the losses of any particular Hong merchant were such as to make him insolvent, the Cohong would assume collective responsibility for the repayment of foreign creditors out of the 'Consoo' fund. This latter, which was financed by a 3% levy on the foreign trade, was used for other collective purposes, such as sending presents to the Emperor and the Government officials.[3] It was not automatically applied in the case of insolvency, but had to be sanctioned each

were known to Europeans generally suffixed with the honorific QUA, together with their real family and business names. Actually the Hongs consisted of firms, not individuals. These often had several partners, generally brothers or other relatives. These were often distinguished by the British merchants as e.g. 'Mowqua number 1 brother', or sometimes facetiously referred to by names of well-known English public figures—thus the elder Chunqua was always called 'Lord Melville' in Jardine's letters to H. Magniac.

[1] *I.L.B.* 27.8.1823.   [2] *P.L.B.* 22.10.1837.

[3] The Consoo Fund was first instituted in 1780 because of the great financial difficulties in which the Hong merchants found themselves. It was originally a 3% *ad valorem* duty (increased in emergencies to 4%-6%) on all goods, both imports and exports, except woollens, calicos and iron. These last exceptions were due to the fact that when the Fund was first instituted, Puankequa the First, the then head of the Cohong, had a monopoly in these articles and was able to secure their exemption from the tax. It was a perpetual source of grievance that this Fund was often raided by the Mandarins for other purposes, to finance the repair of the Yellow River dykes, or build fortifications, etc.

time, and only if the debt were above 100,000 taels.[1] The Cohong was hardly a gild merchant and not quite a Regulated Company. It was a loose association of merchants given the monopoly of the foreign trade in order to control it by means of the 'security' system. They were often termed 'security' or 'mandarin merchants', and acted together in enforcing control but not in carrying on trade.

The few merchants who were members of the Cohong[2] (their maximum number was 13, but they were often depleted, sinking to four in 1782, five in 1791, and in 1828 to seven, of whom only three were really solvent) were the only legal means of carrying on foreign trade at Canton. But their monopoly was limited to staple articles. There were, in addition, a large body of 'outside' merchants, called 'shopmen', who were permitted to retail small personal articles to the foreign traders. Now in practice, while the agents of the East India Company kept to the law, the 'private English' and the Americans began to find it profitable to deal with these 'shopmen' in staple goods such as silks, nankeens, and even teas. Since, however, the Hong merchants were obliged to be *fiadors* for every ship which came to Whampoa and be responsible for the customs duties on every article of cargo, the shopmen had to carry on their illegal trade under cover of a *bona fide* Hongist 'security merchant'. This was made possible by the fact that the junior Hong merchants who lacked capital often formed connections with shopmen and allowed shipments from their own Hongs on account of these 'outsiders'.[3] In one of the earlier surviving letters of Reid and Beale, a Madras merchant is informed that his Indian piece goods, including muslin, and his redwood have been disposed of 'to outside people who do not wish to appear in the business; the duties are paid by the security merchants who charge them to us'.[4] In 1801 the firm wrote to its then Bombay agent as follows: 'It has

---

[1] This limit was not adhered to. *S.C.H. of C.* 1830, Q.683.
[2] *Chronicles*, II, 82, 190; IV, 173, 209.
[3] *S.C.H. of C.* 1830, Q.683.   [4] *L.B.* 10.12.1800.

been a long and universal custom here to purchase goods from outside merchants, but more particularly the articles commonly called "Drugs"[1] in which they deal much more than the Hong merchants; from whom we cannot get these things with the same advantage. There have often been temporary stoppages to this trade, which is certainly not fully authorized by the laws of this port—an outside merchant must always ship off his goods under a Hong merchant's *chop*, or name—yet custom sanctions it, and application is made even in the name of the real vendor of the goods to the Linguist and Hong merchant who is to ship them off, and who both connive at the business from the fees they receive by it'.[2] Chinaware was likewise bought directly from 'the China-Street people', and a letter of 1804 speaks of a cotton contract with an outside man 'of considerable property and respectability'.[3] William Jardine's diary of 1822 shows that when he first settled in China he bought more goods from the outside men than from the Hongists. Matheson, who had direct connections with the 'Chinchew men', certainly bought a good deal from the unauthorized shopmen in Canton.[4] It was the Americans above all who dealt 'very extensively' with the outside merchants.[5] The great Boston firm of Perkins had a particularly large business in silk piece goods with an 'outside man' named Yeshing.

From time to time the Chinese Local Authorities, the Viceroy or less often the *Hoppo* (Customs Officer), took action to stop this violation of the legal monopoly of the Cohong. The shopmen were able to sell 'China goods' more cheaply than the Hong

---

[1] 'Drugs' means rhubarb, cassia buds, camphor, etc., in which the firm were carrying on a flourishing trade, and not 'opium', which is often referred to as 'the drug'.

[2] *L.B.* 6.11.1801, to A. Adamson, Bombay.

[3] *Ibid.* 14.11.1804.

[4] Y. & Co. 18.7.1825. The ledgers of Magniac & Co. show considerable accounts with shopmen were kept, though I have not worked out what proportion of total purchases they formed.

[5] See evidence of Coffin and other Americans. *S.C.H. of C.* 1830, and Hunter, *Fan Kuae*, p. 35. *I.L.B.* 26.7.1830.

merchants because they were not subject to as many financial impositions as the latter. In 1817 over 200 'outside' shops were closed down and their goods confiscated.[1] In 1820 Matheson wrote to his Calcutta agent: 'A serious blow has been given to the Country trade from India by a resolve on the part of the Hong merchants to refuse passing for exportation, as customary, the goods of outside merchants, who have for a long time had a principal share in the trade for manufactured articles, carried on especially by the Parsees. In consequence three Bombay ships have been detained for three months, but a compromise has been reached ... hereafter these individuals (shopmen) will only be permitted to transact such business as the Hong merchants shall deem to be inconsiderable for themselves'.[2] In fact, however, during the next four years the foreign trade of the shopmen increased, partly because the Americans began to import quantities of British manufactures which they bartered with the shopmen for teas.

This last development angered the East India Company, because it touched a sensitive spot. British manufacturers who were clamouring against the Company's monopoly were soon using the American success in selling British goods to the Chinese as a stick wherewith to beat it. In March 1828 the Committee of Supercargoes decided to take up this question of the illegal trade with the shopmen — 'a system pernicious to our interests'. An agreement was reached with the rump of seven Hong merchants that whichever of them should cover a shopman's dealings should lose a share of his tea contract with the Company.[3] But the American and 'private English' were now strong enough to force the Hong merchants to continue their old practice. Whereupon the Select Committee addressed the Viceroy and *Hoppo*, urging them to pronounce on the legality of the outside trade; pointing

[1] *S.C.H. of C.* 1830, Q. 1263.
[2] *L.B.* of Taylor and Matheson, 14.11.1820.
[3] *Chronicles*, IV, p. 169 *et seq.*

out that a decision favourable to that trade 'materially alters the character of the commerce of this port', but one which supported the old system would strengthen the hand of the Cohong. The Americans, Talbot, Olyphant, Russell and the rest, retorted with a rival address to the Viceroy and *Hoppo*, accusing the Select Committee of instigating action prejudicial to all but the Company's interest. It begins: 'We have always been in the habit of buying teas, silks, nankeens and other articles from shopmen or Hong merchants as we pleased', and goes on to argue that the Hongists have not sufficient capital to carry on all the foreign trade of Canton. The Viceroy replied rejecting the American petition, and confirming the old rule that shopmen were to sell only the petty articles originally allowed them, which included neither tea nor silk nor nankeen cloth. However, further pressure, exerted by both the Americans and the 'private English', was sufficiently strong to force a compromise. A 'Proclamation concerning trade carried on by Shopmen' from Le, Governor of Canton, and Yen, *Hoppo*, was issued on 14 July 1828, which modified the existing law.[1] Hong merchants were to retain their monopoly of most of the leading articles of foreign trade. There were now enumerated 24 categories of exports, including tea, raw silk, nankeens, etc., and 53 of foreign import, including woollen and cotton goods, raw cotton, furs, etc. All other commodities might be handled by the shopmen, including, as a concession, two major articles—Chinese silk piece goods and imported white (cotton) goods. But the shopmen were still to trade under the aegis of the Hong merchant, who could thus ensure the collection of the customs and the 'security' of the ship. The edict concluded by warning foreigners that the Cohong was not responsible for the debts of insolvent shopmen as it was for those of Mandarin merchants. Both the Americans and the 'private English' continued to trade extensively with the 'outside men', to the

---

[1] It is printed in full in *The Canton Register* of 2.8.1828. The American memorial is preserved in MS. in the J.M. archives.

anger of the Company and the detriment of the Hong merchants. In this way, the restrictive Cohong monopoly was in practice modified by regular recourse to the 'outside' merchants, just as the confinement of trade to Canton was modified by the use of the 'outside' anchorages—both breaches being forced by the 'free' foreign merchants.

But there were other restrictions in the Canton System, commercial and personal, which were not always so easily evaded. First, there were the minute rules regarding shipping in the Canton river; the necessity for getting permits to sail up the river, of using only official 'chop-boats' to convey goods over the twelve miles between the anchorage at Whampoa and the Factories at Canton, of securing the 'Grand Chop' from the Customs Officer (the *Hoppo*) before finally leaving. Then there was the compulsion to employ official 'linguists' to interpret and to make up lists of goods shipped, etc.; and 'compradores' for managing domestic arrangements and safeguarding the 'treasure'—each private merchant having his own strong-room in those bank-less days; and the inevitable 'shroff' to test the touch of bullion and coin. These regulations and others more detailed are given with a wealth of loving detail in the contemporary 'commercial handbooks' written by men with personal experience of the China trade, such as Milburn and Phipps.[1] Of the restrictions on particular commodities we have noted the most important; the import of opium was always, the export of silver sycee generally, prohibited, as was that of most metals. Saltpetre could be sold only to the Hong of the salt merchants; silks could be exported only in small quantities, the maximum being 100 pieces per ship, and when the European demand was brisk there was feverish competition among the foreign merchants to buy up each other's 'privilege'. Rice imports were endowed by a paternal Government, mindful of China's periodic famines, with the magic quality of giving immunity from the chief ('measurement') port duty—provided

[1] A succinct account may be found in Morrison's *Commercial Guide*, pp. 9-18.

nothing but rice was brought.[1] This immunity was ingeniously used, by the device of transhipment at Lintin, to secure exemption for many most varied cargoes.

Finally there were those irksome personal restrictions, the famous 'Eight Regulations'.[2] Briefly, they defined the conditions of residence in the Factories and the method of communicating with the Chinese authorities; they forbade loans to be granted to Chinese merchants, foreign women and guns to be brought to Canton, or warships to enter the Bogue. These points were vigorously taken up as grievances by the private merchants in their efforts to persuade the British Government to demand redress. They have accordingly received expatiatory treatment from every writer on China's international relations. From the commercial standpoint, however, the crux of the matter was the actual mode of trading within the Canton System.

Outstanding feature of the manner of trading was the sharp distinction between the practice of the East India Company and that of the private merchants. Both bought and sold and contracted for exports and imports without written agreement from the Hong merchants at prices which included all duties. The extent of these charges were often unknown to the foreign merchant;[3] and when the Hong merchants acted as brokers—as they did to an increasing extent in the last days of the system—they acted as guarantors for both the Chinese and the foreign parties. But whereas the Company tended to treat the Cohong as a unit, apportioning its tea contracts in twenty-one shares among the Hongists according to seniority, and fixing the same price for all,[4] the private traders on the other hand dealt separately

---

[1] *I.L.B.* 15.3.1831, and elsewhere.

[2] These regulations are printed in full in *The Canton Register* of 15.7.1831.

[3] *S.C.H. of L.* 1830, p. 459. For Hong merchants as brokers, see *I.L.B.* 21.4.1831, etc.

[4] *S.C.H. of C.* 1830, Q.1213. 4 shares of its contract teas went to the Chief Hongist, 3 shares to each of the next four, and 2½ shares to the two junior. This scheme varied according to the numbers and solvency of the Hong merchants.

for each ship's cargo with whichever Hongist would give them the best price. Morse is wrong when he suggests that consignees could sell only to the Hong merchant who 'secured' the ship.[1] In fact, many of the Country ships had on board goods consigned to different Canton agents, who were free to sell their consignments to any of the Hong merchants; though the practice grew up of compensating the security merchant with a fixed sum ($700) for his expenses and risk in securing a ship without being able to profit from its cargo.[2] Certain Hong merchants who had established a close connection with a particular foreign agent might secure the same ship season after season. Naturally, certain foreign merchants would in time come to establish special relations with one or more Hongists. Thus, the Magniac-Jardine-Matheson House was especially friendly with Mowqua, Manhop and, later, Hangtai, until the failure of the two latter Hongs in 1828 and 1836 respectively. Howqua was their *bête noir*, because he preferred to trade with the Americans and was wealthy enough to command the market, and at times do what few Hongists were ever prepared to do—send goods directly to Europe in chartered ships on his own account.[3]

Secondly, the Company would in practice barter its British and Indian imports for teas. Though the representatives of the Company in their evidence before the Select Committee of 1830 attempted to deny this 'trucking', as it was called, yet it is evident from the *Chronicles* that the prices paid by a Hongist for, say, woollens were determined by the prices the Company paid him for his teas.[4] In the 18th century the Company actually shared out the proportion of its various imports, the practice being

[1] *International Relations* I, Chapter 4.   [2] *I.L.B.* 5.1.1825, 2.7.1832.
[3] Howqua had business relations with Baring Brothers, London; but his main agents were the Boston house of Perkins through its Canton partner, J. P. Cushing, and after 1829 Russell & Co. For the hostility with which J.M. & Co. regarded Howqua, see the evidence of Alexander Matheson in the *Report of the S.C. of the H. of C. (opium)*, 1840.
[4] *S.C.H. of C.* 1830, Q.342, 573, 2137.

later dropped.[1] But the private merchants, mainly because their chief import, opium, was almost always sold for cash, and also because their tea purchases until the end of the Company's monopoly in 1834 were negligible, rarely practised 'trucking'.[2]

Thirdly, whereas the Company's goods which were branded with the Company's mark were accepted without question, the Country traders, whose numbers increased annually, were not always trusted by the Hong merchants to deliver good-quality goods. It therefore became the practice for the private merchants to sell less by contract and more by muster.[3] Finally, the Company, in obedience to the Chinese law, dealt entirely through the Hong merchants. The 'private English' on the other hand carried on the major part of their business outside the Cohong, in the 'outer' anchorages; while at Canton they dealt extensively with the shopmen.[4] Thus, in practice, their manner of trading militated against the private merchants' fitting as snugly into the Canton Commercial System as did the Honourable Company.

How, then, did the Canton System as a whole, with its modifications of practice, appear to the foreign merchant? Almost all the witnesses before the all-important Select Committee of the House of Commons on the China Trade of 1830 were agreed that business could be despatched with greater ease and facility at

---

[1] Thus in 1795 Puankequa, head Hong merchant, was required to have two-thirds of the tin and one-quarter of the woollens which the Company had brought that season. *Chronicles*, II, 268.

[2] At times when the opium market collapsed, the drug was occasionally bartered for goods, but mainly by the Parsees—Y. & Co. 26.10.1823. In the Patna crisis of 1822, Matheson reported to Calcutta that Charles Magniac was underselling him by 'trucking'.—4.9.1822, Y. & Co.

[3] This led frequently to 'no little altercation', as in the case of Cowqua in 1806. *L.B.* 8.9.1806.

[4] On only one or two isolated occasions did the Hong merchants have direct connections with opium, after the definitive prohibition of 1799. Thus in 1819 Manhop was security for Davidson's notorious opium vessel *Mentor*, and in 1830 Mowqua is mentioned as having a share in a large opium concern at Canton. *P,L.B.* of W.J. 7,12.1830, and *S.C.H. of C.* 1830, 2577.

Canton than anywhere else in the world.[1] This unanimity of Company, 'private English' and American testimony is conclusive. The honesty and commercial integrity of the distant Hong merchants were a byword in the alleys of the City of London as in the bazaars of Bombay. One who traded with them for twenty years wrote: 'As a body of merchants we found them able and reliable in their dealings, faithful to their contracts, and largeminded. The monopoly they enjoyed could not have been in the hands of a more able, liberal or genial class of men'.[2] Written contracts only became necessary in the China trade after the Treaty of Nanking, once the Cohong was abolished.

The system, therefore, worked well normally. But there was one flaw—indeed a symptom rather than a cause—which made the Cohong system undesirable in the eyes of the foreign traders. The Hong merchants very frequently became insolvent. Bankruptcy was considered by the Chinese Government 'degrading and even criminal';[3] in the case of a Hong merchant it involved severe punishment and generally transportation to 'Eli' on the frozen frontiers of Central Asia.[4] There were three major crises of this kind in our period.

[1] *S.C.H. of C.* 1830. Aken (1892), Davidson (1592), Bates (3203), Maxwell (3205) and of course the Company's men, Marjoribanks and Davis.

[2] Hunter, *Fan-Kwai*, p. 40. The only case of dishonesty I have come across was in 1827, when the desperate Manhop on the brink of ruin fraudulently removed $60,000 worth of cotton belonging to Magniac & Co. to pay off his Chinese creditors. See *I.L.B.* 1827, 3 Feb.—an angry letter written by Jardine at 2 a.m. in which he declares his intention of addressing himself to the Viceroy directly on the subject. In a letter of 27.6.1828 it is mentioned that the Viceroy had answered by threatening Jardine with every manner of rough treatment should he again venture to address His Excellency on such a subject.

[3] Hunter, *op. cit.*, p. 38.

[4] For a case of severe punishment of a bankrupt Hongist which resulted in death, see *Chronicles*, II, 278. But Manhop in 1829 took his departure for 'Eli' 'with two or three wives, a large retinue of servants, from 90 to 100 packages containing gold, silver and opium'. *P.L.B.* of W.J. 7.4.1830. In the same year the bankrupt Chunqua married his fourth wife in jail.

In 1810-5, four Hong merchants were in great financial difficulties—Conseequa, Manhop, Exching (Patqua) and Poonequa. They were forced to appeal to their foreign creditors, to whom they owed almost a million taels. The creditors were always reluctant to 'break' insolvent Hongs, because it would reduce the number of available Hong merchants and therefore the competition for the foreign private trade; and because, as Matheson once pointed out to an impatient Calcutta creditor, there would be considerable delay in referring the matter to Pekin and in receiving the instalments from the Consoo Fund *without interest*.[1] The Company, which depended entirely on the Cohong for its teas, was usually prepared to take every possible step to help the credit of the weaker Hongs which were in difficulties. In January 1814 the Select Committee therefore advanced 250,000 taels to enable these Hongs to pay off the pressing demands of the Government for payment of duties,[2] which could never be postponed. Their private debts were placed in the hands of three trustees, Messrs. Moloney, Pearson and Magniac,[3] who were to collect 'regular instalments at interest'—usually 15% per annum. The Hong merchants continued to transact business, though by 1819 the seven junior Hongists still owed just under one million taels, of which Conseequa alone owed a quarter.[4]

The second crisis was in 1827-9, when Manhop was 'broke' and Chanqua deeply embarrassed, the former owing his foreign creditors over a million dollars, the latter over half a million, including interest.[5] The Company paid out almost a million

[1] Y. & Co. *L.B.* 14.6.1825.

[2] *Chronicles*, III, 223. In both the previous and the following year the Company found it necessary to advance means of paying the duties, and in 1813 two Hongists, Kinqua and Fatqua, who were still solvent, had to apply for this credit. In the same year Howqua and Mowqua helped their weaker brethren by means of transfers of balances in the Company's books.

[3] The correspondence of these trustees is preserved in the J.M. archives.

[4] *Chronicles*, III, 352.

[5] *P.L.B.* of W.J. 7.4.1830. Morse, using the Company's documents, says Manhop failed for $1,900,000.

dollars in 1827 to help the weaker Hongs pay their duties.[1] But these enormous failures shook the credit of every Hong merchant except Howqua; even Mowqua, the second senior merchant, was embarrassed and had to be assisted, at interest of course, by Magniac & Co.[2]

In 1836-7 the third crisis took place. Hentai failed, owing 16 lacs of dollars to Jardine Matheson alone.[3] At a rough estimate the total of insolvent debts over the eighty-two years in which the Cohong operated amounted to over $16\frac{1}{2}$ million dollars. These remarkable 'failures' of Mandarin merchants who had a monopoly of a growing foreign trade require an explanation.

The Imperial decree of 1780 which reconstituted the Cohong alleged that the cause of the recurrent financial state of the Hong merchants was the high interest they paid on loans from foreigners. These were henceforth to be prohibited. The foreign merchants, on the other hand, always asserted that the cause of financial weakness of the Hongists was their lack of capital and especially the heavy exactions which were periodically 'squeezed' out of them by rapacious Mandarins (the local officials).[4] Both parties only partially explained the problem.

Of course the heavy periodic 'squeezes' did contribute to impoverish the Hongists. In particular the crisis of 1810 and the following years was primarily due to the burden of 'singsongs' and other compulsory gifts, which were particularly heavy at that time.[5] But squeezes in aggregate could hardly compare with the many millions of pounds paid by the East India Company

[1] *Chronicles*, IV, 150.

[2] *P.L.B.* 15.6.1832, marked 'private'. Mowqua had large property locked up in land which brought him in 6%-8% per annum; but he paid 12% interest on over 1\frac{1}{2}$ million owed to Chinese and foreign creditors.

[3] *P.L.B.* 8.11.1837. See Chapter VII below.

[4] In his *Commercial Guide*, J. R. Morrison, who interpreted for the Company's Factory and sometimes for the private merchants, compiled a table which showed that 425,000 taels per annum were paid by the Hong merchants in 'presents', etc.

[5] *E.L.B.*, 1810-1, various letters.

annually to the British Exchequer and to bondholders out of the proceeds of the China trade.

Since the 'private English' were loud in their denunciations of the squeezes and exactions levied by corrupt Mandarins, it will be instructive to examine how China tea was taxed in England.

Up to 1784 the taxes levied on tea were an extraordinary jumble of duties, imposts, subsidies and surtaxes, so that it is difficult to say what the *ad valorem* duty was. Morse, after elaborate calculations in the *Chronicles*, arrives at the conclusion that the duty on tea consumed in England ranged from 75.9% to 127.5%. Some 13 million lb. of tea were consumed yearly in England, but of this amount only some 5½ million lb. paid duty. The remaining 7½ million lb. consisted of tea imported into France and other countries on the Continent for the express purpose of being smuggled into England. In 1783 a House of Commons Committee was set up to enquire into 'Illicit Practices Used in Defrauding the Revenue'. By the Commutation Act, passed in 1784, the duty on tea was reduced to a simple 12½%. Smuggling then became less universal because less profitable; but some twenty years later the import duty had advanced from 12½% to 100%, at which figure it remained until 1833. Tea from China (as noted in Chapter I above) provided about one tenth of the total revenue of England.

As to the Hongists' debts, the greater part were not ordinary trading liabilities but the accumulation of loans at compound interest. The lack of liquid capital in China and the consequent high rates of interest attracted foreign investors. In particular, many fortunes acquired in India were sent to the Canton 'private English' to be invested with one of the Hong merchants, usually at 12% per annum. The early ledgers of Beale and Magniac show that more profit was derived from their interest account than from their trade commissions. As late as 1837, Jeejeebhoy, the wealthy Bombay merchant, wanted Jardine to place $100,000 at interest with the Hong merchants.[1] We have noted in the previous chapter how the very earliest 'private English' charged sometimes as much as 20% per annum on the *debts* of the Chinese merchants. Hunter remarks that just after Manhop's failure and consequent exile to 'Eli', he came across his promissory note for $60,000 bearing interest at 5% per *month*.[2]

This high rate of interest was, of course, an expression of the inchoate state of capital accumulation in China (as in medieval Europe), which was the fundamental reason why the Cohong could not cope with the expansion of British trade. A report[3] by one of the trustees of the four insolvent Hong merchants in 1813 came to the conclusion that 'they may be stated to be of no original capital, little connection and too often under par in point of respectability'. William Jardine, writing in 1830[4] on the consequences of the abolition of the Company's monopoly in the near future, declared: 'Should the trade be thrown open it will still be carried on by European or rather English capital. Howqua is old and cautious, too much disposed for quiet to advance his very large capital in distant speculations.[5] Mowqua has large landed property but not enough of ready cash to carry on the

---

[1] *P.L.B.* of W.J. 30.8.1837.　　　　　　　　　[2] *Fan-Kwai*, p. 39.
[3] The report, by A. Pearson, is preserved in the J.M. archives.
[4] *P.L.B.* W.J. to J. H. Gledstanes, London, 29.3.1830. It is significant that about the same time leading members of the Company's Factory were giving a rather different sort of estimate to the S.C. of the H. of C. J. F. Davis declared that the Hong merchants were generally wealthy men (Q.451). 'Howqua is a man of large property', Mowqua is 'still considered a very sufficient merchant'. Puankequa and Cumqua 'are both men of opulence as is Gowqua' (or Goqua). They admit the two junior merchants, Kinqua and Fatqua, were, 'we believe, both poor men and indifferent merchants' (Q.672). The new Hongs created in 1830 as a result of pressure from the Country merchants (see Chapter VII) were not known to Davis or Marjoribanks. It was as much in the interests of the Company to minimise the weakness of the Cohong as it was in the interests of the 'free traders' to magnify it.
[5] In fact Howqua did charter ships from the American firm, Russell & Co., to send his teas to Europe even after this date. But he would only venture on profitable shipments, not caring to deal in British imports.

Company's trade allotted to him without borrowing from Europeans. Tenqua, who conducts the business of Ponkequa Hong, is too timid to embark on uncertain speculations; and has ever since he took charge of the Hong confined himself almost entirely to the Company's business. Chunqua is neither solvent nor is the Hong broken up. I have this forenoon been requested by his creditors to draw up a chop or petition against this Hong, the Viceroy having been under a promise to bring the head of the Hong, old 'Lord Melville',[1] back ever since September last; but has hitherto failed doing so. Old Kinqua is still poor, and in debt, though his credit is good. Fatqua has neither money nor character. Gowqua has money, but knows nothing of business beyond supplying Teas for the Company, who generally pay him cash and *burden* him with as little import cargo as possible . . . So much for the old Hongs. We have now four or five new Hongs, one conducted by a Tea merchant, one or two men from Macao, who have some money and some character but who have been engaged in the opium trade—and one of them has visited the cold country passage free.[2] The others are mere adventurers without money and without character—or rather with so very so-so character—broken down opium brokers, dismissed Hoppo's pursers, etc. What is to be the result of this newfangled nonsense I know not'.

Hengtai, who failed in 1836, owing Jardine Matheson $1,600,000, attributed his fall to over-trading, miscalculation of markets, and misappropriation of funds for family expenses. But in fact it was mainly the consequence of his treatment by the Mandarins and his lack of capital. He wrote[3] to Jardine, his principal creditor: 'In 1830, I began business with a limited capital; after deducting expenses of hanging out my signboard beginning business, and buying packing houses and furniture, not a *cash* remained to me. In that year on account of the English

---

[1] See p. 51, n. 6   [2] I.e. has been transported to Eli.
[3] Hengtai (or Yen) to W.J. 19.4.1837.

ladies coming up to Canton,[1] I was confined to prison for more than a month and found myself minus a lac of dollars. In the fifth year happened Lord Napier's affair.[2] I was detained several months in prison and did little business. My expenses at the offices of the Viceroy and Hoppo and other places were not less than another lac'.

Yet neither 'squeezes' nor lack of capital will explain fully the financial weaknesses of the Mandarin merchants. There were always several 'Seniors' who were really wealthy men. According to Hunter, Howqua estimated his fortune in 1824 at 26 million dollars, probably the largest mercantile fortune of the epoch. The 'extortions' of the Mandarins fell most heavily on him. Thus in 1841 the Hong merchants were called upon to contribute $2 million towards the 'ransom' of Canton demanded by the English military authorities. Howqua's share was $1,100,000, Puanke-qua's $260,000, and all the rest together only $640,000.[3] There were occasions, indeed, when the foreign merchants had to borrow from the Chinese! The young and struggling firm of Reid Beale & Co. found itself in difficulties in 1801 and borrowed $50,000 from Pinqua (Howqua), $30,000 from Puankequa, and $20,000 from Chinqua.[4] Howqua even acted as banker to the Company's Factory, on one occasion (1813) advancing it a quarter million taels.[5] Clearly the great Howqua, Mowqua, Puan-kequa, and occasionally others, had more than enough capital to give ample flexibility to the private foreign trade. But they were reluctant to do so more than was necessary, because *it was a losing trade for them.*

The private merchants, as a result of the Company's monopoly, could buy little tea. Their imports consisted primarily of Indian

[1] The attempt by the President of the Select Committee to introduce his wife into the Factories provoked a stoppage of trade.

[2] See Chapter VII. Hengtai was imprisoned because he 'secured' the ship, *Fort William*, on which Napier came up the Canton river.

[3] *Fan-Kwai*, pp. 45, 48.

[4] *L.B.* 13.3.1801, to D. Reid.   [5] *Chronicles*, III, 249.

goods, of which the two dominant items were opium and raw cotton. Opium was sold illegally and only to 'outside' traders for cash; cotton, from about 1818, fell catastrophically in price, because of the competition from an increased supply of the native China crop from the Nanking district.[1] Thus in 1821-2 and again in 1827 Magniac & Co. complained to its Indian correspondents that the only solvent Hong merchants, 'greatly smarting under the losses of last season', refused 'repeatedly' to buy Indian cotton except in truck for teas from the Company.[2] On British manufactures the Hong merchants generally lost; according to J. F. Davis, who ought to have known, they took them from the Company only because they were obliged to.[3] One of the main sources of loss to Hengtai was his large speculation in British piece goods. Those Hongists whom financial stringencies did not compel to unwise transactions were ever reluctant to undertake the (to them) losing trade of the 'private English'. Howqua, the shrewdest of them, concentrated on selling teas to the Americans for cash. The Americans brought specie as their major import cargo, or Bills on London which they sold for Spanish dollars to the eager English private merchants.[4] The latter paid the large sums of dollars and sycee derived from the sale of their opium not to any Hong merchant for China goods, but into the Company's Treasury or to the Americans for Bills of Exchange. That is why we have in 1828 a remarkable case of a prosperous Chinese salt merchant who tried to form a Hong to deal with the Americans only.[5] It was generally those Hong merchants involved in the private British import trade who got into financial difficulties, because it was a losing trade. Manhop and Hengtai, the two

---

[1] See below, Chapter IV. The declining profitability of Indian cotton in the China market was one of the underlying reasons for the rapid expansion of opium shipments.

[2] *I.L.B.*, 5.3.1821 and 1.7.1827 especially.

[3] *S.C.H. of C.* 1830, Q.408.

[4] See Appendix for the amount of specie and Bills brought by the Americans.

[5] *Chronicles*, IV, 168.

largest bankrupts, had both dealt heavily with Jardine's in British piece goods.

Another cause of loss sustained by the weaker Hongs arose from the smuggling of goods, other than opium, from the Lintin ships. The Hong merchants had to compete, both in the internal Chinese market for foreign imports and in selling China goods to foreigners, with unauthorised dealers who had illegally evaded the duties which they, the Hong merchants, always had to pay. The extent of the injury they thus received cannot be estimated precisely, but Davis, who was perhaps not altogether unbiassed, asserted that it was large.[1] Moreover, while their foreign imports might lie in the warehouses for months awaiting a sale, the goods had to be paid for within a fixed time—often with money borrowed from the foreigners themselves![2] With the special reasons which brought on a final crisis in the affairs of the Hong merchants in 1835-7—their struggle with a 'combination', the 'Black Tea men'—we shall deal in a later chapter. Enough has already been said to show that the financial instability of the Hong merchants arose from the nature of their trade with the foreigners, as well as from their lack of capital resources and 'squeezes'.

There were aspects of the 'bankruptcy question' which actually favoured the foreign traders at Canton. Firstly, by Imperial decree all debts to foreigners had in case of insolvency to be repaid out of the Consoo Fund. This latter was indeed sustained by a levy on foreign trade (which in the last analysis was *not* paid by the individual foreign merchants at Canton, but by the Chinese and British consumer); but it provided the 'free' merchants with a unique guarantee against losing their money—a guarantee which was all the more valuable in those days of great risks (and great profits) in the Eastern trade. When the largest British agency houses in Calcutta collapsed in the financial crisis of 1830-3, and brought their most respectable London houses down with them,

[1] *S.C.H. of C.* 1830, Q.480.   [2] Kuo, *First Anglo-Chinese War*, Ch. 7.

there was no Consoo Fund to repay, even in instalments, the £15,000,000 sterling which was the estimated total of the liabilities.[1] When the failure of their old-established Calcutta and London agents, the Fairlie and Fergusson firms, was followed in a few years by Hengtai's heavy bankruptcy, Jardine was able to reassure Hollingworth Magniac in London as to the stability of the firm by pointing out that the Consoo Fund was legally bound to repay the foreign debts of a 'broke' Hong. This appeal by Jardine to the despised laws of China is an ironic instance of the devil having a use for the Scriptures.[2] The fact was that the Hong merchants had no similar guarantee against *foreign* 'failures'; not merely swindlers like the notorious Armenian G. M. Baboum,[3] but speculative Presidents of the Company's Select Committee of Supercargoes such as Sir James Urmston, who was for many years in debt to several Hong merchants on private account. When the latter, headed by Howqua, applied to the Court of Directors to pay off the debts of its Canton President in the same way as the Cohong repaid the debts of 'broke' Hong merchants in all cases, the Court refused and contented itself with removing Urmston from office.[4] Though, in truth, the bankruptcy shoe was but rarely on the other foot, it did pinch.

A second and more surprising way in which the 'bankruptcy question' favoured the 'private English' at Canton was disclosed in the evidence of W. S. Davidson before the Select Committee of the House of Lords in 1830. He declared[5] that he had received great advantage from dealing with the bankrupt Hong merchants

---

[1] See Chapter VI.

[2] *P.L.B.* W.J. 18.11.37.

[3] This 'villain and swindler' succeeded in robbing Reid and Beale in 1801 of $30,000, and a Hong merchant of over $100,000. He was sufficiently plausible a scoundrel to induce old Robert Taylor (James Matheson's first partner at Canton) to invest over $60,000 in one of his adventures in 1819. The money was never seen again and Taylor 'nearly went off his head' and died shortly afterwards. See *L.B.* of James Matheson, 1821, and *L.B.* 2.12.1801, and see Chapter IV.

[4] See Jardine's letter to Urmston, *P.L.B.* 30.3.1830.

[5] *S.C.H. of L.* 1830, p. 456.

in his time. 'I often selected bankrupts to deal with because I could seldom deal with the merchants on fair terms; some of them were satisfied with the certain profits on the Company's business and did not covet other business very much ... They [the bankrupt Hongists] gave much better prices; too often (I suspect) they gave higher prices than they could afford to in the actual state of the market.' He went on to say that he conducted business with an insolvent precisely in the same way as with a solvent merchant, since they held the same rank (only as long as they were not 'broke' by the Government) and conducted their business in the same manner. He contracted with them 'constantly and in large sums entrusted money to them'. Though no rich Hongist was individually responsible for a poor one (though the Cohong was collectively), yet 'I knew they had shares in the Company's business and I felt assured they would be able to pay me, which they were'. This was due to the fact that selling teas to the Company at fixed prices was very profitable to the Hong merchants. The insolvent Hongist was very anxious to deal with people like Davidson and gave better prices for obvious reasons— 'he wishes to continue or his insolvency will become apparent'. Davidson was able to carry out his transactions with individual Hong merchants because they shared in the Company's heavy tea purchases and received the Company's advances. The ultimate security was the Company, and with the end of the Factory at Canton, this method of deriving advantage from the financial weakness of the junior Hongs was no longer at the disposal of the private English trader.

Davidson was the spokesman of the older generation of 'private English' at Canton.[1] For the next and more aggressive generation such advantages as might be derived from the insolvency of Hong merchants were petty and completely outweighed by the restrictive character of the Canton System as a whole. That

---

[1] He left China in 1824. In fact, his firm was the only one established besides the Beale and Magniac house and Parsee firms until the later 'teens of the century.

was the gravamen of their charge against the Cohong. The frequent bankruptcies of the Mandarin merchants were in themselves not fatal to the foreign trade. The foreign traders still continued to make fortunes in spite of them, and, as Davidson revealed, to a certain extent because of them. But these bankruptcies not only thinned the ranks of the Chinese merchants who were legally expected to cope with an increasing foreign trade; they demonstrated the inability of a stereotyped régime, whose object was restriction, to adapt itself to rapidly changing conditions which called for expansion.

What the breakdown of the Cohong really indicated was the gulf between the level of China's economy, with its low state of capital accumulation and its 'domestic' industry, and that of the rapidly developing British economy in this period of what is conventionally known as the 'Industrial Revolution'. But Jardine and his fellows were too close to the actual development of an as yet only half-completed process to be able to understand this fully.

The Honourable Company, after the failure of its diplomatic efforts—the Macartney and Amherst Embassies—was prepared to accept the Canton System. Occasionally the Court of Directors in London had to restrain an impetuous Committee of Supercargoes at Canton. Thus in 1832 it wrote to the Canton Factory as follows: 'We cannot approve of the support you gave to a continued disobedience of the laws respecting foreigners at Canton. The commerce between Great Britain and China is too valuable to be put to hazard without the most urgent and imperious necessity'.[1] The over-riding consideration for Leadenhall Street was the continued steady supply of tea. The Americans, too, were well satisfied with the Canton System. Hunter's enthusiasm for the 'old' system and especially the perfection of the Cohong,

---

[1] 13.1.1832, quoted *Canton Register*. This despatch forms part of the triangular struggle between the C. of D., the S.C. and the 'private English' over policy in regard to the Canton System, which is more fully discussed in Chapter VII below.

pervades his memoirs. Jardine complained that the Americans 'obstinately refused' to join in common action to bring pressure on the Chinese authorities to change the Canton System.[1] A letter to the Editor of *The Canton Register* over the signature of 'An American' began as follows: 'The American Government requires of us to submit peaceably to the laws of the country we may visit; hence we consider ourselves bound to obey the laws of China. Other foreigners may take a different view of their obligations and their governments may uphold their resistance. We do not question the propriety of their conduct. We well know the terms on which we are admitted to trade'.[2]

The 'private English', however, took a different attitude to the Canton System. The first generation thought themselves lucky to get, surreptitiously, into the China trade at all. They had ventured the hazardous voyage to China to make money as quickly as possible and return home. So long as they could do that within the Canton System, they were prepared to endure the personal discomforts of Factory life at Canton. (Incidentally, Hunter's picture of the genial social life in 'old Canton' suggests that the woes of the Old China Hands have been exaggerated.) The nature of their Country Trade, however, made them adept at evading the rigour of the Canton System by smuggling and bribery. Beale had written contemptuously, as early as 1806, 'Indeed there are few things in China that cannot be had by paying for them'.[3] The second generation of 'private English' continued to extend the illicit 'outside' trade which circumvented the Canton System. The *Chinese Repository* of June 1835 quotes an E.I.C. servant as follows: 'It could safely be stated that there was no officer of the Canton Government whose hands were clean ...' It could likewise be broadly stated that from 1829 no foreign merchant except the East India Company had traded in conformity to Chinese proclamations.

---

[1] *I.L.B.* 10.10.1829. [2] *Canton Register*, 2.10.1830.
[3] *L.B.* 10.11.1806.

But the second generation of 'free merchants' went further than evasion of the Chinese regulations. They took the offensive. Become a stronger and more numerous group, economically able to stand on its own feet and reach upwards towards a vision of unparalleled expansion, in which there remained monopoly to neither the Honourable Company nor the venerable Cohong; armed with a theoretical knowledge derived from Adam Smith and his followers[1] that a restrictive commercial system was irrational and ingenious; they formed a compact body, which found allies in the manufacturing towns of England, and a leader in the Scotsman, William Jardine, a man equipped by dominating personality and mercantile position to lead the frontal attack on the Canton System. Already by 1830, while still subject to the Company's rule, they had formulated their demands in a petition to Parliament. What they called for was 'a new commercial code', which would place the China trade on a 'permanent and honourable basis'; that is to say, which would liberate it from the fetters of the existing Canton Commercial System.[2]

[1] James Matheson, in an interesting letter to his stationers, Smith Elder & Co., orders the works of Smith, Ricardo, McCulloch, and their less-remembered disciples to be sent out to him in China. Cf. also the prize offered by *The Canton Register* for a work on 'Political Economy', reproduced after the title-page.

[2] See Chapters VII and VIII. That it was a partial fallacy to believe that only the artificial restrictions at Canton prevented the rapid expansion of the British trade was not realised till well after 1842, when disappointing statistics proved that the real limitations of the trade were rooted in the nature of China's economy.

Chapter IV

THE DEVELOPMENT OF THE
CANTON TRADE TO 1834

Hitherto we have been considering the framework of the China trade, the general conditions within which the British merchants at Canton operated. We must now turn to the trade itself and examine its constituents and its lines of development. It is intended to analyse trends rather than describe 'typical' voyages or cargoes. Descriptive accounts of ports and ships, lists of articles of export and import, often with interesting details of the more exotic commodities in the Eastern trade, are given in such contemporary compilations as Milburn's *Oriental Commerce*,[1] J. R. Morrison's *Commercial Guide to Canton* of 1834 and similar handbooks. The inadequacy of the merely descriptive is insisted upon by James Matheson himself, who in his third season at Canton wrote to a Singapore friend that 'the most minutely written description could scarcely suffice to give you anything like an accurate idea of a market singular and different in many respects from all others'.[2] Not to give a general survey of the movements of import and export figures at Canton, but rather to look into the actual operations revealed in the surviving books of the firms concerned is the purpose of this chapter. The subject of opium, on account of its special importance, will be treated separately in the following chapter. Separate treatment will likewise be given to the organisation and financing of the trade and its ancillaries, such as shipping and insurance.

In the period prior to 1834, when the advent of free trade into the China commerce modified its character, there can be separated

[1] Vol. II, pp. 216, 497-545 describe the main articles of Eastern trade.
[2] J.M. 2.7.1821 to J. Morgan, Singapore.

two broad phases. Up to about 1815, when there were but few private merchants established at Canton, and these treading warily within the Company's ambit and under war-time conditions,[1] the character of the trade was fairly simple, its scale small and its expansion slow. Towards the end of the second decade, important changes took place which complicated the trade and subjected it to sharp crises. There followed rapid but uneven development in several new directions.

When the letter books open, in November 1800, the sole private British firm at Canton is Reid Beale & Co., previously Hamilton & Reid, and in 1804 to become Beale & Magniac. The firm, though young, is a going concern; its lines of business already display a certain routine. It is conditioned by the obvious limiting factors, the Company's monopoly and the Canton Commercial System. Its main preoccuptaion is, of course, with the Country Trade; but it is noteworthy that direct trade with England is possible in spite of the Company, and that it becomes sufficiently important to warrant a separate letter book.

Indeed, for several years Reid Beale & Co. made a remarkable attempt to carve out for themselves a slice of the forbidden Anglo-Chinese trade, in what were known as 'Drugs'. These were certain Chinese products—rhubarb, cassia and camphor were the chief—for which a strong demand had sprung up in England. A 'Drug Concern' was formed in London in which Cleland White & Co. and D. Scott & Co. were the principals; a partner of the Canton firm, Alexander Shank, being given a share in the syndicate in 1802. Each season the Concern sent out specie and about $50,000 worth of miscellaneous European goods—lead, Prussian blue, cochineal, etc.—to the Canton firm, which advanced over a lac of dollars to the Hong merchants and shopmen, wherewith to buy the 'drugs' from up-country dealers. They were then shipped in the Company's direct tea fleet from Whampoa to

[1] Some effects of the Napoleonic Wars on the China trade are considered later in this chapter.

England by means of the 'privilege tonnage' of the ships' officers, which the Drug Concern bought up. This drug business was very profitable; soon the Company's officers were 'falling over one another' to buy up drugs. There was a 'perfect scramble' for camphor; but Shank was able to write to the Drug Concern that he was still 'from my interest with the Hong merchants by far the greatest purchaser of drugs here', sufficient to give the syndicate a command of the London market.[1]

But this very success revealed the limits of what was possible in English trade to the private merchant at Canton. There were three obstacles to their prosecution of the drug business. First, they had to be paid for very largely in cash, since the Chinese demand for European imports was very limited. A moderate importation of any particular Western article would soon satisfy the demand and send down the price to an unprofitable level before the prospective but distant English shipper could be informed. Therefore 'it is always precarious and dangerous to speculate on European articles' Shank wrote to William Lennox, of D. Scott & Co., London.[2] Secondly, any such goods could be undercut at Canton by the commanders and officers of the Company's ships, who were able to 'truck' or barter their imports for teas, which, unlike the private merchants, they were allowed to export to England. 'Teas being the grand staple export from hence in which the Chinese make their greatest profits, every [Chinese] merchant almost deals with them [the officers] and is on constant look out to dispose of them, especially at the end of the season, when they will make great apparent sacrifices to get rid of them.'

The third and greatest handicap was lack of tonnage to England. There was never sufficient 'privilege tonnage' available. When the officers of the Company's ships were short of cash they sold their 'space' to Reid Beale & Co. at £20-£25 per ton;[3] but they often preferred to trade themselves and would refuse even £40

---

[1] *L.B.* 28.2.1801, 20.10.1801.　　[2] *Ibid.* 30.4.1801.　　[3] *Ibid.* 20.4.1801.

a ton. The Drug Concern was always pressing Reid Beale & Co. to buy more of the drug supply. On one occasion Shank, who handled the English business for the firm, since the other partners were 'Prussian', wrote a despairing letter to David Reid, the partner gone home to London: 'For God's sake point out to them how impossible it would be to purchase more than we have done even were it practicable, upon the assumption that the commanders and officers would not fix up their tonnage on finding some articles dear and others scarce. I have already more goods than I shall get tonnage for'.[1] Want of cash was a difficulty, but 'tonnage seems the great desideratum and until that is provided for in a far more certain mode than hitherto, we fear Mr Shank will never be free from anxiety'. An attempt was therefore made to get Parliamentary permission for an annual 'free' ship between England and China. In 1802 Shank was sanguine: 'A private ship is again promised with much confidence, from the private trade and India shipping questions being before Parliament and expected to be favourably decided'.[2] But permission for a private ship was refused. The free traders were as yet too weak to persuade Parliament; and when the East India Company proceeded to tighten up its regulations concerning 'privilege tonnage', the death-blow was given to the 'Drug trade'.[3] The private merchants were driven back to the Country Trade. Though Francis Magniac and Daniel Beale continued to send $100,000 worth of 'singsongs' to Canton each year,[4] from 1804 onwards the Canton private merchants were effectively excluded from trade with Europe.

Asiatic trade was from the beginning the mainstay of the private business. The produce brought to China on Country ships was highly miscellaneous, coming from a variety of regions. From the Persian Gulf and Araby were brought, through Parsee intermediaries, such articles as putchuk, cutch, olibanum, myrrh. Bombay and the western coast of India supplied raw cotton, piece

[1] *L.B.* 25.2.1801.
[2] *Ibid.* 24.1.1802.
[3] *Ibid.* 10.2.1802 and 9.6.1802.
[4] *Ibid.* 2.1.1802.

goods, elephants' teeth (ivory), sharks' fins. Bengal contributed cotton, opium, rice; Madras and the Coromandel Coast, cotton piece goods, pearls, woods (redwood, blackwood, sandalwood). Fom the Malay Peninsula and the East Indian Islands came a huge assortment of 'Straits produce'—birds' nests, betel nut, rattans, pepper, mother-o'-pearl, tortoiseshell and the like. Tin was picked up at the island of Banka; rice taken aboard at Batavia, or Manila. Isolated ships, venturing off the regular India-Malaya-China run, scoured the seas for articles of import to Canton, bringing sandalwood from Hawaii or 'Fidji' (sic); skins from North America, and from other sources of supply such as New Holland and Botany Bay; bèche de mer, coral, amber from nameless islands in the Pacific Ocean. But partly because the miscellaneous Straits trade had to meet competition from Chinese junks,[1] the bulk of the Country merchants' business was with India, especially in the two 'grand staples'—raw cotton and opium.

Most of the cotton came from Bombay or Surat; little was exported from Bengal in these early years, none by private merchants. Until 1820 Bombay cotton was the more profitable; in 1815, for example, it yielded $56\frac{1}{4}\%$ over prime cost compared with $39\frac{1}{2}\%$ profit on the Bengal crop.[2] The Hong merchants' margin of profit was fixed at 0.2657 taels per picul; but they were constantly incurring losses, their stock remaining unsold whenever the Chinese cotton dealers refused to buy, while they—the Hong merchants—were obliged to pay the European importer three months after delivery of the cargo.[3] Each shipload was treated as a separate venture, and was usually contracted for by verbal agreement six or seven months in advance. But in spite of the contract, the price to be paid was often the subject of lengthy disputes with the Hong merchants, who demanded reductions on

[1] Thus in 1806 pepper was unsaleable owing to the very large imports in the junks. *L.B.* 25.10.1806.

[2] Milburn, *op. cit.* In 1806 Charles Magniac wrote 'a speculation in Bengal cotton will, generally speaking, lose'.

[3] *Canton Register*, 18.11.1829.

account of the inferior quality of the cotton. Thus in 1805 Beale & Magniac had contracted with Howqua to sell him cotton, consigned by Alexander Adamson of Bombay, who sent the firm cotton ships each season, at 13 taels 6 mace per picul. When the cotton arrived Howqua refused to discharge the cargo because the cotton was old. 'None of the other Hong merchants would touch a bale . . . altho' they are always importuning to make a sale to them . . . We appealed to Howqua as a gentleman to agree to a reduction of only 4 mace from the contract price'. Howqua agreed, and lost over $10,000 on the deal.[1] Subsequently the Hong merchants insisted on purchasing by muster from the ship side— 'a practice we always wish to avoid'.[2]

But the major variations in the price of cotton—in one season it varied by nearly $33\frac{1}{3}\%$—were irrespective of quality. The price of cotton at Canton turned on the nature of the China crop rather than the amount imported from India. This was especially true of Bengal cotton, which was little used in Canton provinces, but was sent into the interior when the 'Nanking crop' failed, since it resembled the latter in texture.[3] The season 1805-6 is illustrative. In that year there was 'an unheard of importation' of about 140,000 bales (310,000 piculs), the normal importation in the first decade being about 60,000 bales. Yet, in spite of this 'unexampled' quantity, rarely exceeded throughout the next thirty years, prices were very high, right throughout the season. Bengal cotton attained the new high level of 14 taels 5 mace per picul; Surat cotton of 'execrable quality' fetched 11 taels 5 mace—'more than it deserved'.[4] The reason was a catastrophic failure of the China crop. The Bengal cotton sent up-country as a substitute for the Nanking staple was sold locally in the Nanking area at 32 taels (including a profit of 5 taels per picul to the Chinese dealers), i.e. more than double the Canton price—incidentally a reflection of the enormous charges of land transport in the interior.

[1] *L.B.* 7.8.1805 to A. Adamson.   [2] *Ibid.* 20.4.1801.
[3] *Ibid.* 17.1.1806, 21.2,1806.   [4] *Ibid.* 3.2.1806, 20.2.1806.

This dependence of the China price of Indian cotton, and therefore its profitability, upon the state of the China crop made it impossible for the British importers to anticipate with precision the demand of the next season. They therefore preferred to act as commission agents rather than principals, and tried always to place the burden of possible loss upon the Hong merchants by engaging them in long-term contracts. Along these lines they were able to develop the import of cotton into a regular and lucrative business. But the fact that China was itself a great cotton-producing country constituted not merely a limit to the possible expansion of the India cotton trade but also an ever-present threat to the foreign merchants who depended upon it as 'a grand staple'. This threat, however, did not become serious until after 1815.

Cotton imports were not overtaken in value by the second staple—opium—until 1823. The spectacular rise of the latter is analysed in the following chapter. Equally spectacular but spasmodic were speculations in rice. It will be remembered that the Chinese authorities offered a special incentive to the importer of rice, relieving his ship from measurement duties. In March 1806 the *Hoppo* had issued a chop reaffirming this old-standing facility. The result was extraordinary; no less than 33 ships were sent from Calcutta bringing 235,000 bags of rice. Beale & Magniac were taken aback by these 'immense, unlooked for and, to us, incomprehensible speculations which have been lately undertaken from Calcutta to this part in the article of rice . . . and which nothing short of absolute certainty of a famine would warrant'.[1] In fact the China crop was unusually abundant. Prices naturally collapsed; the rice could not be warehoused except with Hong merchants, who, under pressure from the East India Company's Select Committee, agreed to bear part of the huge losses.[2] Beale

---

[1] *L.B.* 6.8.1806 to Fairlie Gilmore & Co.

[2] The Hong merchants agreed to buy the rice at $3 a picul though it could only be resold at $2½. *L.B.* 16.10.1806.

wrote to one of his constituents, J. Scott & Co., of Calcutta and Penang: 'We are happy you were not in the secret of our supposed want of grain . . . you escaped a most glorious opportunity of losing money'.

The risks of the Country Trade were thus large and commensurate with the large profits of successful ventures. The main difficulty, however, was not with imports to China but with returns to India. The India market for China goods was varied but limited. Sugar and sugar candy were the chief articles, constituting about one-quarter of the total during the period. Next came raw silk, tutenag and woven silks. These were followed by small quantities of numerous articles—camphor, cassia, nankeens, vermilion, lacquer and chinaware, grasscloth, fans, writing paper and other 'sundries'—produce of the Cantonese craftsmen, exported mainly for the use of Europeans in India. These goods were troublesome to obtain, involving contracts with the Chinese manufacturers; while their high cost together with the limited demand frequently made for losing sales. But they continued to be shipped as a means of remitting at least part of the proceeds of the cotton and opium imports back to India. Moreover, the Chinese authorities insisted that every foreign importer purchase a proportion of China goods before his ship be granted the 'grand chop' permitting her departure; a regulation which provoked Thomas Beale to an early outburst against 'this diabolical Government'.[1] Country ships, however, often returned to India virtually empty, with a cargo of alum as ballast to comply with the Canton regulation. The problem of finding 'a saving remittance which is all that can be expected from hence' was a perpetual headache to the Country merchants. Alum was 'better than paying for stones'.[2] But with the expansion of the import trade, the problem became increasingly difficult to solve, and they had to resort more and more to purely financial methods of effecting

[1] *L.B.* 30.9.1808.
[2] *Ibid.* 30.12.1821.

remittance.[1] Again, this tendency, observable in the earliest years of the private trade, only came to a head in the period after 1820. Other problems of this first period arose from the temporary circumstance of the Napoleonic Wars. The extension of conflict from the European battlefields to the Eastern seas had several consequences for the China trade. First, the status of the British merchants protected by continental papers was ambiguous. Reid Beale & Co. were unable to ship goods to India or Europe in their own name; invoices and bills of lading were made out in the name of Alexander Shank. 'From the disturbances in Europe, it has been feared that property appearing in the name of Mr Reid or Mr Beale (the one a naturalised Dane, the other holding a commission from the King of Prussia) might be liable to seizure or some embarrassing detention from the English Government or ships of war'.[2] On the high seas, the protection of the British Navy was vital and the Country ships had to be convoyed together with the East Indiamen. Relief was expressed when French frigates were captured. Satisfaction was felt when rival merchantmen, especially Dutch and Spanish, were taken; for 'these misfortunes must prove very distressing to the Dutch and Spanish [East India] Companies'.[3] On the other hand, the conflicts between European nations caused considerable inconvenience at Canton. Holding Danish papers, Beale & Co. were painfully torn between patriotic exultation at 'the glorious news of the destruction of Copenhagen' and commercial discomfort caused by the rupture of relations with the Northern powers.[4]

The most serious effect of the War was the depletion of shipping in the Eastern trade. Country merchants found it more profitable to charter their ships out to the East India Company to

[1] See Chapter VI below.
[2] *L.B.* 22.12.1801.
[3] *Ibid.* 8.9.1806, Beale to A. Adamson, on the capture of a Spanish ship from Manila carrying $700,000 worth of cargo, and two Dutch merchantmen loaded with the annual products of the Moluccas valued at £600,000 sterling.
[4] *Ibid.* 4.11.1801.

D

take rice to Europe, and, in 1801, for purposes of the British expedition to Egypt fitted out from India.[1] On this occasion there were no private British ships between Bengal and Canton for the whole season; and the Country merchants had to use Portuguese bottoms from Macao—-though the possibility of war with Portugal made English goods liable to confiscation.[2] Even a stray Arab ship was pressed into service by Beale & Co.—to return opium proceeds to Parsees at Calcutta.[3] Freights and insurance rates were naturally higher under war conditions.

Lastly, perhaps the main effect of the War was to encourage American traders at Canton. As neutrals, they were able to engage in 'a highly profitable and deeply irritating' carrying trade from Europe and South America, as well as that from the United States.[4] Beale & Co. obtained a little business with such American firms as did not have their own Supercargoes or resident agents at Canton. In some years they carried on trade—mainly shipping teas—with William Rogers of New York. But this interesting development was interrupted by the outbreak of the Anglo-American War in 1812.

Throughout the war years communication of commercial intelligence was uncertain; letters were sent in triplicate by different ships, sometimes in quadruplicate. The British merchants at Canton, operating so far from the main theatre of political events which yet affected their own trade, suffered 'a most unpleasant state of suspense' at the delay in the arrival of ships. 1815 was a year of exceptional anxiety—which perhaps explains the extravagant language which news of the 'Hundred Days' evoked at Canton. 'Congratulations on the peace between your country and ours', Beale wrote to A. Hosack, Jnr., of New York, 'we have at the same time to lament both for the sake of humanity and commerce that a war more bloody and dreadful perhaps than ever has again broken out on the Continent of Europe'.[5] To

---

[1] *L.B.* 25.7.1801.   [2] *Ibid.* 4.10.1801.   [3] *Ibid.* 6.11.1801.
[4] *Chronicles*, III, 108.   [5] *E.L.B.* 12.12.1815.

Fairlie Bonham & Co., their London agents, Beale & Co. wrote, 'the astonishing and lamentable changes that took place in Europe leave us only to deplore that the fair prospects of peace should so speedily be darkened by the most extraordinary event that ever took place in the history of the world, we believe . . . with anxious expectation we look for the next news from Europe, our latest as yet being only very general accounts of the dreadful battle in June between Napoleon and the Duke of Wellington near Mons'.[1] The result of Waterloo, though it arrived six months later, was all the more welcome at Canton both 'for the sake of humanity and commerce'.

By 1816, in spite of the difficulties of war-time conditions, the private merchants at Canton had succeeded in establishing a flourishing trade on regular though simple lines. During the next few years a number of influences combined to unsettle the trade and modify the lines of its early development. From 1818 until 1827 we have the additional evidence of the papers of the small firms with which the young James Matheson was associated, to corroborate the impression derived from the records of the Magniac House that, under changing conditions, the China trade was passing through a period of crisis.[2]

Perhaps the most important new factor was the influx of new-comers into the Country Trade consequent on the Peace of 1815 and the opening of the India trade in 1813. In 1815 there were 18 British commercial houses in Calcutta; five years later there were 32. For Bombay the figures are 11 and 19 respectively.[3] Many of these were mushroom firms, eager to try their hand at the fabulous China trade. The result at Canton was increased competition, over-abundant stocks, falling prices and general depression. Some of the small firms were able to survive only by supplying the

---

[1] *E.L.B.* 5.1.1816.
[2] R.T. and J.M., 2.10.1820 and passim.
[3] *E.I. Register*, 1815, 1820.

increased requirements of the exiled Europeans in the way of strong drinks and more solid provisioning.

Secondly, the Hong merchants proved themselves unable to cope with this expansion of the private trade. Already in the early 'teens, several of them had become insolvent and had been put under foreign trustees. In the '20s there were only four Hongists with whom it was reckoned safe to deal. Their difficulties were aggravated by the great fire of 1822. Charles Magniac, after vividly reporting the outbreak, which destroyed 10,000 Chinese houses and many lives, continued: 'So dreadful a conflagration is not on record in Canton . . . Some of the Hong merchants have suffered terrible loss of property. Howqua has lost about 200,000 taels, Mowqua 350,000 taels, Cheonqua a large sum. Poonqua had a large quantity of woollens, the loss of which will greatly distress him.' He added that he was afraid of the effect of 'the extensive ruin which must have fallen on a number of Chinese dealers and brokers of every description . . . At present mercantile transactions are in a state of suspension'.[1] Merchandise belonging to the foreigners was stored in the warehouses of the Hong merchants, at the latter's risk. There was no fire insurance in old Canton.

Thirdly, there were market changes at Canton which undermined some of the older bases of the private trade. Primarily an import trade, it was especially hit by the decline in the Chinese demand for certain articles of import. That old stand-by, the 'singsong' trade, had fallen off after 1815, both on account of the embarrassed state of the Cohong and because Chinese merchants had learned to copy them at half the cost. An additional reason may be found in an Imperial sumptuary edict published in 1815, which survives in translation among the Jardine Matheson papers: 'It is very lamentable that for these things [singsongs] which can neither feed the hungry nor clothe those who are perished with cold, the valuable property of our country is gradually almost

[1] *I.L.B.* 2.11.1822.

totally expended'. Charles Magniac wrote his father: 'hopeless of sale as the clocks may now be, considered in the ordinary mode of disposal, we have determined to sell the first three pairs to Poonqua, Conseequa, and Kingqua for $3,000 each, payable within two years, with an interest of 1 % per month. We assure you that these merchants consider they have done us a favour in thus taking them even at these ruinous rates, for they could actually have gotten Chinese clocks . . . for exactly half the money'.[1] The firm did not finally close its singsong department until 1824.

Several other imports fell away for one reason or another. Thus, Prussian blue, a favourite article of the early days, became unsaleable when the Chinese discovered a process for manufacturing a substitute dye. Especially marked was the depression in 'Straits produce'. This branch of the China trade had always been precarious because the limited demand for these miscellaneous articles was apt to be supplied by the native junks. With the commercial growth of Singapore in the 1820s, the import of Straits produce into Canton increased to the point of glut. 'You know from experience what a delicate market this is for Straits produce in the face of any fresh importation', Matheson had to warn his Singapore agent.[2] There was a sharp fall in the Canton prices of these articles, pepper in particular touching its lowest point ($6½ per picul) for many years in 1827. Even tin, which had appealed to James Matheson in 1821 as 'the most steady article of Straits produce', was six years later having to be sold off by auction at a loss.[3] Some of the Singapore traders tried to escape loss by shipping adulterated tin. Their Canton agents observed acidly 'we fear there is little chance of the Chinese being reconciled to a bad article by the arguments of the "Singapore Chronicle" '.[4] Rattans were the only article of Straits produce to

[1] *E.L.B.* 5.2.1815.
[2] *P.L.B.* of J.M. to Charles Thomas, 31.10.1831.
[3] R.T. and J.M., 2.6.1821; *I,L,B.* 12.7.1827.   [4] *I.L.B.* 24.2.1832.

escape the collapse, 'their bulk preventing the market from being glutted'.[1] The season 1827-8 was perhaps the nadir of this branch of the trade, when the market for Straits goods was 'as depressed as it well can be'.[2] The result was many failures among the small firms dependent upon this trade. The remainder owed their survival mainly to the growing use of Singapore as an entrepôt for private trade between China and England. But the old trade in Straits produce to China became increasingly 'a bad and losing business'.[3]

Other imports into Canton, prominent in the early phase of the trade, fell off later. The quantity of furs imported reached its high level in 1808-12, declining rapidly in the 1820s.[4] Sandalwood, shipped in large quantities from the Pacific islands for a decade, suddenly dropped to insignificance.[5] In both these cases, the cause of decline was depletion of the source of supply by rapacious traders. These two articles chiefly affected the American trade. That which above all else was of concern to the 'private English' was the collapse of the cotton market, the foundation of their early prosperity.

From about 1819 for a decade, the state of the Canton market for India cotton was one of acute and chronic depression. In October 1819 Charles Magniac wrote a puzzled letter to his principal shipper of Bombay cotton: 'It is somewhat singular that our cotton market, even under the very limited importation from your quarter and the almost total failure from Bengal, is by no means high or brisk.'[6] In the following June he had to report his 'considerable mortification that there is no change in our depressed

---

[1] *I.L.B.* 7.6.1826.
[2] *Ibid.* 26.4.1828.
[3] *P.L.B.* of J.M. 10.7.1837.
[4] Forbes in *Remarks* gives the following data:
        1812—11,500 sea-otters, 1730,000 seal skins.
        1831—   300   „   „   6,000   „   „
[5] Forbes in *Remarks*.
[6] *I.L.B.* 13.10.1819 to Remington Crawford & Co.

cotton market in spite of holders withholding sales of recent importations'.[1] In September there was a further sharp fall in the price of cotton. 'It could hardly be credited that a Parsee, the consignee of the *Byramcore*'s and *Good Success*'s cargo of old Bombay cotton was actually offered 17 taels—the highest price offered for Bombay cotton during an experience of twenty years —and that he rejected it. Now he cannot obtain 14 taels 5 mace for this quality.'[2] A year later, the cotton market was 'the worst for 20 years'; over 100,000 bales were lying unsold in Canton, and a further 70,000 due to arrive. Some sales were taking place, but at a loss and under extraordinary terms for which Magniac & Co. expressed their 'excessive mortification': at a price of 9 taels and long credits of 5-6 months—the usual period was 3 months— and 'trucked away' in part for return cargo.[3] In December Magniac had to write to the largest exporter of Bengal cotton, Mercer & Co.: 'We cannot encourage you to speculate in cotton next season.'[4]

The records of the smaller firms, in which Matheson was partner, tell much the same story. In 1820 the cotton trade was 'completely at a stand'; in 1821 it was in 'irretrievable depression'.[5] In January 1823 Yrissari & Co. wrote to Mercer & Co., Calcutta: 'It is with heartfelt sorrow that we have to commence our correspondence for another year by announcing the continued depression of the staple in which you are so much interested'.[6] Bengal cotton was selling for 8 taels 2 mace, payable in 4 months. In 1824-5 there was a temporary improvement owing to the partial failure of the Nanking crop. This was followed by a further short-lived rise in price on the report that large stocks had been destroyed by fire—the cotton market had become dependent on such adventitious fillip.[7] In 1826 Bengal cotton was

---

[1] *I.L.B.* 10.6.1820, to Fergusson Clark & Co., Calcutta.
[2] *Ibid.* 30.9.1820, 4.10.1820.   [3] *Ibid.* 15.10.1821.
[4] *Ibid.* 9.12.1821.   [5] R.T. and J.M., 17.2.1821.
[6] Y. & Co., 9.1.1823.   [7] *I.L.B.* 1.4.1825, 22.7.1825.

unsaleable—'a complete drug'.[1] In the following season cotton
was in 'a most deplorable state . . . The dealers are smarting under
their losses of last season: while the Hong merchants avoid purchasing from individuals, knowing they must each take his
proportion of Company's cotton . . . The low price of cotton
[7 taels 5 mace] has thrown speculators into consternation . . . No
human exertion can save the speculators in that article from a
heavy loss.'[2] In 1829 cotton reached a new low figure, 6 taels
9 mace for the worst quality. At one point there were ten Country
ships lying at Whampoa for months with their cargoes unsold.
The Hong merchants refused to buy a single bale on their own
account, preferring to act as brokers only.[3] The cotton crisis hit
the Bombay merchant community so hard that they demanded
Governmental intervention to alter the whole commercial system
at Canton;[4] a slight improvement in 1829 was followed by a
further collapse in 1830, when the cheapest cotton sold at 5 taels
7 mace! The Canton consignees attempted to prevent Country
ships from landing their cotton. 'We have never witnessed a
greater stagnation' wrote Jardine.[5] In a letter to several new
British firms at Bombay eager to establish a correspondence with
China, Jardine wrote 'cotton is generally so much run upon by
shipowners for the sake of keeping their ships in employ that it
seldom answers those speculators who have no such interest at
stake'.[6]

What had happened to the 'grand staple' of the early years? No
comprehensive explanation was attempted by the foreign merchants, but several arguments were thrown out *en passant*. At
first, the 'disadvantageous speculations' in cotton were attributed
to the 'unwarranted' rise in India, 'the enormous prices which the
article seems almost permanently to have there attained.'[7] But

[1] *I.L.B.* 5.6.1826.
[2] *Ibid.* 11.8.1828.
[3] *I.L.B.* 24.7.1830.
[4] *Ibid.* 20.10.1819, 10.4.1820,

[2] *Ibid.* 1.7.1827, 4.7.1827, 15.7.1827.
[4] See Chapter VII below,
[6] *Ibid.* 4.10.1831,

when the cotton crisis continued in China and the India price consequently fell, the brunt of criticism fell on the Hong merchants. 'It is truly lamentable that out of only eleven individuals licensed by the Chinese Government to deal openly with foreigners there should be seven reduced if not to a state of insolvency, at least of extreme embarrassment; the effect of this is that the wealthy four, by combining together and being free from competition, often control the market as is at present happening in the article of cotton.'[1] In fact the Hong merchants were not 'free of competition', and in their less prejudiced moments the foreign merchants admitted that the Hongists were equally suffering from the cotton crisis—that some had been ruined in consequence of the fall in prices. 'The unprecedented scarcity of money among the Hong merchants is partly caused by the large capitals locked up in cotton'.[2] 'The general stagnation that prevails in the internal trade of this country is the cause [of the low price of cotton] ... One cause is the scarcity of money, which prevails to a degree we have seldom witnessed here ... The Chinese purchasers of your earlier consignments of cotton are rather slack in their payments, at which, under want of cash in circulation, we are not surprised; but we shall oblige the parties, if possible, to pay interest on the lost time.'[3]

Of China's internal trade (or anything that went on in the interior) they knew little,[4] except that the Chinese demand for Indian cotton was dependent on the produce of the Nanking crop. One frequently meets with the following comment in the market reports: 'our cotton market, in consequence of the exuberance of the native crop, has continued unfavourable to foreign importation'.[5] One remarkable suggestion was, however, thrown out, that the main cause of the changed demand for cotton was an alteration in the method of internal transportation ... 'The

[1] *I.L.B.* 24.7.1823.   [2] Y. & Co., 10.4.1822.
[3] *I.L.B.* 10.6.1820.   [4] *Ibid.* 5.3.1821.
[5] *Ibid.* 13.4.1820 to Mackintosh & Co., Calcutta,

unusually abundant native Chinese crop which was brought to Canton, on junks, contrary to former custom, instead of by land carriage, has come into market so greatly cheaper than heretofore, selling now at 15 taels instead of 25 and 30 taels; and being of so far superior quality to Indian cotton it has terribly interfered with the sales of the latter to such an extent that they [50,000 bales] are now unsold by the Hong merchants.'[1] There is another reference to internal conditions to explain the fall in the price of cotton— 'the cause assigned by the Chinese dealers is poverty among the consumers of the article owing to their country having been inundated and the price of rice consequently high.'[2] The isolation of the foreign merchants from Chinese life made it impossible for them to probe deeper. But the shrewd James Matheson does have significant comment to make on the cotton crisis: 'Cotton seems under an irretrievable depression, which I suspect is connected with large importations of British manufactures interfering with the native manufacture.'[3] Again, he speaks of 'a stagnation of manufactures arising from an extraordinary mortality, and in some degree I suspect from the influx of British cotton, is the cause of the depression.'[4] This opinion was some years later seconded in a minute of the Select Committee of the Company's Supercargoes: 'The foreign [Indian] cotton is principally consumed as we understand in the provinces of Canton, and the market is of course materially affected by the importation of the manufactured cotton goods and cotton yarns from Great Britain'.[5] Considering that the import of Lancashire cotton manufactures into China was still in its infancy the future seemed unpromising for the old staple import of the Country Trade, raw cotton.

The cotton slump was the most important aspect of the general depression in the Country Trade in the 1820s. But there were other difficulties, a most pressing one being the question of return

[1] *I.L.B.* 5.3.1821.   [2] *Ibid.* 28.7.1824 to Leckie & Co., Bombay.
[3] R.T. and J.M. 17.2.1821.   [4] *Ibid.* 27.12.1820.
[5] *Chronicles*, IV, 186.

cargoes to India. This had been a problem from the beginning; but from about 1820 it was aggravated by a decline in the Indian demand for several of the regular China goods. Sugar, the most considerable of these, now suffered from the competition of Manila sugar; though the latter was generally ordered by India importers through Canton agents. Chinese tutenag, a favourite of the early period, was completely ruined as a 'return' by the introduction of European spelter into India at a far lower cost.[1] The decline in 'China goods' was such that in 1825 Charles Magniac could write, 'The Parsees are now the only speculators in China goods to India'.[2] This in turn produced a fall in freight rates to India: 'The return freight is so low that even a full ship would do little to defraying the heavy expenses of a China voyage.'[3] An additional shipping complication arose out of the growth of the opium trade at the 'outer anchorage' of Lintin.[4] It became difficult to procure tonnage for non-contraband goods up to Whampoa, 'and when goods are shipped for Lintin it is very uncertain when there may be an opportunity for trans-shipping them to an inward-bound vessel—an operation which is seldom accomplished without loss of weight and some risk of damage'.[5]

Finally, its increasing financial independence of the East India Company compared with the earlier period made the Country Trade susceptible to credit disturbances in London and even America.[6] After the financial crisis of 1827 in America, Magniac & Co. sent out the following circular letter to their India constituents: 'Accounts from the United States must lead us to anticipate a material falling off in this branch of the commerce of our port, *so important to its general prosperity*.'[7]

The season 1827-8 was probably the nadir of the depression in the Country Trade, when, with the all-important exception of

---

[1] *I.L.B.* 24.11.1826, etc.   [2] *Ibid.* 13.3.1825.
[3] *Ibid.* 4.7.1827.   [4] See next chapter.
[5] *I.L.B.* 24.7.1830.   [6] See Chapter VI.
[7] *I.L.B.* 26.4.1828.

opium, there was 'scarcely an article of import yielding prime cost, and charges, nor one of export that has the prospect of paying even a remittance.'[1] Yet the 'private English' at Canton were flourishing more than ever. This was because in the face of depression they had been able to develop the China trade along new lines and in new directions.

The most obvious as well as the most important consequence of the general decline of the old bases of the Canton trade, especially of the cotton staple, was the concentration on opium. At a time when the profitability if not the volume of other imports had shrunk, the import of opium expanded enormously and consistently. The mass of new correspondents and agents which the Canton firms acquired in the 1820s, especially those in Bombay, were opium shippers.[2]

Secondly, there was a tendency to reach outwards, to bring new markets into direct connection with the Canton trade—Spanish America, Australia, Java, Siam. In South America the struggle for liberation against Spain was watched with sympathetic interest by the British merchants. 'Our good wishes are on the side of liberty and independence against despotism and oppression, though we agree with you in doubting if the patriots have sufficient energy and public spirit to give success to their cause', wrote Charles Magniac in 1819 to his agent in Manila, itself a Spanish colony.[3] Chinese silk piece goods were in demand in South America, which in turn supplied metals, especially copper and Peruvian silver, which the Canton merchants could make use of as returns to India. A small but very profitable trade developed with Chile in the 'thirties, though by then the bigger Canton firms were too preoccupied with opium and the newly-freed trade with England to undertake more than a casual correspondence with Valparaiso.[4] More regular were the 'speculations'

---

[1] *I.L.B.* 26.4.1828.   [2] See next chapter.   [3] *I.L.B.* 30.11.1819.
[4] *P.L.B.* of J.M. 28.4.1827, 23.10.1827.

to Mexico. Matheson's early Spanish connections[1] were useful at Mazatlan and San Blas, and for some years his firm, Yrissari & Co., consigned an annual ship from Canton to Mexico.[2] The growing Australian colonies of Botany Bay and Van Dieman's Land offered a natural though limited outlet, especially for China teas, once the East India Company had been persuaded to license private English ships bound for that quarter. New South Wales was 'a colony from which foreign vessels are excluded'. Wherefore for purposes of Australian trade the Canton agents conveniently put aside their foreign papers. In 1819 James Matheson, newly arrived in China, despatched one of the first cargoes of teas from Canton to Port Jackson, New South Wales, in the *Marquis of Hastings*, an opium ship from Calcutta which had been unable to secure freight for a profitable return to India. By 1830, when Captain Ladd, an old shipmate of William Jardine, took a cargo of teas and silks in the barque *Austin* to Hobart Town and Sydney, the Canton firms had regular agents in these ports, to which they were sending several ships every season. But an impediment to the further advance of this trade was the absence of a suitable return from Australia. In 1830 a trial consignment of 15 bales of wool was shipped by John Bell of Hobart Town to Magniac & Co., who reported unfavourably on the experiment: 'It will be long before the Chinese will be able to bring wool into extensive use sufficient to render it an object of traffic. They possess none of the implements necessary to bring it to a manufactured state, and no idea of making cards beyond the rude model of sticking nails into two pieces of wood, and are perfectly ignorant of the manner of cleaning it.' A little was finally made into wool cloth by silk workers in Canton, but most of it had to be disposed of to carpenters to stuff couches with![3]

---

[1] From 1821-7 James Matheson was in partnership with F.X.J. de Yrissari, a native of Aragon with relatives in Calcutta, Manila and Mexico. The correspondence with the two latter places is in Spanish.

[2] Y. & Co., 1.7.1824.

[3] *I.L.B.* 8.9.1830, 12.4.1831.

Other ventures were made to Rangoon for teak, Mauritius for ebony, Siam for rice. But more important were the regular 'speculations' which developed with Java and Manila. The former besides being a source of Straits produce was also the mart for Japan copper, since the Dutch had the monopoly of foreign trade with Japan. On one occasion Magniacs bought up from the Dutch their whole season's supply of Japan copper for the all-important remittance to India. In 1823 Matheson, hearing of the arrival of a fellow Scot 'among the mynheers at Batavia', wrote strongly urging him to take up trade with China. In the late 'twenties a very extensive trade was developed in rice from Java and Manila to Canton.[1] Rice, it will be recalled, carried valuable exemption from the Canton measurement duty; wherefore rice ships would make several voyages between Manila and Java in a single season. These rice operations were on such a large scale that, in the '30s, Jardine Matheson & Co. set up what was virtually a branch firm at Manila to carry them out.[2] Manila, in addition to rice, supplied sugar, tobacco and hemp—the first especially being useful to Canton merchants as remittance to India.

Another development of this period was the revival of private trade with Europe. After the failure of the 'Drug Concern' of 1802 to obtain a 'free' ship between England and China, that trade had lapsed to insignificance for want of 'tonnage'. But in the 1820s the situation was radically altered by the establishment of Singapore. It was illegal for private British subjects to ship goods from China to England; but how if China goods were landed at Singapore, a 'free port', and transferred to another ship, a 'free trader' bound for England? Accordingly, although the legality of the procedure was doubtful,[3] a technique of trans-shipping at Singapore was devised; for the supervision of which the newly-established British firms at Singapore were eager to make an easy

---

[1] Thus in 1831-2 over 1¼ lacs of piculs of Java rice were imported into Canton. *I.L.B.* 24.3.1832.

[2] Otadui & Co. See Chapter VI.   [3] *I.L.B.* 7.4.1827.

1% commission. Cargo taken aboard at Lintin or Macao was landed at Singapore; fresh bills of lading were made out to London consignees, and the cargo taken aboard again on the *same* ship, which then proceeded to England. By this legal fiction a serious inroad into the East India Company's monopoly of the Anglo-Chinese trade was made possible.[1]

In May 1819, when Singapore had hardly been taken possession of by Sir Stamford Raffles, its commercial possibilities were foreseen by the 22-year-old James Matheson, making his second voyage to China as Supercargo of the opium ship *Marquis of Hastings*: 'As far as two or three observations and conversations enable me to speak, I have formed the highest opinion of Singapore as a place of trade. Its principal staple article at present is tin, for which there is a melting house belonging to the Sultan of Johore. It is procurable at $15 per picul. As yet however no trade can be carried on to any great extent there being no merchants to deal with; but this is a disadvantage which, as there are no duties or port charges, will soon vanish. I am of the opinion that a person settling here for a few months with a few thousand dollars as a circulating medium (which they greatly want) might carry on business to great advantage . . . the situation of the settlement is truly delightful, being within 4 miles of the direct tract for China; and the mild sway of Major Farquhar has attracted settlers from all parts of the village, which consisted of 200 houses and containing now upward of 2,000; and the Sultan of Johore, attracted by the protection of the British Government, means to establish his residence there . . . Singapore will certainly be retained, the Java Government having declined interfering with our possession.'[2]

However, for several years the commercial development of Singapore was slow, mainly because of uncertainty as to its political future and the low state of the trade in Straits produce.

[1] *I.L.B.* 12.10.1825, 24.3.1827, 3.11.1827, 1.1.1829.
[2] R.T. and J.M., 24.5.1819.

It was not until January 1825 that the 'first authentick statement' of the Dutch Government confirming British possession of Singapore reached Magniac & Co. in Canton.[1] It was about the same time that a sudden rise in the English demand for China goods made apparent the rôle which Singapore could play as an entrepôt between Canton and London. This time the 'China goods' in question were not 'drugs' but silks. The lowering of the English duty on silks in 1825 produced a remarkable boom at Canton. Baring Brothers, of London, through their agents, A. L. Johnstone, of Singapore, and Dents, of Canton, placed a contract with the Hong merchants for 900 piculs of Nankin raw silk at $480 per picul.[2] This created a 'sensation' and was followed by a remarkable run on this article (the best-quality China silk), the price of which rose at once to $500. The Hong merchants demanded two-thirds in advance as bargain money for silk contracts. Matheson combined with J. Purvis of Singapore and Gregson, Melville & Knight of London to effect silk 'speculations'. The 'gentlemen of the Company's fleet' joined in the scramble. Such was the competition for ship room that 'privilege tonnage' rose to its old high price of £40-£50 per ton.[3] To meet the demand the Chinese Government's limitations on the quantity of silk that could be exported had to be overcome by regular smuggling via the Lintin ships.[4] Magniac & Co. were able to use their special connections with the 'outside shopmen' to advantage, until the restriction on their dealings of 1828.[5] Though the boom did not last, this silk trade was no passing thing, because it represented the capture of a section of Anglo-Chinese commerce by the 'free' merchants.[6]

By 1831 there were four 'free traders' a season plying between

[1] *I.L.B.*, to Napier & Scott, Singapore, 28.1.1825.
[2] Y. & Co., 10.8.1825.
[3] *Ibid.* 21.1.1836.
[4] *I.L.B.* 10.6.1825, etc.
[5] *Ibid.* 3.1.1828. For the crisis over the 'outside shopmen' see Chapter III.
[6] *Ibid.* 31.10.1831. The figures for the exports of China raw silk in British

Canton and London, all 'trans-shipping' their cargo at Singapore. The innermost preserve of the Company's monopoly, the tea trade, could not yet be invaded; but from about 1831 there are instances of the 'private English' at Canton shipping teas to various parts of Europe—Hamburg, Bordeaux, Lisbon—on non-English bottoms.[1] By 1833, 'Jardine tea mixture' was already a celebrated blend in England.

Finally, there was a complementary development of private trade from Europe to Canton. The decline in certain of the old articles of import led to an attempt to introduce new ones—such as cochineal, cudbear, British copper and, above all, British cotton manufactures.

Early shippers of Lancashire goods to China met with an unpromising response. One of the first attempts to dispose of cotton piece goods was made by James Matheson, who in 1819 sold a trial assortment by 'public outcry', i.e. by auction. 'A public sale held on the 18th ult. [July] was attended by a pretty numerous concourse of dealers from all parts of the town . . . The shirting seems quite unsaleable—they call it an imitation (and of course an inferior one) of their grasscloth. Stripes were not liked. They seem altogether insensible to the beauty of these.'[2] Chinese vessels from 1826-31 show a remarkable increase:

	CANTON SILK (piculs)	NANKIN SILK (piculs)	TOTAL (piculs)
1826-27	1,332	2,854	2,749
1827-28	1,736	1,834	2,806
1828-29	2,714	4,181	6,336
1829-30	2,224	3,746	4,831
1830-31	3,670	2,918	6,588

[1] *I.L.B.* 23.8.1831, 6.2.1833, etc.
[2] R.T. & J.M. to MacIntyre & Co., Calcutta, 14.8.1819.

taste preferred 'small separate flowers thinly interspersed, and if on a white ground the better'. To avoid losses, it was necessary to evade the heavy duty on piece goods. 'I could by this time have smuggled up the whole of them in the ship's boat and sold them gradually by auction, but was obliged to desist on finding that my house servants were not to be trusted and had indeed given information of contraband proceedings to the Mandarins.' Nevertheless Matheson was optimistic. 'We augur favourably of the future consumption of British cottons in the Chinese dominions from their present abundance and cheapness: we conceive by attending to their suggestions as to pattern (which seems more looked to than texture) considerable advantage may accrue to the manufacturer, even though the trade should be a losing one to those speculating on credit, as many of those in the Company ships, who are at present the principal importers, do. But a know-ledge of the most approved patterns continues a secret to most of them ... Mr Matheson carries with him [to Calcutta] a few musters which may be relied on as eligible.'[1]

Magniac & Co. were less sanguine. On receiving a small quantity of printed calicoes from Ritchie Stewart & Co., Bombay, they reported that it was 'difficult to sell ... and in our opinion a bad speculation', which was 'fortunately bought up by a man who wished to ship to Manila'.[2] They were equally doubtful about some cotton yarn, received a year later, arguing that it could not be introduced owing to the arrangements of Canton domestic industry. 'It is usual between the master manufacturer of cotton cloth and the spinner of yarn for the former to supply the people with 2 catties of cotton and receive back half the quantity of yarn; and therefore the very low price of cotton and yarn can be of but little value; and tho' your parcel is firmer and better than the Chinese, yet they have a strong objection to all novelty ... However, we have it in contemplation to cause a small piece of

[1] R.T. and J.M., 16.12.1819, to MacIntyre & Co., Calcutta.
[2] *I.L.B.* 1.10.1820.

cloth to be made from yours, to try what value it may have among the natives.'[1] A year later bleached calicoes exported by James Finlay & Co., London and Glasgow, were selling at Canton—but profitably only when duty was evaded.[2]

With the use of Singapore as a trans-shipping depôt for the China trade, increased quantities of Manchester goods were sent out. At first the many enquiries from Singapore agents as to the prospects of Manchester manufactures in China met with the reply: 'no encouragement for adventure to this quarter'.[3] But lowered cost consequent on increased production and persistent pressure by the Canton agents forced a passage. Matheson was soon able to report that 'the Chinese demand for British piece goods, hitherto limited, will probably increase, on account of the low prices. We know some instances of wealthy merchants dressing their children in chintzes, previously only used for bedcovers, and if the taste becomes fashionable, as is by no means impossible, *the field which it opens up for British industry is immense*.'[4] The vista was made even more splendid by the successful adaptation of British cotton yarn to Chinese manufacture.

In November 1828 Jardine reported that cotton twine which previously had been sold in Canton only for resale to India, or in small lots to the Canton manufacturers, was now being sent to the interior. He added: 'The Chinese cannot spin cotton yarn so cheap as we can import it from England, but they find considerable difficulty in using it for woof and generally use it in the beam as warp. Time may overcome this difficulty, however, and if so the consumption must increase very considerably'.[5] 'Time' was not remiss. Within a year, report was made to the Singapore agents that 'the Chinese are now bringing into use

[1] *I.L.B.* 31.10.1821.
[2] *Ibid.* 2.10.1822. 'The duty is very large—$3 per piece if classed as No. 1, but we got them entered as No. 2 by giving a present to the Mandarin'.
[3] Y. & Co., 14.4.1824, to Syme & Co., Singapore, and others.
[4] *Ibid.* 28.7.1824.   [5] *I.L.B.* 20.11.1828.

some of the finer numbers of cotton twist. There are considerable enquiries, though the application of the articles to the native manufacture is still in its infancy, and success therefore depends on cheapness.'[1] Piece goods, too, were selling—long clothes, cambrics and chintz 'of good bright colours . . . but the patterns must be confined to those of flowers, as those representing houses, birds and beasts, are very objectionable and the formal pillar pattern is not admired'.[2] Numerous letters in 1830 reported that 'cotton twist is daily growing in estimation among the manufacturers', and the sale of Dutch piece goods was 'constant and very considerable'. By 1831, Jardine Matheson & Co. found it worth their while to set up a special 'piece-goods department', and to appoint a permanent 'confidential agent' in Manchester, a Mr John MacVicar.[3] The latter, a prominent member of the Manchester Chamber of Commerce, brought the Canton merchants into direct contact with the principal cotton manufacturers of Lancashire, including such famous firms as Horrocks of Preston.[4] Already by 1833, British cotton manufactures had become a major branch of the China trade.

But there were two obstacles which were felt to impede an even more rapid expansion of the Lancashire trade. First, 'we must have some great change in the duties and the mode of collecting them [at Canton] before we can calculate on any extension of the trade in this market. Unless we adopt the American plan of bribing the examiners of cargo and linguists to defraud His Celestial Majesty of half the established dues'.[5] Secondly, as long as the Company's charter lasted, the 'private English' could only ship cotton goods to China indirectly, via Singapore or India, at an additional cost of about $8\frac{1}{2}\%$, and then only in limited quantities. Under these conditions the Americans were able to engross

---

[1] *I.L.B.* 3.10.1829. [2] *Ibid.*
[3] *P.L.B.* of J.M. 17.1.1831. There was a subsidiary agency in Glasgow, under a Mr Paton.
[4] The political importance of this is discussed in Chapter VII.
[5] *I.L.B.* 2.1.1833.

the trade in British manufactures to China. But the increasingly important manufacturing interests were not going to be content to remain within the old bounds. The development of the trade in British cotton goods had brought a new and powerful urgency to the critical affairs of the Canton merchant community in the 1830s.[1]

By 1834 the China trade had become something very different from what it was in 1800. It had multiplied in volume and value; but it had also increased in range and altered in emphasis. The great tea monopoly was still the perquisite of the Honourable Company. But tea no longer stood by itself. Finally, the advent of the steamship provided the technical pre-requisite for the fusion of the two branches of the China trade, the 'Country' and the English trade. In April 1830 the steamer *Forbes*, consigned to Magniac & Co. (now Jardine and Matheson), chugged up the mouth of the Pearl river to the astonishment of the natives.[2] A few years later, the 'overland route' via Suez was becoming the normal means of communication between England and China. Affairs at Canton were about to enter a new and quickened phase.

Before enquiring into this, it is first necessary to supplement our account of the early development of the China trade by examining its largest constituent—the trade in opium.

---

[1] See Chapters VII and VIII.

[2] *I.L.B.* 11.9.1830. The first steamer to go right up the river was the little 58-ton *Jardine* in 1835. The Mandarins refused to allow it to ply up and down the river as a passage boat, but the curiosity of the Chinese was unbounded. Wherever the *Jardine* appeared 'the engine could not be seen for masses of Chinese'. Forty years later a similar experience befell the firm when it built the first railway from Shanghai to Woosung, and the local Mandarins ordered the rails to be torn up.

Chapter V

OPIUM

'A pipe of old Patna, that soother of all sorrows,
the manna of the mind.'

A. *The Importance of the Opium Trade*

Thomas de Quincey, in his *Confessions of an Opium Eater*, had
one criticism to make of all that had been previously written on
the subject of opium—lies! Since he wrote, much ink has been
spilled on the subject, as well as blood. Opium became a 'question'.
In China it occasioned several years of warfare, in Victorian
England half a century of moral conflict. It is not here intended
to add to this hoary ethical, medical and legalist controversy; but
because of the unique part which opium played in the Old China
Trade, an examination of the *economic* side of the subject is
necessary. Opium was no hole-in-the-corner petty smuggling
trade, but *probably the largest commerce of the time in any single
commodity*.[1] In 1840 William Jardine defended his character as
the leading opium merchant by citing the repeated declarations
of both Houses of Parliament, 'with all the bench of bishops at
their back', that it was financially inexpedient to abolish the trade.[2]
The men directing British policy at the time were not of more than
average cynicism. They were helped in overcoming moral scruple
by an appreciation of the size of the material interest involved.
The opium trade was important not merely *per se*, for its magnitude and its lucrative character; though such considerations
were by no means ignored. Phipps, the contemporary compiler

---

[1] J. Phipps, *A Practical Treatise on the China and Eastern Trade*, 1836,
Introduction.

[2] Evidence before *S.C.H. of C.* 1840, 1498.

of commercial handbooks, held that the extent of the trade in opium 'can scarcely be matched in any one article of consumption in any part of the world'.[1] Jardine once wrote from Canton to a friend in Essex urging him to invest in opium, 'the safest and most gentlemanlike speculation I am aware of'.[2]

The full economic significance of the drug, however, was not to be measured by the profits it brought to the China merchants. It was to be found, rather, in its connection with the affairs of the Honourable East India Company, territorial and commercial, in India as well as in China. The Bengal opium monopoly was one of the prizes of Clive's victory. In 1773 the British Government in India assumed a monopoly of the sale of opium in their dominions, and in 1797 of its manufacture. This monopoly came, in the next century, to yield one-seventh of the total revenue of British India, 'one of the most unique facts that the history of finance affords'.[3] The production of Indian opium, in Bengal directly under the aegis of a Governmental administrative monopoly, in the Native States controlled by means of transit passes, became an essential and permanent element in the Indian fiscal system.[4] Of this the Parliamentary Committees *never lost sight*. Its wider repercussions on Indian economic life are difficult to measure, but Phipps, writing in 1835, stated that the increased opium production of the previous ten years 'has enhanced the value of the land fourfold, enriched the *Zemindars*, maintained thousands of people employed in collecting and preparing the drug, and benefited the commerce and shipping of Calcutta'.

Secondly, the tea investment at Canton depended for adequate

---

[1] Phipps, *loc. cit.*
[2] *P.L.B.* of W.J. 3.4.1830. There were some lean years in which opium dealers, especially the smaller ones, lost money. But in the good years, I have calculated that gross profits were sometimes as high as $1,000 a chest.
[3] Owen, *British Opium Policy*, preface.
[4] Owen has a good account of the mechanism of the Company's opium monopoly in India; *op. cit.* Chapters 2 and 4. For official documents stressing the importance of the opium revenue, see *S.C.H. of L.* 1840, Appendix I.

funds upon the supplies of the Country Trade (as explained in Chapter I). The two 'grand staples' of that trade were Indian raw cotton and opium. But the demand at Canton for Indian cotton was always limited by the supply of the Nankin cotton crop; and for many years after 1819 the market for Indian cotton was in a state of chronic depression.[1] After 1823 the value of opium imports consistently exceeded that of cotton. Moreover, whereas cotton was sold to the Hong merchants separately under conditions of barter, opium, being contraband, was smuggled to outside brokers, almost always on a cash basis.[2] Most of its proceeds could be remitted, as a rule, only by being paid into the Factory's Treasury in return for Bills of Exchange. Opium thus became the chief India product upon which the Company relied for its tea investment. Already in March 1801 the Court of Directors had explicitly suggested to the Governor-General of Bengal that the production of opium be increased to avoid the necessity of shipping bullion to China.[3] All who were connected with the tea trade were vitally interested in the progress of the opium traffic.

A contemporary pamphleteer[4] wrote: 'From the opium trade the Honourable Company have derived for years an immense revenue and through them the British Government and nation have also reaped an incalculable amount of political and financial advantage. The turn of the balance of trade between Great Britain and China in favour of the former has enabled India to increase tenfold her consumption of British manufacture; contributed directly to support the vast fabric of British dominion in the East, to defray the expenses of His Majesty's establishment in India, and by the operation of exchanges and remittances in teas, to pour an abundant revenue into the British Exchequer and benefit the

[1] See above, Chapter IV.

[2] In spite of W. Jardine's assertion that opium was never sold except for cash, the J.M. papers reveal quite a number of cases when, in an unfavourable market, opium was bartered for China goods. But this was the exception not the rule.

[3] Owen, op. cit., p. 67.

[4] S. Warren, Opium, 1839.

nation to an extent of £6 million yearly without impoverishing India. Therefore the Company has done everything in its power to foster the opium trade.'

The opium trade had the further significance of being a private trade. It was the economic foundation of the rise of the foreign merchant community in China. 'Holly' Magniac told the Lords' Committee of 1830 that his firm, the largest in Canton, was concerned 'almost entirely in opium as a matter of business, and in goods, as far as remittance required, from China only'.[1] W. S. Davidson, the former head of the only other large Canton firm declared that 'nine-tenths of his agency business was in cotton and opium'. Both James Matheson and William Jardine transacted almost nothing but opium business during their first years in China. The same is true of the Parsees. When in 1839 Commissioner Lin effectively checked the drug trade, the commercial communities of Bombay and Calcutta suffered great distress.[2] And Jenks has pointed out that owing to its close credit relations with the China trade, the news of the opium crisis in 1839 was sufficient to cause high tension in Anglo-American mercantile relations.[3]

Finally, the opium traffic was completely outside the Canton Commercial System, being conducted at other places than Canton and through other channels than the Hong merchants. This characteristic of its procedure, together with the financial effects of its huge increase, precipitated the final crisis in which the entire commercial and political relations of China with foreigners was put to ordeal by battle.[4] Opium was no small, incidental question, but the central fact.

[1] *S.C.H. of L.* 1830, p. 429.
[2] *S.C.H. of C.* 1840, 1796-8. There were several suicides among the Bombay Parsees.
[3] L. H. Jenks, *Migration of British Capital*, Chapter 3. The triangular structure of Anglo-American-Chinese exchange and credit relations is examined below in Chapter VI.
[4] See Chapter VIII below.

The development and organisation of the opium trade can best be traced from data in the actual books of the various Canton firms. There were three main sources of supply—Bengal, the 'native provinces' of Central India, and Turkey. Occasionally, during a boom, adventurers would attempt to pass off 'Ispahan juice', cutch, and other mongrel kinds of drug, which even the Canton entrepreneurs designated as 'rubbish'.[1] The poppy was indeed, indigenous to China, and there appears to be evidence that the Arabs imported opium as early as the fourth century. But authorities are agreed that it was not smoked nor its import prohibited by the Chinese Government until the 18th century,[2] and the demand remained small and local until the 19th. The Europeans did not introduce the drug to China; but they organised its production and distribution upon a large scale for the first time.

In this enterprise the East India Company took the lead. The Company had the monopoly of the manufacture and sale of the 'Patna' and 'Benares' varieties of Bengal opium, and managed its production so well that the Company's trademark was accepted by the Chinese as a hallmark of quality in this contraband article as in the legal commodities.[3] 'Malwa', an inferior opium produced in the Indian Native States, was at first shipped in small quantities and only by the Portuguese, through their settlements on the north-west coast of India, Goa and Daimaun. Turkey opium from Smyrna (in practice generally imported *ex bond* from London), being prohibited to British speculators, was taken to China by American traders. Though its import alarmed the Company, its quality was inferior and its source was distant. Turkey opium was used only for mixing with the costlier Bengal and until the 1830s

---

[1] *I.L.B.* 3.8.1824, to a Bombay Parsee. Magniac writes sharply: 'There is little use in forcing this kind on the market when there is so much competition among sellers of that opium which is really good, including Company's.' The Chinese edicts periodically designated all opium as 'vile and pernicious dirt'.

[2] The first anti-opium edict was issued in 1729. See Edkins, Owen, Morse, *International Relations*, for the early history of opium.

[3] *S.C.H. of C.* 1830, 3742, 2027.

it never sold more than 900 chests a year.[1] Early statistics on
opium are even more unreliable than later ones,[2] but practically
all the 4,000 chests per annum which China took on the average,
in the first years of the 19th century, were Patna or Benares, i.e.
Company opium.

It was the Company's policy to confine itself to the production
of opium in India and not to participate in its distribution in China.
The single exception was in 1782, when, the Canton Supercargoes
being unusually short of funds and no treasure coming from
Europe because of the Spanish War, Warren Hastings, then
Governor-General of Bengal, cut the Gordian knot and shipped
two vessels with opium on Company's account.[3] Though it
afforded relief to the Company's finances by enabling the Canton
Government to draw for 20 lacs of rupees, the speculation was a
failure, and was not repeated. The Company developed its alternative method of providing funds at Canton, and left the distribution of the opium in China to private Country merchants.
The latter bought the opium at the Company's public sales in
Calcutta, and carried it to its destination in their private Country
ships, which sailed by licence of the Company. From 1816 there
was a clause in that licence declaring it to be void if any opium
other than the Company's were carried. But in the sailing orders
of every Company's Indiaman bound for China was embodied
a strict prohibition against carrying opium, 'lest the Company be
implicated' with the Chinese![4] By 1800, the East India Company

[1] Its imports averaged 230 chests per annum in 1811-20, 141 in 1821-7, 857 in
1828-33. Morse, *International Relations*, I, 209. Jardine occasionally handled
Turkey opium in the later 1820s and the '30s; it was consigned until 1834 on
foreign bottoms.

[2] On the unreliability of opium statistics see Morse, *op. cit.*, I, 174. When it is
remembered that opium was a contraband article after all, with several centres
of distribution and several sources of supply, the discrepancies in the various
statistical compilations are not surprising.   [3] *Chronicles*, II, 76, 89.

[4] *Chronicles*, II, 316, 325. But Jardine alleged, before the 1840 enquiry, that
Company ships sometimes carried opium, presumably on 'privilege' account.
S.C.H. of C. 1840, Q.1405-22. This is borne out by Y. & Co., *L.B.* 22.10.1822,

had perfected the technique of growing opium in India and dis-
owning it in China.

In China, the destination of the opium,[1] the drug was prohibited
both from being imported and from being smoked, by repeated
edicts, Imperial and local. The first edict appears to have been
issued in 1729 and the later orders generally drew attention to a
prohibition long in force. A definitive prohibition was embodied
in a decree of 1799 (it is printed in the *Chronicles*, Vol. III,
Appendix M) which speaks of the spread of 'the destructive and
ensnaring vice' beyond the coastal provinces of Kwangtung and
Fukien. But the trade continued illegally. The Hong merchants
of course did not deal in opium;[2] but they continued to 'secure'
ships at Whampoa which were known to have brought opium
until 1820, when, being required by the Government authorities
to guarantee that no opium was aboard any ship in their charge,
they declined to 'secure' such ships. Sales were effected through
the medium of Chinese brokers, who acted at a commission of $2
per chest on behalf of the 'dealers' who were agents for the real
'adventuring parties' in Canton.[3] Deliveries were made possible
by the notorious connivance of the local Chinese officials, who
received a fixed fee per chest. In 1815 there was actually a
corruption fund, started by the Portuguese at Macao, with a levy
of $40 a chest, which must have amounted, at the then volume of
sales, to about $100,000 per year.[4] When, in the 1830s, opium was
smuggled 'by a regular system' up the East Coast of China, the
fees to the Mandarins were even higher. The contraband traffic in

when the Company's ships were used to take opium up-river to Whampoa.
Moreover J.M. & Co. were occasionally applied to by the Government of India
Board of Salt and Opium for musters of opium.

[1] A proportion, which varied from year to year, but was never above one-
seventh, was sold in Java, Malaya and in the islands. Singapore became, within a
few years of its foundation, a fair-sized opium mart; though not of course on a
scale comparable with the Chinese centres.

[2] For the rare exceptions, see above, Chapter II.

[3] *Canton Register*, 12.4.1828.

[4] *Chronicles*, III, 323.

opium was generally carried on quite openly; when *The Canton Register* was started in 1827, prices of opium were published with every issue. The Chinese buyers were responsible for securing the connivance of the local officials (which, incidentally, gave some of the more disingenuous foreign dealers who brought the opium to China an opportunity for self-righteousness).

W. S. Davidson declared that in his day nothing could be more simple than to smuggle opium in China.[1] Nevertheless, the trade was still illegal and difficulties were frequent. Not all the Mandarins could be bribed all the time. The anonymous 'Censors' whose function it was 'to guard the guardians' periodically reported to Pekin on the corruption of the Canton officials. The Jardine Matheson papers definitely prove that few years passed without 'persecution' of the Chinese opium dealers, who were fined, imprisoned and sometimes even transported to 'Eli'. These drives were generally short-lived, but often succeeded in stopping opium sales for several weeks or months. In 1821 there was a more than usually vigorous drive; all dealings were stopped for over two months, and the opium ships successfully driven out of the Canton river. Davidson admitted that he was 'in a constant sea of trouble and anxiety' when smuggling at Whampoa; while in the 'outer anchorages' the opium ships were better able to defend themselves.[2]

Two obstacles in the way of any effective suppression on the Chinese side were a corrupt Mandarinate and naval weakness. Corruption went to such lengths that the 'smug boats' which delivered the opium were often Mandarin boats whose function it was to prevent smuggling. Likewise, a favourite means of conveying opium to the northern provinces was the annual Imperial junks, which left Canton for the Pekin river loaded with presents for the Emperor.[3] In 1826 the Select Committee

[1] *S.C.H. of C.* 1830, 2536.
[2] *Ibid.* 1830, Q.2526, 2548.
[3] *I.L.B.* 14.14.1824. Cf. evidence of Jardine to S.C. 1840.

recorded: 'The Chinese war vessels have for some days past collected at Macao and among the islands and have shown a disposition to interfere with and embarrass the opium trade at Lintin by preventing smuggling boats from going alongside the ships, which have been in consequence obliged to disperse. As the war vessels are at all times prevented from attacking the smuggling boats, from the latter being manned by desperate people, who, if apprehended in offering resistance would probably be put to death, while the crews of the former are persons hired at low wages and often very ignorant of all seafaring matters, it is not probable that any violent measures will be adopted or that the interruption will be of long continuance.'[1] The opium vessels belonging to the foreign merchants were of course heavily armed with European weapons. Until the final Chinese effort to suppress the trade, after 1837, the foreigners were themselves not subjected to punishment for partaking in the smuggling, apart from verbal attacks. The 'persecution' was reserved for the Chinese agents. With this reservation, it is a fallacy to believe that before the advent of Commissioner Lin in 1838 the opium trade was not subjected to frequent and vigorous interruption by the Chinese authorities. The incidence of these efforts was one of the chief factors contributing to the remarkable fluctuations of the trade.

B.   *The Business History of Opium*

The 'business history' of opium between 1800, when the letter books of Reid Beale & Co. begin, and 1838, the eve of the Opium War, falls into three separable phases. During the first period, until 1821, when the trade was driven out of the inner Canton river, imports of all kinds of opium rarely exceeded 5,000 chests per year, and averaged less than 4,500[2] The second phase between 1821 and 1830-1, which was marked by the rapid increase in the consumption of Malwa and a smaller expansion in that of Bengal,

[1] *Chronicles*, IV, 133.   [2] See statistical tables in Appendix.

was accompanied by a sharp struggle between the British merchants and the inhabitants of Macao for control of the trade. Smuggling was carried on entirely from ships stationed in the 'outer anchorages' (especially Lintin), except for some premature attempts by James Matheson to open a traffic up the East Coast. During this period total sales fluctuated almost as much as prices, but averaged about 10,000 chests per annum, of which over half were Malwa. In the third phase, during the '30s, there was an enormous expansion in imports from 16,550 chests in the season 1831-2 to over 30,000 in 1835-6, and 40,000 in 1838-9. This was due to a number of forces—an expansionist production policy in India, a new organisation of distribution by means of clippers from India and a fleet of boats up the China coast, an influx of private merchants to Canton upon the abolition of the Company's charter. Smuggling ceased to be confined to Lintin, but developed rapidly along both the East and South Coasts, and in the last three years before the war (really a separate phase) it was carried on once more in Canton waters, as before 1821, only on six times the scale. But these broad trends must be analysed in detail.

When the letter books open, Patna was being sold at Macao for $560 to $590 a chest. 'De Souza is down there manoeuvring and Parry being greatly pushed is selling at 580.'[1] In that year Thomas Beale sold 20 chests to Manhop, who was about to be made a Hong merchant. During this first decade, Macao was the opium mart. Beale warned his Calcutta correspondents that it was imprudent to consign opium to Whampoa, where they were liable to detention and to cause embarrassment.[2] Opium was often consigned to the firm in Portuguese bottoms, but the first mention of Malwa is in 1805, when a quantity of some 300 piculs per *Asia* of 'very bad quality' was 'scarcely saleable at $400 per chest'.[3] This

---

[1] *L.B.* 13.3.1801.
[2] *Ibid.* 3.11.1804, to Mackintosh & Co., Calcutta, and other letters.
[3] *Ibid.* 5.5.1805. Patna was at this time scaling at $1,400.

quantity was brought up to Whampoa; whereupon the Senate of Macao complained to the Select Committee. 'The Select' commented to the Indian authorities that they did not object to Whampoa being preferred to Macao, but to the fact that non-Company opium was being brought to China. Already they could anticipate the future struggle. A year previously the 'jealousy of the Macao Senate' had been noticed.[1] They were afraid of the opium trade slipping out of Portuguese control. When in 1805 the East India Company put a heavy tax on Portuguese vessels resorting to Calcutta, the Government of Macao retaliated by refusing to allow any opium to be landed at the port except from Portuguese ships.[2] This dispute, however, did not flare up into a bitter conflict for another decade. But Beale & Co. were obliged to employ Portuguese agents in the Macao opium market: first 'our friends' Senhor Januario de Almeida and Sur Manoel des Barros, and later a B. Barretto, who was paid a regular commission on sales.

In these early years the opium trade was largely in the hands of Armenians from Calcutta, though Scotsmen and Parsees were beginning to compete. Beale & Magniac were agents for some of these Armenians, Johan Sarkeis, Sarkeis Owen, S. P. Bagram, H. Chatoor, etc. But many of them came over annually with the Portuguese and Country ships, and, being forced to realise their opium quickly in order to return to Bengal before the monsoon's turn, undercut their competitors in the opium market. Beale wrote: 'We must inform you that the depreciation of opium for some months past, and our consequent difficulty in realising sales are in a great degree owing to the Armenians, who have been retailing it at such low price as has proved prejudicial to the Portuguese . . . and their conduct has been thought so improper and hurtful to Macao that we understand the Senate has positively forbidden the Portuguese ships to bring any Armenians as

[1] *L.B.* 26.7.1804, to Fairlie Gilmore & Co., their Calcutta agents.
[2] *Ibid.* 3.12.1805, 26.7.1811.

passengers next year.'[1] The firm of Beale & Magniac, then the only British house besides the semi-official Baring Moloney concern, acted solely as agents in the opium trade at this period, being content with a commission on sales. It was already of sufficient importance to the firm for the senior partner, Beale, to devote his whole attention to it. In 1806-7 he stayed on at Macao for over ten months for the 'sole purpose of awaiting the most favourable opportunity of making [opium] sales'.[2] The demand for opium was found to be very inelastic. 'Opium is an article which cannot be forced', the Calcutta shippers were warned repeatedly. On one occasion Senhor Januario was actually obliged to re-ship 100 chests back from Macao to be disposed of in the Straits of Malacca.[3] Opium at this period was 'a very precarious article which is liable to sudden and often unaccountable fluctuations'; in another letter, written two years later, 'the price of it is of all commodities the most precarious'.[4] At times the prospects of the trade were very discouraging. Beale wrote to Sarkeis and the other Calcutta Armenians: 'We never before last season speculated so much in your opium, gentlemen, and the result holds out no inducement for us to do so again.'[5]

Since the amount sold at the Calcutta sales during this period remained fairly steady, while imports of Malwa and Turkey were small, the price fluctuations depended very largely upon conditions in China. Among contributing factors were periodic combinations among the Chinese opium dealers, and among foreign agents; occasional 'persecutions' by the Mandarins; the attitude of the Macao Government; and miscellaneous influences

---

[1] *L.B.* 26.11.1801. The egregious G. M. Baboum, who was an Armenian, was possessed of little more capital than his compatriots. Yet in 1799 he offered to buy up the whole of the Company's supply of opium at 550 Sicca rupees per chest if granted a monopoly for three years. The Company refused to be tempted. *Chronicles*, II, 325.   [2] *Ibid.* 25.9.1806.
[3] *Ibid.* 16.2.1806. It is not clear whether these were on his own account or on that of Beale & Magniac.
[4] *Ibid.* 22.11.1801, 25.9.1803.   [5] *Ibid.* 26.11.1801.

E

of a political character, such as a rebellion in Formosa or piracy in the Macao waters. Both in 1801 and in 1805 'rings' of Chinese dealers forced up the price of opium—up, not down as might be expected, for the following reason. Opium was at that time generally sold on credit, four or five months being allowed for payment and a deposit of $50 per chest required as 'bargain money'. The foreign merchants were continually in fear of the Chinese buyers not being able to make good their sale, though the deposit would thereby be lost. The latter often forced up the price to a fictitious high level; 'a finesse the Chinese often have recourse to, to enable them to realise what they have been purchasing'.[1]

In the season 1805-6 there was a severe depression on the market and not a chest could be sold. This was partly because for some months past pirates had succeeded in 'surrounding Macao';[2] secondly because 'a great rebellion has broken out in Formosa, which has decreased the demand for opium and cotton from the province of Chinchew [apparently Fukien], where rice is now very dear; it is said the Chinese have lost nearly the whole of their possessions [in Formosa]';[3] and thirdly, because the Chinese dealers at Macao had been obliged to conceal themselves for a time 'owing to the persecutions of the Mandarins'.[4] A fourth reason for the stagnation was the tendency for the captains of Country and Honourable Company ships to bring up opium to Whampoa with orders to sell at any price.[5] A fifth and less

---

[1] *L.B.* 22.11.1801.

[2] *Ibid.* 8.11.1805. The Chinchew merchants, who came down in junks every summer to the Canton river, and brought back large quantities of opium, got the Macao Government to convoy their junks with armed European ships, which the *ladrones* were less eager to attack. *L.B.* 26.7.1805. A year previously Beale had reported 'opium completely at a standstill owing to the number of *ladrone* pirate junks off Macao'.   [3] *Ibid.* 20.3.1806.

[4] *Ibid.* 26.7.1805; the writer continues 'but we hope they will soon reappear and transact their business openly'.

[5] *Ibid.* 31.8.1806. They sold $150-$200 below the market price, because they were forced to realise at once.

accidental reason was the inelasticity of demand. In 1804-5 the price of Patna had practically doubled, rising to $1,400 a chest. (Benares, 'ever unsaleable in itself without Patna', always fetched about $100 less than its fellow unless their respective qualities varied considerably from the normal, as in some later seasons.) In the summer of 1806, in spite of a combination led by William Baring to keep up the price, Patna fell to below $1,130, and was unsaleable at that. Beale, who had been unable to sell more than a few chests in his ten month's stay at Macao, wrote to his Armenian principals, asking to resign charge of their future transactions in the drug: 'no advantages accruing to us from the agency of this business can compensate in any degree for the trouble and anxiety'. In a further letter he declared that the continued and rapid depression (in opium prices) was the most sudden and extensive ever remembered, adding that the exorbitant price of the last two years had 'rendered it necessary for numbers who were in the habit of using this destructive drug to abstain from indulging their propensities'.[1] Not all seasons were so unfortunate as that of 1805-6, when the difficulties of the pioneer smugglers were multiplied by a conscientious Mandarin and a jealous Senate. 'The present *Foyan* is so strict that it is impossible to sell within the Bogue, while the Portuguese will not allow it at Macao.'[2] Beale expressed his 'chagrin' and remarked that 'such adventures are and ever have been hazardous in the extreme', but continued to persevere.

From 1806 to 1819 we have only one fragmentary *Indian Letter Book* and two *Europe Letter Books;* none of these throw additional light on the mysteries of the opium trade. Neither do the few letters of this period which are preserved in the 'Correspondence In'. But the ledgers suggest that in the second decade of the century the firm's opium business expanded considerably. This impression is confirmed by the Company's *Chronicles*,[3] which record the fact that in November 1819 Thomas Beale

[1] *L.B.* 28.5.1806, 8.9.1806.   [2] *I.L.B.* 26.7.1805.   [3] *Chronicles*, III, 208.

applied to the East India Company's Supercargoes for Bills of
Exchange to the value of 8 lacs of dollars to be paid in advance of
receipt of cash, 900 chests of opium being given as security. The
Select Committee were sufficiently confident of Beale's talents as
an opium dealer to accept chests of opium as collateral security
for so large a sum. Beale had, apparently, caught the gambler's
fever and was indulging in large-scale opium operations on his
own account under secret arrangement with the chief Judge of
Macao, Senhor Arriaga. The latter became indebted to Beale for
no less than $1,780,000; Beale, unable to repay his debt to the
Committee, absconded.[1] These transactions were certainly not
typical; but they give an indication of the new scale of operation
in the opium trade.

After 1819 we have evidence from two sets of letter books, those
of Magniac & Co. and those of the Taylor-Matheson concern and
afterwards Yrissari & Co. During the first two or three years
they both reveal certain new features in the opium trade. First,
there was a heightening of tempo as new merchants entered the
field. Taylor and Matheson formed an agency which dealt almost
entirely in opium. The ships consigned to them—the brig *Tweed*
in 1818, the *Marquis of Hastings* in 1819, the *Hooghly* in the
following year—were all opium ships sent by Calcutta firms,
J. Scott & Co., D. MacIntyre & Co., and M. Larruleta & Co.
respectively. There was an 'opium rush' on. Old Taylor wrote
in 1818: 'Opium is like gold, I can sell it any time'.[2]

After a hesitant start, in which Taylor was obliged to barter a
few chests for sugar ('a dangerous expedient'), the merchants

---

[1] *Chronicles*, III, 238, 248-50, 307-8. J.M. ledger 1815-6; and see below, Chapter
VI, for discussion of the relations between partners. Nearly twenty years later,
Thomas Beale, now the oldest foreign inhabitant and living at Macao in such
penury that his former partners had to raise a fund by subscription on his behalf,
still occasionally indulged in a mild opium gamble with borrowed money. This
brought down upon him the wrath of William Jardine, now head of the firm.
I.L.B. 6.10.1832.

[2] *L.B.* of R.T. 4.11.1819.

beat up the market into a boom. In July 1819, Patna was to be had for $1,170 a chest. In August, Magniac & Co. began buying up everything they could lay their hands on. In October they wrote to a timorous Baboo of Calcutta who had ventured to send some 25 chests: 'We sincerely wish you had sent ten times the quantity'.[1] They continued to buy up the new season's opium imports, since cotton was in a state of depression. By the following winter they controlled all the opium in China. In December 1820, $1,800 was being offered and refused for Benares. By the following February, Patna had reached a new high level of $2,500 a chest. Taylor had made a profit in selling to Magniac for $1,390! Malwa, which at the beginning of 1819 had 'got up to $730', was selling at $1,320 a year later, and at $1,800 in 1821. Turkey had been forced up to $1,200. At this stage the Magniacs sold out. The 'rigorous measurements just commenced by this Government to *impede* the consumption of opium in China' caused a sudden fall in prices. Magniac & Co. sent urgent despatches to Calcutta cancelling orders for future purchases. The *Topaze* affair,[2] which produced a temporary stoppage of the legitimate trade, had little effect on the smuggling trade; and once the severity of the opium 'persecution' had been relaxed and 'store-ship' system developed at Lintin, prices of opium recovered rapidly. In March 1822, Patna was selling below $2,000, and Malwa had fallen to $1,200. By August, Patna had passed the $2,500 mark and Malwa was selling at $1,500. Parsee dealers and English ships' captains joined in the scramble to get opium to China. 'Ispahan juice' and cutch were being hopefully shipped to Lintin.[3] A Portuguese named Pereira

---

[1] *I.L.B.* 13.10.1819, to Baboo Ramdololl Day, one of the wealthiest merchants in India.   [2] See *Chronicles*, IV, p. 18.

[3] See footnote 1, page 108, above. Writing on the causes of poor quality of much of the seasons's opium, the youthful Matheson remarked solemnly: 'I would in almost every case attribute it to disintegrity on the part of the agent ... the article having for some time been attended with such large profits as to hold out more than common temptation to the weak passions of our nature'. 'Disintegrity' was the sin; the adulteration of the drug, not its distribution to the Chinese.

was asking $3,000 for a chest of Patna. Then came the collapse. Within a few months (by June 1823) Patna was unsaleable at $1,800, Malwa had fallen to $1,120. In September Patna was priced at $1,420. Yrissari & Co., who had tried to emulate the feat of the Magniacs two years previously in cornering the market, found themselves faced with ruin.[1] The chief causes of the collapse, apart from over-speculation by numerous smallholders, were a renewal of the anti-opium campaign on the part of the Mandarins and the Company's new Malwa policy in India.

This bare account of the first great opium 'boom' illustrates the increasingly speculative character and fierce tempo of the trade. A second major feature of these years was the radical adjustment of the opium merchants to a new manner of conducting their commerce in consequence of a very vigorous campaign on the part of the Chinese Government which succeeded in forcing the trade outside the Bogue. When in 1815 the Macao Senate had judiciously renewed its old restrictions against opium from non-Portuguese shipping being landed at Macao, the British Country merchants proceeded to bring the bulk of their Bengal opium up-river to Whampoa. This was too close to Canton to be really safe.

James Matheson, on arriving at Whampoa on the *Marquis of Hastings*, had reported to its owners that 'the Hong merchants have commonly an objection to securing opium ships and require to be coaxed into the measure.' In October 1819 a small boat belonging to a Company ship, the *Essex*, was discovered, on its way from Whampoa to Canton, to be carrying opium. Manhop, the ship's 'security' merchant, was able to buy off the Mandarins with a bribe of $6,000. The following March W. S. Davidson was ordered by the Viceroy to remove his opium ship *Mentor* from Whampoa and 'no money could reverse the decree'.[2] In April and

---

[1] The situation was saved by James Matheson, junior partner of the firm, finding a new outlet by venturing along the East Coast.

[2] R.T. *L.B.* 4.4.1820.

July the Viceroy and *Hoppo* issued edicts requiring the Hong merchants to search all ships for opium and bear full responsibility for any ships they secured.[1]

The following July, Howqua himself was implicated by the officials, who had obviously received a sharp order from Pekin. Apparently, a certain opium dealer at Macao named Asee, who had been imprisoned by a local official on a criminal charge, had avenged himself by exposing the corruption of the officials, for whom he had acted as bribe collector. 'The same caitiff Asee, the late principal dealer at Macao, has received sentence of transportation to the cold country, but is still in prison here. He has it seems made representations to Pekin, laying open the venality and corruption of the Mandareens and offering proofs by the production of his book of accounts of the bribes he has been paying them for several years . . . It is expected a special commission will be sent from Pekin to adjudge the matter.'[2] There followed what Charles Magniac called 'the hottest persecution we remember'. In November and December 1821 the local officials promulgated severe edicts against the opium ships, calling upon them to quit the river. The Hong merchants told the foreigners that they would refuse to 'secure' any more ships with a part cargo of opium.[3] Four opium ships were specially named, the *Merope*, *Hooghly*, *Eugenia* and the American *Emily*. With the first three Matheson was connected. His ships quitted the port, but once outside the Bogue anchored off the island of Lintin, at the mouth of the river. The *Merope* was to remain there for three years.

The British opium importers, driven from Whampoa, were forced to seek a new depôt for their ships. Their solution was to station at Lintin armed floating 'hulks' to serve as 'receiving ships' in which the opium was stored on arrival from India, and

[1] Printed in *Chronicles*, Appendix W.
[2] Y. & Co., 17.5.1822.
[3] *Chronicles*, Appendix Z,

from which the Chinese 'smug-boats' took delivery. (Other 'outer anchorages' were also used—Kumsingmoon off Lantao Island, and later Hongkong. The anchorage at Lintin was only a roadstead, and unsafe during the typhoon season.) The Country ships would deliver their drug to these receiving vessels before proceeding up-river to Whampoa with their legitimate cargoes, which the Hongists could then 'secure'. Demurrage charge of $7 per opium chest per month (soon reduced to $5 on account of competition) provided an additional source of income to receiving shipowners; and the example of Matheson's *Merope* was quickly imitated by the Magniac and Dent houses, who jointly purchased the *Samarang* to serve as a receiving vessel. The *Eugenia, Jamesina* and the Spanish brig *General Quiroga* soon followed.

For some time, however, it was by no means clear whether this system would work. The expenses were heavy: demurrage, maintenance, wages of the crew, and a large insurance premium of 1% per month, soon, however, reduced to $\frac{1}{2}\%$. Matheson wrote to Larruleta, his Calcutta agent: 'On the *Merope's* first going out, our neighbours declined entirely insuring her. The effect of a few months' experience has however induced their swerving from their determination. Then [in July 1822] 1% for sea risk was charged for Mr Calvo's *Quiroga*, and even at the present diminished rate of $\frac{1}{2}\%$, it appears to us a heavier tax than, with the demurrage, the trade can well bear'.[1] The insurance was against storms or pirates, and not against the Mandarins. Matheson was optimistic on all three heads. 'Our experience after one of the most tempestuous seasons known here is that the sea risk is in fact so inconsiderable as not to require insurance'; on account of the special equipment of the *Merope*, and because of the 'knowledge the commander has acquired of the soundings and various places of safety on each side of the river (the safest river in the world), and other ships to render her assistance in case of need . . . The idea of seizure by the Chinese we consider out of the question.

[1] Y. & Co., *L.B.* 22.9.1822.

The only danger on that score would be from an organised band of pirates making an attempt on the property; but for some years there have been no pirates in the Canton river. Nor however great the prize can it be considered a tempting one, since [it] . . . could not fail to lead to their detection and punishment, as in the case of the plunderers of an American vessel in Macao Roads in 1817, who were executed in front of the American consul'. It was a case of the smuggler relying on the policeman to protect him against the robber!

Still the insurance was expensive and the system not qiute satisfactory . . . 'It is important to avoid this heavy charge, since it is extremely improbable that we can by any means for the present bring back the trade to Whampoa.' Other solutions were therefore sought.

Macao was ruled out from the first. In 1820 Davidson's brig *Mentor*, being forced to quit Whampoa, had intended going to Macao, 'but upon mature deliberation it was judged imprudent to venture into a port where the Chinese are lords paramount, the Portuguese being only tenants-at-will. Nothing was to be done but to go to Singapore or remain at Lintin. The latter was adopted'.[1] Taylor's opinion was echoed two years later by Matheson: 'As for Macao, the increased restrictions by the Portuguese as well as the Chinese, and the unsettled state of its Government render it a far from desirable depôt for so valuable a trade.' This was written in September 1822 at the time of the revolution in Macao, whose significance will be examined below. A year later the problem was still unsolved. 'You will have noticed our proposal of storing opium at Manila to save insurance and demurrage—a proposal which but for the present ferment in men's minds at that colony, and the recent war in Europe, we should reiterate[2] . . . Some change from the present system of

[1] R.T. *L.B.* 23.3.1820.
[2] The Filipinos had just massacred some Spaniards, and the French had marched into Spain.

floating depôts must sooner or later take place; the following plan from Messrs Uriarte [a Spanish firm in Calcutta] coincides with our views—that the general warehouse for the drug be Manila or Singapore, keeping China supplied by small but swift, good vessels making periodical trips every three or four months to the various parts of the Coast best calculated for getting rid of the article. The distance of Singapore is a great drawback if not an insuperable objection, in consequence of the difficulty and delay of a passage up the China Sea in the N.E. monsoon.'[1] In fact the difficulties of any alternative were insuperable, and the Lintin system remained, with some modification in the 'thirties, until the outbreak of the Opium War.

C. *Malwa and Damaun*

Another problem which the opium traders had to solve during this period arose from the enormous increase in the consumption of Malwa, and its effect upon the East India Company's policy in India. Until 1815 the imports of Malwa by Country merchants were small and difficult of sale. In that season the high price to which the Bengal opium had been forced by 'a combination among the foreign merchants' led to the introduction of cheaper substitutes.[2] In 1817 the imports of Malwa and Turkey jumped to 1,100 and 1,900 piculs respectively, and in the following season to even greater quantities. The effect of these Malwa imports upon the price of Bengal opium was immediate. Patna, which had sold for $1,300 a chest in 1817, fell to $840 in the following season, in which Malwa sold at $680. The cheapness of Malwa, and the high rate of profit compared with the monopolist Bengal opium, attracted the small speculators. But the possibility of large-scale operations outside the control of the Company invited the attention of the largest dealers.

In 1819 James Matheson, still in his early twenties, conceived

---

[1] Y. & Co., 26.9.1823, J.M. to Mackintosh & Co., Calcutta.
[2] *Chronicles*, III, 339.

the plan of sending a special ship secretly to the West Coast of India, to bring supplies of Malwa directly to China. On 23 December 1819 he sailed from China on the *Hooghly* (owned by Larruleta & Co., Calcutta) under Danish colours, nominally to supply Tranquebar (the Danish establishment south of Madras) with sundry China goods, in fact to proceed to Portuguese Damaun and Goa. (Matheson was about to be appointed Danish Consul; British, i.e. 'Country', vessels required the licence of the Company, which would of course not have been granted in this case.) The exact details of what happened are not clearly expressed in Matheson's letters,[1] and can only be guessed at from veiled allusions. But apparently he fell foul of the Portuguese authorities at Damaun and Goa, who were bribed by rival Portuguese opium shippers to refuse the *Hooghly* permission to load.[2] Large stakes were at issue. Jardine was connected with the affair. Magniac & Co. were heavily interested and were working through a rival agent, an Anglicised Portuguese of Bombay, Sir Roger de Faria.

---

[1] R.T. and J.M., February-June 1820.

[2] Matheson wrote Larruleta from Goa, 31.5.1820: 'I beg to mention that those opposed to us are in the first place Sir Roger de Faria of Bombay (who gave 16,600 rupees to the Governor and Council of Damaun for their unjust decision), secondly Don Lorrenco de Navorrha, the Governor of Damaun. On the other hand, Senhor Vincente Salvador Rozario, Judge at Damaun (formerly at Macao) made a stand in our favour against all the rest of the Council. The Viceroy [of Goa], Conde de Rio Pindo, has had his feelings strongly excited by the events, and Don Lorrenco has been appointed Governor by the King [of Portugal] in supersession of a previous appointment by the Conde . . . The Adjutant General, Don Joaquim de Silvare, behaves to us with great complaisance, but is said to be a friend of Faria's. I fear he will be bought over to the other side. Bernardo Aleire, a former Governor of Macao, has promised to watch our interests in consideration of my paying him an old debt of *Baboum's*, of a small amount if the event was not a success—an honest way of offering a bribe. I mention these names in the probable event of your being able to exert a favourable influence on any of the parties. Our destination is now Tranquebar, in order to influence the Danish Government in our behalf and in support of the honour of their flag. By them complaint will probably be made to the Royal Government in the Brazils.' This experience of Portuguese justice did not enamour Matheson of the claims of Macao as an opium depôt.

Matheson took legal action, appealing from the head of the Portuguese authorities in India, whom his opponents had bribed, to the Superior Portuguese Court in Rio de Janeiro, Brazil. The result is not mentioned in any surviving document, but Matheson was apparently unsuccessful.

In spite of the failure of the *Hooghly* venture, large speculations by British Country merchants in Malwa continued. In November 1820 the Magniacs co-operated with Davidson and the Dent brothers in forming a Malwa syndicate with their Bombay agents ('and I have great hopes that your influence will prevail on several wealthy natives to join us in an extensive purchase'). At this point the East India Company was reluctantly forced to change its opium policy and enter the Malwa market itself.

The steady revenue brought into the Bengal Treasury from opium depended upon the Company's Bengal drug retaining its ascendancy in the Chinese market. The rise of Malwa presented a challenge which the Directors had to meet. In 1813 the first shipments of Malwa had excited the fear of the Select Committee at Canton. The Government of Bengal at once considered steps for 'the prevention of the further growth of that commerce and for its ultimate annihilation'. Accordingly, the export of Malwa from Bombay was forbidden to vessels sailing under the Company's licence. The Country merchants then chartered ships under the Portuguese flag to carry Malwa to Macao; but they could not consign it to Whampoa, since Portuguese vessels were not allowed up the Canton river. From 1816, as we have noted, Malwa was imported on an increasing scale. In 1816 and 1818 the Select Committee again sounded the alarm and the Company decided to take action. In January 1819 the Court of Directors wrote to the Governor-General-in-Council at Bengal as follows:[1] 'We have received your political letter of 4 January 1817, representing the injury which the opium branch of the Company's

---

[1] C. of D. to G.-G., Bengal, 27.1.1819, printed in Appendix to *S.C.H. of L.* 1840. Owen, *op. cit.* Chapter IV, gives a fuller account.

revenue is likely to sustain from the traffic in that article, which is stated to be carried on between Goa and other ports of India not subject to British jurisdiction and the Portuguese settlement of Macao . . . suggesting an arrangement between the Governments of Great Britain and Portugal, under which the latter would prohibit the import into Macao of non-monopoly opium . . .' The letter goes on to doubt whether the Portuguese would agree and expresses confidence in the superiority of the Company's article, which they urged should be cheapened. This was one of the methods adopted to deal with the challenge of Malwa—the cheapening of Patna by an expansion of poppy cultivation in Bengal. But the effect of this could not be felt for some time, and immediate action was considered necessary.

Between 1821 and 1831 the Company tried to control Malwa shipments by a variety of methods. First it tried to buy up the whole crop itself. In 1821-2, 4,000 chests of Malwa were purchased *on Company account* and sold by public auction to agents in Bombay in the same manner as Patna and Benares were sold in Calcutta. The result of this measure was to double the China import of Malwa; for 'smuggled opium' (i.e. non-Company opium) continued to be brought from Damaun. (Magniac & Co. had no less than 5 ships carrying Damaun opium consigned to them during the first season of 'Company Malwa'.) This caused the collapse of the opium boom in 1823. Malwa transactions, encouraged by the Company's action, had been very extensive. The grand total of the net proceeds of Malwa sold April 1822 to March 1823 by Magniac & Co. on joint account with Remingtons and Jamsetjee Jeejeebhoy of Bombay came to not less than $2,403,834.[1] The collapse of the market from an excessive supply caused great distress among the Country merchants, who blamed the Company. Magniac wrote with bitter eloquence to Mackintosh and Co., Calcutta, as follows: 'The unfortunate state of the opium market . . . (is) . . . a natural consequence of the extraordinary

[1] *I.L.B.* 22.7.23.

proceedings of your Government, incomprehensible to us on every ground of wisdom of policy, in offering a premium on the production of *Malwa* by purchasing 4,000 chests, and thus overlaying and stifling the drug produced in Bengal from whence the Company were deriving a profit which in respect of first cost is almost unequalled in the annals of commerce, a profit which in one season . . . actually rose to such a pitch as nearly to pay for the whole Chinese investment for cargoes for 20 ships of 1,400 tons—a profit which no person in their senses would have dreamed of until it exhibited in itself symptons of decay. To such a profit, by fostering a production that should have called only to have it put down and if possible annihilated, the Government have given a death blow; and this under the vague idea of guarding against some distant, undefined and, we have no doubt, unreal danger of Turkey opium interfering with that of India, and even under the more contradictory notion in the beginning of preventing Malwa coming through Damaun, while they are offering a bounty for the additional production of it by annual purchases . . . of 4,000 chests.

'We really do think the Company's operations in Malwa opium (from which by the way we have good reason to believe loss rather than the contrary has arisen) offers a most striking anomaly in commercial proceedings—and we feel persuaded an injury has been done the revenue which will not be suddenly repaired; unless relief be afforded next season, we expect to sell opium at the price of nearly 22 years ago—namely $350-$500 per chest. But we must apologise for detaining you by this long rhapsody.'[1]

The Country merchants also demanded compensation for the bad quality of Company Malwa. When the Company refused compensation, Magniac wrote: 'The faith and credit of the Company's stamp have received a blot among Europeans, . . . and [it] has shaken that implicit reliance with which the Chinese have been

[1] *I.L.B.* 12.11.1823. Malwa did drop to 550 in August 1824, *I.L.B.* 1.1.1825.

hitherto in the habit of accepting all merchandise under the seal of the Company.'[1]

The East India Company's experiment in purchasing opium had failed. The flooding of the market with supplies from both sides of India had increased the consumption but lowered the prices, as the following figures for the years in question reveal.[2]

	Patna and Benares		Malwa	
	Chests	Value in $	Chests	Value in $
1821-22	2,910	6,038,250	1,718	2,276,350
1822-23	1,822	2,828,930	4,000	5,160,000
1823-24	2,900	4,656,000	4,172	3,859,100

Early in 1824[3] the Select Committee sent a strong representation to the Supreme Government at Calcutta, recommending a reduction of supply. The Company stopped buying Malwa.

But it had to devise some new policy because Malwa consumption continued on the increase. Its quality, though inferior to good Patna, was improving and in addition it yielded a greater proportion of smokeable extract than the Bengal drug. 'It has now become the favourite drug of the great mass of Chinese with the

[1] *I.L.B.* 7.11.1823.
[2] From *Canton Register*, 5.4.1828. These figures include sales at Macao and on the East Coast.
[3] Reported by Matheson, 6.2.1824—Y. & Co., *L.B.*

exception of the wealthy, and is certainly safer to speculate in.'[1] The Company changed its tactics. The growth of British power in Central India, following earlier military operations against the Pindari and Marathi, in proximity to the Malwa areas, enabled the Company to force agreements upon the native princes for restricting cultivation of the drug.[2] But this policy of restriction was unable to prevent the Bombay agents of the Canton opium dealers[3] from continuing to make large shipments of Malwa through the Portuguese ports. In every season 1826-31 except one, imports of 'smuggled' Malwa from Damaun exceeded that which the Company now allowed to be bought at Bombay.[4] By 1829 it was clear that their policy of restriction had failed.

In 1831 a new and lasting method was devised of dealing with the Malwa problem, indeed of turning it into an asset. Malwa was now permitted to be shipped through Bombay to any extent by private purchasers *on the payment of a transit duty* of 175 rupees per chest, (later reduced to 125 and subsequently again raised). The route from the Malwa area to the sea via Bombay was so much better than that through Damaun or Goa that 'smuggled' Malwa

[1] Reported by Matheson, 6.2.1824. This opinion was confirmed by Hollingworth Magniac (*I.L.B.* 19.4.1826): 'It has now become clear that as a general rule Malwa is the safe and satisfactory kind of opium to speculate in, both because it usually yields an equal profit upon a smaller amount of capital employed, and because it is an article that can always be realised to a considerable extent upon deduction from the market price, in case any sudden information should render it a matter of importance for the speculator to get out. Patna on the other hand, except for 3 months in the year, and under casual and uncertain ships in the market, remits slowly. No sacrifice will suddenly run off 50-100 chests against a limited demand, however desirable for the holder to do so'. Hence from the season 1823-4 to 1834-5 Malwa imports exceeded those of Bengal in every year but two.

[2] Owen, *op. cit.*, Chapter IV.

[3] Magniac & Co., Yrissari & Co. and the other Canton firms were no longer limiting themselves to selling the opium of others on commission. They were buying on their own account at the Calcutta and Bombay sales to the extent of their capacity to place funds in India for the purpose. Magniac & Co. entered into arrangements with the largest Parsee dealers in Bombay, Motichund Amichund, Hormusjee Dorabjee, and of course Jamsetjee Jeejeebhoy.

[4] See Morse's statistics in *International Relations*, and in *Chronicles*, *loc. cit.*

ceased to be worthwhile. Whereas previously two-thirds of the Malwa was carried by the circuitous route of Damaun and only one-third via Bombay, after 1831 nine-tenths passed through Bombay.[1] The duty on the transit passes brought in a new revenue—£200,000 in its first year. 'The Rothschild of Malwa,' Bedahur Mull, who sent 10-12 lacs of rupees worth of opium to China, paid nearly the same amount in duty to the Bombay Government.[2]

Thus, the Government of India, which was the Honourable East India Company, faced with the competition of Malwa, had gradually and reluctantly been forced from its policy of restricted production and high prices into a policy of maximum production in both British India and the Native States. This of course meant the flooding of China with cheap opium from both sides of India.

The Canton private merchants welcomed the new Company system of open trade in Malwa. It made for a greatly enlarged supply of cheap opium to China. In 1832-3, 11,000 chests of 'pass Malwa' which had paid Company transit duty were shipped from Bombay. The enormous expansion in the opium trade, which followed upon the Company's new policy in India, had remarkable repercussions in China.

D. *The Struggle against Macao*

One of the most visible effects of the Company's new Malwa policy was the further decay of Macao. That the Malwa question involved a life-and-death struggle for economic existence on the part of the tiny Portuguese settlement in China has not been adequately appreciated.

In decline since the 17th century, by the beginning of the 19th Macao had already ceased to be an important trading station—a direct consequence of the decline of the mother country. It exhibited 'in its spacious dwellings, warehouses, churches,

---

[1] *Revenue Report*, August 1832, S.C. 1840, Appendix C, 1.
[2] Phipps, *op. cit.*, 277.

fortifications, the remains of former opulence and prosperity' and was 'in a fair way to recover in fashion and elegance what it had lost in commerce'.[1] The growing British community escaped from the confines of the Canton Factories for the 'season' to indulge in those very British 'gay and inspiriting amusements'—musical parties, masquerades, horse-racing, amateur theatricals—'in this dull land of form and ceremony'. One great attraction of the place was its remarkable superfluity of women; and many a ship's officer or merchant thousands of miles away relied upon Magniac & Co. to pay regular sums for the maintenance of his 'pensioner' at Macao. The population of Macao in 1822 was:

Freemen, over 15 years of age	=	604
„ under „ „ „ „	=	473
Slaves	=	573
Women	=	2,693
Chinese men and women	=	45,000

These figures reveal that the oldest Western trading post in East Asia had become a very curious urban community.[2] The majority of its Portuguese inhabitants lived in penury; its officials on corruption. There were one or two wealthy mercantile houses, the 'Widow Payva & Sons', managed by Veiga, and A. Pereira & Co., which were associated with the Jardine and Dent houses respectively.

Besides the slender income it earned as a kind of seaside resort, Macao had one other resource—opium. It was a safer distribution centre than Whampoa. Portuguese ships, which were the only carriers of Malwa after the Company's prohibiting it on Bombay ships in 1815, could under the Chinese regulations unload only at Macao. But the Portuguese need for as high a revenue as possible from opium, and their insistence that foreigners must deal at Macao only through Portuguese agents, drove the British dealers in Malwa to Whampoa. Alarmed for their livelihood, the Macao Government put forward a project in 1819 for equalising

---

[1] *Canton Register*, 1.12.1827.   [2] *Ibid.* 1.6.1830.

the duties it charged on British and Portuguese shipping if the
Company would agree to hold Malwa sales in Bombay and
compensate the Macao Custom House for loss of the Damaun
trade.[1] Nothing came of the proposal.

The campaign of the Mandarins against the opium smugglers
in 1820-2 involved Macao. When the vigilance of the officials was
at its height, it was impossible to move a chest from one building
to another unless disguised in packages made to resemble other
goods.[2] The drug trade was brought to a standstill; and Magniac
& Co., who were deeply involved in Malwa, which had been
brought to Macao through its leading citizen, the old Baron de
St José de Porto Allegre, had the stuff exported to the islands on
the Spanish brig *Quiroga*, in spite of the $25 per chest export duty
charged by the Portuguese. The firm thereupon wrote to its India
correspondents recommending them to avoid consigning their
opium to Macao.[3] In consequence the Macao Government 'lost
all credit and at length was subverted ... Symptoms of discontent
against foreigners, particularly those concerned in opium, were
exhibited by the populace'.[4] But this domestic revolution could
not save Macao from economic ruin.

When the problem arose of finding a permanent depôt for
opium storage and distribution, the new Macao Government
eagerly put in its claim: 'The most respectable merchants sanctioned by the Government at Macao are making strong endeavours
to induce foreigners to deposit their opium at that place, offering
us the same privileges with themselves, that we shall pay no more
duty. Exclusive of the duty, they propose levying an impost on
each chest to form a fund of about $200,000 per annum for the
purpose of bribing the mandareens, and keeping them always
contented. But our opinion is that it is impossible to content the
mandareens, who are continually increasing the exorbitancy of
their demands, the more they receive; and Macao is so completely

---

[1] *Chronicles*, III, 357.   [2] *Canton Register*, 19.2.1831.
[3] *I.L.B.* 25.9.1823.   [4] Y. & Co., 1.9.1822.

in subjection to them that we can scarcely form a hope of the scheme being practicable.'[1] When this offer of the Macao Government was rejected by the British merchants, who preferred the islands, the Portuguese became 'incensed against the Lintin squadron'.[2] But they were helpless because the British controlled the sources of opium in India. By the summer of 1825 the Chinese brokers had practically abandoned Macao, because 'with the exception of a limited quantity for its own consumption the sales are almost wholly confined to Lintin and the receiving ships outside'.

There was one last hope for Macao—'smuggled' opium, i.e. Malwa from Damaun. It will be remembered that the East India Company after 1824 attempted to restrict the export of Malwa through Bombay, as a result of which large quantities of the drug were taken from the native states by way of the Portuguese port of Damaun, in ships sailing under Portuguese colours. These ships had to land their cargoes and pay duties at Macao harbour. But the British merchants at Canton preferred Lintin. They therefore launched a successful attack on this last remnant of Macao privilege by driving a wedge between the Portuguese authorities in India and the Government of Macao. Acting through the agency of Sir Roger de Faria of Bombay, they were able to obtain, at a price, certificates from the Government of Goa or Damaun allowing the ships to go to Lintin instead of Macao. But the inhabitants of the latter settlement, though under the jurisdiction of the Viceroy of Goa, did not yield without a struggle. 'You will be disappointed to hear of the failure of Sir Roger's arrangements for exempting Damaun opium from Macao duties. The inhabitants considered such an arrangement a death blow to their revenue and ruin to their shipowners, and were determined to do everything in their power to prevent it being carried into effect.'[3] A further letter from Magniacs elaborates the nature of this final struggle.

[1] Y & Co., 26.4.1823.   [2] Magniac to his Singapore agent, *I.L.B.* 27.1.1824.
[3] *I.L.B.* 24.7.1828.

'The inevitable ruin of Macao, if deprived of this trade—now their only resource—has been represented to the Viceroy of Goa as well as to the Court at Lisbon; until the decision of the latter shall have been received, it is not likely the people and Government of Macao with ruin staring them in the face will attend to any orders of the Viceroy should he venture an opposition to their strong remonstrances . . . The Macao authorities are actuated in their measures by necessity, the most powerful of all motives, of all laws.' For a time the Senate of Macao was able to defy its Goan overlord. Jardine, now head of Magniac & Co., advised his constituents 'to pay such extra duty at Damaun as shall place the vessel beyond the control of the Macao authorities.'

A further argument which the British merchants were able to urge for boycotting Macao was the corruptness of its justice. Matheson wrote: 'Since the death of Arriaga there has been no regular judge in this place. If you wish for justice here you ought to use every possible interest at the Court of Lisbon to have a respectable judge sent out.' Magniac & Co. warned the Bombay shippers of Damaun opium against consigning it to Macao 'lest some detriment should accrue through that [i.e. Macao] Government which is conducted upon principles which preclude all confidence or safety in the property of foreigners coming under its control'.[1]

The final blow came when the East India Company introduced the transit pass system, thereby destroying the 'smuggled Malwa' trade via Damaun. About 1835 a slight increase in the Damaun drug was countered by a reduction in the transit duty to Bombay.[2] In this way Macao was deprived of its 'only resource'.

[1] *Ibid.* 22.7.1825. One example of the justice prevalent in the Portuguese colonial world at this time is the extraordinary litigation which followed the death of 'the Baron', Macao's leading citizen, in 1825. The Baroness (de St José de Porto Allegre) fought the creditors of the estate, including several Indian correspondents of Yrissari & Co. and of Magniac & Co., for many years; the case going from Macao to Goa and to Lisbon, its fortunes varying according to bribe and counter-bribe.   [2] *Ibid.* 28.1.1839.

In 1831, the Government of Macao in desperation tried to prevent all foreigners, including the British merchants, from residing at the settlement. The Editor of *The Canton Register* wrote an angry comment, expatiating on the theme of 'the most ancient ally of the British nation . . . the common rights of Christian hospitality'. In the end Macao had to yield, since it could not afford to lose the rents, etc., paid by the British residents.

It is worth recording that the fate of Macao was put to use by the British merchants in their propaganda for a 'forward' policy against the Chinese. 'One of the principal causes of the present deplorable state of a once prosperous colony was . . . a tame submission to the imposition of the Chinese.'[1]

E. *The Coastal Trade*

The conflict with Macao during the 1820s was taken in its stride by the body of British merchants, which was increasing in numbers and wealth. During these years the opium business had developed its organisation to a point at which Jardine could speak of its quiet routine. The procedure was to pay 'bargain money' of $50-$100 per chest, whereupon a delivery note would be given to the Chinese broker, who would collect the drug from one of the receiving ships, after paying over the balance. The drug would then be trans-shipped to a Chinese 'smug boat' for delivery on the shore or to junks which came from a distance. There were intermittent interruptions of the trade by the Mandarins. (On one occasion Jardine wrote: 'We have every reason to believe the Viceroy averse to strong measures but he feels the necessity of checking the open boldness of the smuggling boats. Considerable sums have been raised, a number of fast-pulling boats built, to intercept the smug boats on their way to and from the ships at Lintin. But . . . it is impossible to say whether they will protect the revenue or assist the smuggling. In the meantime, the brokers

---

[1] *Canton Register*, 4.12.1827.

and dealers are a good deal alarmed and some of them have absconded.')[1] There were at times 'unmeaning fluctuations' of price caused by speculators, Chinese and foreign, and by 'combination' of sellers and buyers.[2] But the merchants prospered. Jardine reported to Magniac in London that the firm had turned over $4½ million worth of opium in the 1829-30 season, handling over 5,000 chests—about one-third of the total in China. During these years from Bombay alone over 50 Parsees shipped opium to the consignment of Magniac & Co. After 1831, however, the Company's new policy greatly increased production in India, and China was flooded with cheap opium of both varieties.[3] Prices fell sharply, almost to half. New markets had to be found, and new methods of distribution devised.

The firm, which had now become Jardine Matheson & Co., took the initiative in both directions—the development of a market along the East Coast and the laying down of a fleet of 'clippers' on the Calcutta-Lintin run.

There had been an earlier attempt to sell the drug along the coast. It will be remembered that in 1823 the first great opium boom had collapsed, Patna falling over $1,000 a chest in price. Yrissari & Co., who had attempted to corner the market in Patna, were faced with ruin. Even trucking the drug 'with up-country merchants' at a loss did not suffice to get rid of their large stock; while selling on long credit was extremely risky. 'The practice of the last 18 months has grown into a complete system of delivering

[1] *I.L.B.* 13.12.1826. Again (27.10.1827) 'deliveries and sales are entirely at an end owing to one of the boats having been seized with 21 chests on board and the crew imprisoned . . . the dealers have absconded'.

[2] On one occasion, August 2-3, 1828, the price of Malwa shot up by $100 in one day. *I.L.B.* 11.8.1828. In 1832 there was a 'wild speculation'. 'The general excitement is greater than I have ever seen. It reminds me of what took place in England in 1824, and the result may be the same'.—W.J. in *P.L.B.* 2.11.1832. Malwa had risen from $465 in July to $850 in October.

[3] 1827-8: 9,525 chests were consumed in China.
    1833-4: 21,650   „   „   „   „   „
    Morse, *International Relations*, I, Chapter VI.

opium to the dealers on credit without which they will not buy. The aggregate amount which we know these fellows of no capital to be indebted to various agents is incredible; some of them owe more than 1 lac of dollars in this way, which would never be seen again in the event of any involvement with the mandareens, which happens now and then to compel the dealers to abscond.' James Matheson, junior partner of the firm, wrote despairing letters to his Calcutta principals on his 'gloomy and disastrous prospects'. As a possible solution he decided to experiment by sending 'an expedition to open a smuggling trade on the East Coast of China'. The *San Sebastian,* a 200-ton brig under Spanish colours (Yrissari was a Spaniard), sailed for Chinchew (Fukien) in June 1823. On its return Matheson reported: 'Small as were the fruits of 106 days' labour, yet a prospect was opened sufficiently encouraging to induce us to hazard a repetition'.[1]

Several successful repetitions were made. Ships which had been in the Canton estuary for years now went up the coast. (When Matheson ordered the *Merope* to leave Lintin, where she had been stationed for the past three years, and proceed up the coast, her commander, Captain Parkyns, had scruples, on account of the bond he had signed in Calcutta against trading at any other port of China than Canton. Matheson commented on his 'erroneous conception of the meaning of the bond' [though he admitted opinions might differ], and added that Captain Parkyns' 'tardiness in obeying orders makes him less useful and agreeable to us than formerly.')

But soon rival firms followed the lead. 'It is with extreme regret that our prospects to the East have been overcast by the resort to the same market of Mr Robertson in the *Eugenia,* Mr Blight of Dent & Co. in the *Jamesina,* besides the Portuguese brig *Constitucio.* We have reason to regret that, being the originators of the coasting system, the competition of our neighbours has

---

[1] Y. & Co., 24.9.1823. See also evidence of the ship's Captain, John Mackie, to the *S.C. of H. of C.* 1830. From his second venture $132,000 was realised.

permitted us to enjoy the advantages of it so little.'[1] Matheson found himself obliged to discontinue the trade. 'I was the first to open a chance commerce on the coast of China. It had been customary before to make arrangements at Macao for delivering up the coast, but ours is the first instance of a vessel going for the chance of selling. For the first two or three times it succeeded well, and we began to entertain sanguine hopes of extending the trade to other articles than opium. But the jealousy of the mandarins here and at Macao having been excited, it led to very serious disturbances on the part of the coast we were accustomed to sell, and we have since had to bear the expense of fruitless voyages . . . we are still of the opinion that something can be done on a small scale, but the times are so unfavourable that we have for the present suspended the pursuit.'[2]

Nine years later the times were more favourable for developing the coastal trade on a large scale. As a result of the increased opium production in India, the amount of the drug imported into China rose rapidly, while the price fell. In 1825 the consumption of Indian opium had been 9,621 chests, valued at $7,600,000; in 1830 the figures were 17,760 chests and $12,900,000; in 1835 26,000 chests and $17 million.[3] It was necessary to find new markets outside the Canton river. In 1832 William Jardine sent two small brigs up the East Coast filled with opium and some piece goods. The experiment was only moderately successful; but Jardine determined to send a large vessel along the coast to try farther north. He therefore chartered the new clipper *Sylph* for a voyage to Shanghai and Tientsin, and persuaded the missionary, the Rev. Charles Gutzlaff, to accompany her as interpreter.[4]

---

[1] Y. & Co., 12.2.1824.   [2] *Ibid.* 1.9.1824.
[3] *Canton Register*, 5.4.1828. Kuo, *Anglo-Chinese War*, Chapter II.
[4] Jardine's letter to Gutzlaff was a model of diplomacy: 'Tho' it is our earnest wish that you should not in any way injure the grand object you have in view by appearing interested in what by many is considered an immoral traffic yet such a traffic is absolutely necessary to give any vessel a reasonable chance . . . Gain sweetens labour and we may add lessens very materially the risk incurred in the

Shortly after the departure of the *Sylph*, the *Jamesina* was sent to Foochow and the *John Biggar* to Chinchew Bay, near Amoy. The two latter were remarkably successful, selling their opium at $100 per chest above current Canton prices, and returning with several hundred thousand dollars worth of treasure.[1] Jardine now saw that it was time to make the coastal trade 'a regular system'. For this more ships were necessary; the firm therefore proceeded to lay down a fleet of clippers, brigs and schooners, buying the *Hercules, Lady Mayes, Colonel Young, Fairy* and other ships, in quick succession. More opium clippers were built, the most beautiful and fastest ships of their class, able to voyage against the monsoon and carry three lots of opium from Calcutta to Lintin in a single season. J.M.'s *Red Rover, Sylph, Falcon* and Dent's *Water Witch* were the most famous clippers of the time.[2] 'Our idea [in building a new clipper] is that the opium trade after the expiration of the East India Company's charter is likely to be so much run upon by speculators of every description for the mere sake of remittance without a view to profit that it can hardly be worth our while pursuing on the old plan unless by operating on a large scale, and on the secure footing of always being beforehand with one's neighbours in point of intelligence.'[3] Experiments

eyes of those who partake therein . . . and the more profitable the expedition the better we shall be able to place at your disposal a sum that may hereafter be usefully employed in furthering the grand object you have in view, and for your success in which we feel deeply interested . . . We have only to add that we consider you as surgeon and interpreter to the expedition and shall remunerate you for your services in that capacity'. As additional inducement Jardine guaranteed for the first six months a magazine which Gutzlaff was starting in Chinese 'for the diffusion of useful knowledge to the natives'. In the published journals of his voyages along the coast Gutzlaff tells of how he distributed pills and Bibles to all whom he met, but omits mention of opium, for the sale of which he was employed. Gutzlaff, eager to enlighten the heathen while pandering to their vices, continued for some years to be of service along the coast. James Innes, perhaps the least scrupulous of the smugglers, once wrote: 'I would give a thousand dollars for three days of Gutzlaff'.

[1] *P.L.B.* of W.J. 16.1.1833.   [2] Cf. B. Lubbock, *Opium Clippers* (1933).
[3] *P.L.B.* of W.J. 10.3.1831.

in steamships were carried out in the effort to reduce the length
of the voyage between Calcutta and Lintin to less than the 17½
days taken by the fastest clippers.[1] By 1836 the firm had a fleet of
a dozen vessels of every description.[2]

In the previous year other Canton agents had begun to compete
in the coastal trade. The local Mandarins raised their price for
'protection' to a flat rate of $10 per chest.[3] Dents and Jardines
jointly proposed to pay the Chinchew Mandarins $20,000 per
annum and no others to be allowed to trade in the Bay. Jardine
wrote Captain Rees, in command of the *Colonel Young:* 'If you
could manage to make the mandarins attack everyone but your
own party it would have a good effect.[!] My principal fear is
that *numbers* may bring down the displeasure of the Government
authorities on the dealers and boatmen, while competition among
sellers will reduce prices very much.'[4] The latter difficulty might
be composed by an arrangement with Dents to share anchorages
and fix prices.[5] The 'displeasure of the Government' was a much
more serious question.

F. *Silver and 'Vile Dirt'*

The remarkable development of the opium trade in the 1830s
impinged itself on the Chinese Government in two ways: the
expansion of foreign trade away from the Canton river along the
coast almost as far as Manchuria roused the attention of the Court
at Pekin;[6] while the drain of silver to pay for the opium caused a
shortage of the circulating medium which sent up prices. This
was noted by local officials and reported to the Emperor.[7] So

---

[1] These were not always successful. The first steamer to sail the China seas, the
Forbes, broke down ignominiously. *P.L.B.* 5.5.1830. Cf. G. A. Prinsep, *Steam
Vessels.*
[2] Cf. Chapter VI and Appendix II.
[3] Captain Mackay's report in *C.L.B.* 1.11.1835.   [4] *P.L.B.* 9.3.1835.
[5] These negotiations for complete monopoly broke down. *P.L.B.* 12.4.1836,
and Captain Rees' reports in *C.L.B.*
[6] *Corresp.*, p. 154.   [7] Kuo, *op. cit.*, Chapters IV and VI.

much had the balance of the China trade altered that between 1829 and 1840 only $7⅜ million of silver was imported, while nearly $56 million of treasure—dollars, sycee and gold—was sent out of the country.[1] Morse has argued that the drain of silver from China was far less than the amount which had been brought in by the foreigners in the previous century and a half; and that in any case the change was due in part to the Americans ceasing to import specie after 1827, bringing instead Bills of Exchange on London.[2] This last point is certainly valid; and it is equally true that in the last days of its monopoly the Company's policy was to ship considerable quantities of silver to London. None the less the source of that silver was the opium dealer. In the last analysis, the outward flow of silver was the direct consequence of the increased import of opium. Whether the foreign merchants drained off more treasure than had been brought in before it is impossible to say, since comprehensive statistics of the import of silver in the 18th century do not exist. All that can be stated definitely is that by the 1830s the previous balance had been completely reversed.

This drain of silver was evident to the foreign merchants at Canton. It was observed with satisfaction by a somewhat aggressive writer in the *Chinese Courier* of 1833, who declared that 'perhaps nothing could contribute more readily to the final reduction of the Chinese to reasonable terms with foreigners than this steady, non-ceasing impoverishment of the country by the abstraction of the circulating medium.'[3] Not unnaturally, therefore, it alarmed Chinese statesmen. It is notable that the memorialists to Pekin, who in 1836 initiated the debate on Chinese opium policy, stressed the economic rather than the moral side of

---

[1] 1829-40: Import: $7,303,841 of silver. Export: $26,618,815 coin; $25,548,205 sycee; $3,616,956 gold. *B.P.P.* 1840, 'Statement of Claims of British Subjects Interested in Opium', p. 42.

[2] Morse, *International Relations*, I, Chapter VI. American Bills on London are discussed below in Chapter VI.

[3] *Chinese Courier*, 6.4.1833.

the question.[1] Commissioner Lin himself was 'one of the shrewdest economists of his time'.[2] Before composing his memorial advocating the total prohibition of the opium trade he consulted merchants at Nankow and Hankow, both busy commercial centres. 'All agree that the market is daily diminishing for all kinds of goods in the country. Those which were sold for tens of thousands of dollars thirty years ago find now a market but half as large as before. Where does the other half go? In short, opium.' Ergo it it must be completely destroyed.

The Imperial edict of 1838 appointing Lin Tse-hsu Special Commissioner to destroy the opium trade is significantly worded in economic terms. 'Since opium has spread its baneful influence through China the quantity of silver exported has yearly been on the increase, till its price has become enhanced, the copper coin depressed, the land and capitation tax, the transport of grain and the [salt] gabelle all alike hampered. If steps be not taken for our defence . . . the useful wealth of China will be poured into the fathomless abyss of transmarine regions.'[3]

For thirty years and more the private merchants at Canton had been building up a vast but illicit trade in opium. Its very expansion made it increasingly intolerable to the Chinese Government. The more this unique commerce was extended the more precarious it became. A 'showdown' could hardly be avoided.

---

[1] Kuo, *op. cit.*, Chapters V and VI.
[2] *Ibid.*
[3] *Chinese Repository*, October 1839.

Chapter VI

BUSINESS AND FINANCIAL ORGANISATION

A. *The Agency House*

We turn now from questions of growth to those of structure, to the morphology of our subject. The characteristic unit of private British trade with the East, both China and India, was the 'Agency House'. This type of firm, though primarily a trading house, also acted as bankers, bill-broker, shipowner, freighter, insurance agent, purveyor, etc. It maintained intimate connections, commercial and financial, with its branch houses or agents all over the world. It was, in short, the medium through which 'backward' areas such as China were brought into economic relation with Great Britain.

The Agency System was the outcome, mainly, of geographic distance between the origin of capital and its actual sphere of operations, and of technical difference between two levels of economy. It was of first importance in the 19th-century British expansion overseas. The development of 'large-scale' machine industry involved a constant endeavour to increase output, since profits depended on lowering the cost per unit of production. Large-scale production brought with it the problem of selling more than the domestic market could absorb. Contemporaries recognised that 'this deficiency of ample market at home' could best be met by consigning the surplus abroad to be sold for what it could bring—even if at a loss—in order to maintain the volume of output[1]. Hence the development of 'consignment trade'; an operation in which British manufacturers, especially in the cotton industry, made up goods to stock not to order, and shipped the

[1] Cf. *B.P.P.* 'Report of Manufacturers, 1833', p. 193.

surplus stock to an Agency House abroad to be sold on commission, taking in return long Bills, which, however, could easily be discounted in the London money market. The consignment system formed the essential method of Manchester trade with the East, and the Agency House was its linchpin. At a later period, when British capital sought to invest in industrial undertakings in India and China, the Agency Houses became entrepreneurs. Thus arose the peculiar and remarkable feature of modern British enterprise in India and China—'the managing agency system'.

Early private firms in China were all described as Houses of Agency. As already explained, the 'private English' at Canton derived from the East India Houses. Many of them, such as David Reid or James Matheson, were travelling Supercargoes for Calcutta, or less often Bombay, firms before they became their resident Canton agents. Robert Taylor, whom James Matheson joined on first coming out to China, described himself as half freighter, half shipowners' agent.[1] For his first three years, Matheson was continuously sailing between Canton and Calcutta. Similarly, William Jardine journeyed several times between Bombay and Canton before joining Magniac & Co. in 1825. The line of advance both in personal history and as the norm of the trade was from Supercargo to resident agent: the latter had obvious advantages for his principal. A Supercargo was obliged to realise his goods quickly in order to return with his ship; nor could he become so intimate with the Hong merchants as a resident. But, in our period, the Supercargo was not wholly superseded by the resident agent. The smaller firms from India, especially the Parsees, continued to operate in the old way, as did most of the Americans. The captain-owner, or captain-Supercargo, of a venture was still much in evidence in the Eastern seas. In the more hazardous expeditions to the Islands off the beaten track, his rôle was still indispensable—and his recompense often a share

[1] R.T. and J.M., 8.11.1818.

in the 'speculation'. But as the China trade grew in volume and regularity, so did resident agency become more necessary.

Unlike the East India Company, these agency firms were not joint-stock. A partnership was preferred to individuals because, in the event of death, the firm would not then come to an end—an important consideration in view of the great distances and slow communications. James Matheson in setting up his nephew Hugh as partner with Charles Lyall at Calcutta argues 'greater confidence resulting from not having to rely on a single life will induce your friends to greater business'.[1] The partnership was often rather loose, individual partners being allowed to have separate dealings on their own account. This sometimes proved disastrous to the partnership, as when in 1815 Thomas Beale, senior member of Beale & Magniac, became so involved in private opium speculations with the Portuguese that he had to be expelled from the firm. It is notable that only the individual partner, not the firm, was adjudged bankrupt.[2] Similarly, when old Taylor failed in 1820, young James Matheson was able, with some difficulty, to escape the former's liabilities. On the other hand, something approaching joint-stock is to be found in the periodic combination of 'mutual friends' into syndicates for a specific purpose to secure control of the market in a particular commodity. Such 'combinations' sometimes lasted for many years, as, for instance, the Malwa opium syndicate of Jardine Matheson & Co., Remington Crawford & Co. and Jamsetjee Jeejeebhoy & Sons, the two latter of Bombay. Resources were pooled—in so far as allocated to this one purpose of Malwa operations—and profits were annually divided. It was something more than a cartel, though less than a full joint-stock company.

The supply of working capital provided no great problem for the Canton Agency Houses. As long as they acted purely as

---

[1] *P.L.B.* 7.11.1832.
[2] *E.L.B.* 8.1.1816. *Chronicles*, III, 239, 240-50. See also *C.L.B.* 12.2.1806 for individual transactions.

agents, they needed little,[1] since they operated on the capital of the shippers; and, of course, the Country Trade was primarily one of imports. When they wished to speculate in 'drugs' or opium, they were in the early days occasionally 'pushed for money', and had to borrow from the Hong merchants or others on strict terms at $1\frac{1}{2}\%$ interest per month—'a system which can never answer to our purpose'.[2] But they were soon in funds again, both because of the long-term deposits which, as we shall see, were attracted to Canton by the high rate of interest, and the quick accumulation of commissions and profits. Profits were annually divided among the partners but usually ploughed back again into the business, each partner maintaining a separate capital account. On leaving China for good the partners usually resigned, withdrawing their share of the capital and accumulated profits, but often reinvesting it in the London house.[3] This flow of capital from Canton to London must have been considerable over a period of years, but unfortunately cannot be accurately assessed owing to the surviving account-books being defective for this period. Except in times of credit stringency, as in 1830-3 at Calcutta, these houses did not suffer by the withdrawal of a partner's capital on retirement[4]. The house was not dissolved, though its name was usually changed; other partners were admitted who enjoyed the advantages of the established credit and financial resources of the house, which became a kind of hereditary concern, a commercial dynasty.

The main type of business carried on by the Agency House,

[1] The capital or partners' balance of Reide Beale & Co. in 1800 was only $120,000, each of the three partners—David Reid, Thomas Beale, Alexander Shank—having contributed $40,000. In 1837 the firm's capital was $2,613,000, most of it being sunk in the fleet of ships and in the purchases of opium, in which the firm was a heavy 'speculator'.

[2] *L.B.* 21.4.1801. G. D. Reid.

[3] Hollingworth Magniac, who went home in 1827, did not retire at once but retained his financial interest in the Canton firm as sleeping partner until 1831. But this was due to exceptional personal reasons. *P.L.B.* J.M. 10.3.1832.

[4] In 1832 the financial weakness of Fairlie & Co., Calcutta, was precipitated by the retirement of its senior partner. See below, pp. 165-7.

F

was selling and buying for others on commission. Independent trade on one's own account was termed 'speculation', though apparently without having any of the present derogatory connotation of the word. Nevertheless, the more cautious Country merchants tended to eschew 'adventures'. Thus in 1802 Alexander Shank wrote apologetically: 'This sugar adventure has not been entered from an intention of speculating, but merely to extricate ourselves from Poonqua (who could only pay his debts in kind). We profess as our former firm (Reid Beale & Co.) did, to confine ourselves to Agency business, and the use of our money at interest, both of which from the friendship of our constituents and our situation here, we find sufficiently advantageous'.[1] Nearly twenty years later, the partnership document of Yrissari & Co. stated: 'The attention of the partners (H. Yrissari and J. Matheson) is to be principally devoted to Agency, not, however, excluding safe speculation on the spot, but adventures to other places are to be considered rather as an exception to their line of business than as properly belonging to it. Profits are to go to a joint account, from which it shall be allowed to neither to withdraw for his separate purposes more than $5,000 per annum, leaving the remainder to accumulate until the termination of the partnership, when it shall be equally divided'. In the later '20s, however, with the accumulation of funds, 'speculation' on their own account became more common, especially in the articles of opium and rice, and sometimes in silk to England. In the '30s Jardine Matheson & Co. combined 'handsome adventures' in these articles with the usual commission business. But when James Matheson set up his nephew at Calcutta in 1831 it was 'on the express understanding that the house is one of mere agency, and that above all you must abstain from speculating in that most treacherous of articles, indigo, which has entailed ruin in so many, while a fortunate few have made money by it'.[2] For a young house 'pure commission business' was best, whereby 'income

[1] *P.L.B.* J.M. 4.11.1831.   [2] *Ibid.*

comes to you without asking in the snug way of the China business'.[1]

The agent charged commission not only for making sales or purchases but for every kind of service rendered to his principal. In the early days there was a fixed tariff of rates of commission, but the charges varied according to the prestige of the agent. Beale & Co. usually charged 5 % on sales and purchases, and 2 % for receiving or remitting, though not selling. On 1 March 1825 a meeting of Canton Agents established the following general rates of agency commission, which were confirmed in November 1831:[2]

(1) On *sale* of opium, cotton, cochineal, quicksilver
    and precious stones; and of ships houses   = 3 %
(2) On *sale or purchase* of all other goods   = 5 %
(3) On *returns* cf. in goods   = 2½ %
        cf. in Treasure or Bills   = 1 %
(4) On the *sale, purchase or shipment* of Bullion = 1 %
(5) *Guarantee* of bills, bonds or other engagements = 2½ %
(6) Ship's disbursement   = 2½ %
(7) Effecting insurance   = ½ %
(8) Chartering ships for other parties   = 2½ %
(9) Receiving inward freight   = 1 %
(10) Obtaining outward freight   = 5 %
(11) Settling insurance losses   = 1 %
(12) Negotiating bills of exchange   = 1 %
        loans on respondentia   = 2 %
(13) *Debts*, where a process at law or arbitration is
    necessary   = 2½ %
    Debts if recovered   = 5 %
(14) Managing estates of others   = 2½ %
    Collecting house rents
(15) Acting as Executors for estate of persons
    deceased   = 5 %
(16) Transhipping goods   = 1 %

[1] *P.L.B.* J.M. 9.5.1832.   [2] *I.L.B.* 10.9.1828. Cf. Phipps, *Treatise.*

'On all advances of money not punctually liquidated the agent to have the option of charging a second commission upon a fresh advance'.

In actual practice, when competition was keen these rates were undercut, habitually by the Parsees. But even the most respectable firms made special concessions to those with whom they conducted business 'in terms of friendship'. Some houses had special rules of business policy. Thus Beale & Co. stated in 1805: 'It is an established rule with us to divide our commission with nobody'. They also charged only half commission on losing sales; but demanded extra commission before guaranteeing debts—'Agents in Canton are not responsible for the failure of Hong Merchants, to whom they may have disposed of goods on account of their constituents, as a commission of 3% cannot be considered likewise a premium against bad debts. *No risk whatever* is incompatible with the regular course of Canton Agency and only to be attained by allowing a premium of 1% on sales for bad debts'.[1] 3% on certain sales at Canton might be 'more moderate than any part of India with which we are acquainted'.[2] But, as far as regular agency business went, James Matheson was justified in speaking of 'the snug way' in which 'income comes to you without asking' in the China trade.

Each agent at Canton had many 'constituents', or 'correspondents' as they were called, since almost the main duty of an agent was to maintain a frequent and accurate correspondence. But, in important centres of trade, each Canton agent had one or perhaps two principal correspondents, who enjoyed his full confidence. Thus Jardine Matheson & Co. in 1832 had over fifty regular correspondents in Bombay, and almost as many in Calcutta; but most of their letters, including all the more important ones, were written to two firms at Bombay and one at Calcutta, Remington Crawford & Co., Jamsetjee Jeejeebhoy & Sons, Bombay, and Lyall Matheson & Co., Calcutta (after Fairlie Fergusson & Co.

[1] *L.B.* 5.10.1805; 4.1.1802; 28.9.1806.   [2] *I.L.B.* 6.1.1830.

had failed in 1832). Relations between such houses were always very close. As compared with other constituents, these received priority of information, more advantageous terms of business, moral and financial support. This sometimes raised delicate questions of business ethics. In 1802 Beale & Co. declined to sell 'singsongs' on behalf of both D. Beale and F. Magniac of London 'to whom our best services are pledged'. In 1825 Yrissari & Co. wrote: 'From our connection with Mackintosh & Co., Calcutta, we have hitherto naturally looked to their London establishment for transaction of such business we might have. As however the support of Rickards Mackintosh & Co., of London, is pledged to another House here (Dents) we do not consider ourselves precluded from forming any other connection in London which may be advantageous to us'.[1] Sometimes there was a collision of interest between an agent and his constituents. The most frequent disputes concerned the wisdom of the agent in selling instead of holding or vice versa; naturally, since the agent's percentage was fixed, he had no great incentive to sell at the best possible price, which would affect the commission comparatively little. Recrimination between agents as to the responsibility for an unprofitable deal was not uncommon. Thus, a characteristic letter of Jardine to Jamsetjee Jeejeebhoy ran as follows: 'It was amazing enough to read our Calcutta letters blaming your Bombay *wallahs* for the high prices (of opium), while you were blaming us and the true cause all the while existing among the *Baboos* on the spot (i.e. at Calcutta). I confess to feeling a good deal hurt at your even for one moment entertaining the opinion that we could act so *uncandidly* and unjustly as to conceal from you any information likely to tend to your benefit'.[2]

Such disputes rarely affected the close relations between principal agents. In fact, partly because one of the firms often sprang from the other, or had a personal connection with it, and partly because they often combined into temporary syndicates,

[1] Y. & Co., 21.6.1825.   [2] *I.L.B.* 12.7.1831.

the agent and his chief constituents may be said to have carried on business virtually as branch houses. James Matheson advised his nephew Hugh: 'Nothing will be gained by amalgamating the London and Calcutta Houses into one concern, since neither House will know what they are worth without waiting for the other and each suffer for the other's bad transactions'.[1] In one case something approaching the modern device of interlocking directorates was apparently used. In the 1830s Jardine Matheson & Co. financed the rice and sugar operations of their Manila agents Otadui & Co., whose partners were B. Shillaber, an American, and E. de Otadui, a Spaniard. Alarmed at Shillaber's 'wild and hazardous tendencies'—his schemes included operating a tobacco monopoly under charter from the Manila government, building a lighthouse, starting a Manila bank—Jardine Matheson sent out a member of their firm to join the Board, as it were, of the Manila concern and keep it under control.[2] This was an exceptional plan devised for an emergency. Such formal methods of control were not usually necessary. The intimate relations between the chief firms in Canton, India and London provide the clue to the organisation of the China trade.

B. *Banking*

Banking operations were from the beginning carried on by the Canton Agency Houses. Since there were no European banks in China, the merchants had to be financiers too. The granting of credits was indispensable to the distant commercial transactions of the China trade, in which the time factor was necessarily important. Advances were granted, usually at 1% per month, and in the form not of cash but of accepting Bills of Exchange drawn on themselves or their London agents. Secondly, exchange banking sprang easily from a commerce so dependent on remittance and so subject to currency variations as the China trade. Thirdly, a remarkable deposit and loan business was developed

---

[1] *P.L.B.* J.M.   [2] *Ibid.* 1837-8 passim.

owing to the peculiar nature of the money market at Canton. The lending of money to the Hong merchants, it will be recalled,[1] was the motive for the first 'private English' coming to China in the 1770s. Finally, the China Agency Houses undertook many of the ancillary services of a modern bank, acting as Trustees and Executors, granting letters of credit to travellers, commercial and others, supplying the temporary financial wants of 'the young gentlemen of the Factory', and of the Company's officers, even acting as investment brokers—mainly of course in opium.

The Canton money market was remarkable in that, owing to the lucrative character of the China trade and the scarcity of funds, an extremely high rate of interest obtained. 'Nabobs' sent their private fortunes made in India to the merchants of Canton, and kept them there on deposit until they returned to England or died.[2] Captains of Indiamen did likewise. To a Mr Robertson who left $3,000 in the hands of Reid Beale & Co., $2,000 on account of his daughter, the firm wrote: 'We pay 10% per annum interest on deposits and beg you to inform us if interest is to be remitted annually or to accumulate here'.[3] Similarly, their London agents were instructed to 'pay annually every 1st September, £1,250 to the order of Senor Manoel V. de Baron being interest (at 10%) in money in our hands'.[4] In 1806 Messrs Locatelli of Manila retained the net proceeds of their tin speculation from Penang in the hands of Beale & Magniac at 10% per annum.[5] The Canton merchants, if they did not wish to use the money themselves, could normally obtain at least a 2% margin above the rate of interest paid out, by loaning the money to the Hong merchants. Generally the Hong merchants paid interest at 1½% per month; in emergencies they had to pay an even higher rate, once in 1803 nearly 40% per annum.[6] The value of money was so high at Canton that Reid Beale & Co. were reluctant to grant advances to

[1] Chapter II above.   [2] Cf. Parkinson, *op. cit.*, Chapter XI.
[3] *L.B.* 28.4.1801.   [4] *Ibid.* 28.12.1800.
[5] *Ibid.* 29.1.1800.   [6] *Chronicles*, III, p. 197.

distant constituents.[1] In 1801 the firm reported that 'the interest account is far less than in 1799-1800, and yet affords as near $5,000 *paying us* 18% *on our capital,* and the loans we have are a great accommodation and convenience. However *in this country we certainly ought to make more by interest than the above,* considering the modest terms on which we have our money; our not making more by it proves how unprofitable advancing for our constituents must ever be to us; as although we charge them more than we pay at present for any of our three principal loans, yet such advances have often been the occasion of our borrowing at $1\frac{1}{2}$% per month'. No interest was paid by Beale and Magniac on money left in their hands for short periods since it was 'wholly impracticable to lend our money at Canton for a shorter period than 6 months'.[2] One year's notice was required before depositors could withdraw their money. Thus, though money was in such demand at Canton, the position was very different from that at London or even in the Indian presidencies, where, owing to the development of the discount of 'paper', money could be employed at short notice. But for long-term business the Canton money market was unrivalled.

This happy state of affairs depended primarily on the condition of the Hong merchants, the principal borrowers. When in 1810 several Hongs became embarrassed, this was soon translated in terms of the current rate of interest payable on deposits, which was reduced from 10%-12%, first to 8% and then to 7%. 'The danger and difficulty of employing money in China as usual with the Hong merchants, from the distressed situation of some of them—indeed by far the greater number—have obliged us and all other agents here to reduce our rate of interest'.[3] On the easing of the situation in 1814, when the defaulting Hong merchants were put under foreign trustees, to whom they paid regular instalments, the interest date was again raised to 10% per annum.[4]

---

[1] *L.B.* 10.10.1801.　　　　　　　[2] *Ibid.* 15.2.1806.
[3] *E.L.B.* 10.1.1814.　　　　　　　[4] *Ibid.* 1.1.1815.

In the '20s the general depression in the Country Trade, and the increasing difficulties of a number of Hongs, sharply affected the money market. 'The state of commercial affairs no longer affords any facility for the employment of capital. We are under the necessity of paying off our constituents, and therefore beg to announce our intention on returning to you on the 1st February next, the principal sum of $10,000 plus interest, now in our hands'.[1]

Magniac & Co. continued to charge interest on advance remittance to Indian constituents whose funds were locked up in opium or cotton in China. This led in 1825 to one of the few disputes with the Bombay firm of Remington & Co. An illustrative letter speaks of 'the pain which we have experienced from your accusation against us of a want of due appreciation of the friendly services we have so often received from your firm. The current rate of interest in China is 12%; less than 10% is never charged by agents on advances unless under special feelings towards the parties concerned such as actuate us in regard to you. In charging you 8% while we allowed the same, we conceived ourselves to be making a sacrifice to our consideration for you, as we ourselves were paying 10% interest on a portion of those very advances made to you. We could not afford to continue this system (of the previous season) in not charging you interest—a system which would have reduced to about ½% our commission upon opium sales—a retail trade, the most troublesome, anxious and above all the most attended with risk of any that is conducted in Canton . . . upon which trade it is generally admitted the special rate of 3% is a very inadequate recompense for his anxiety and risk to the fair-dealing agent. At the same time we have no right to force our advances, and we will therefore remodel your interest

[1] *I.L.B.* 15.10.1824. To Martha Van Mierop, Macao. Cf. R.T. and J.M. 14.6.1821. 'Money is at this moment very scarce in China but good security is also scarce. And although until lately in possession of considerable funds of your firm (M. Larruleta & Co., Calcutta) I have never realised a dollar of interest, preferring unquestionable security to any such advantage'.

account at that rate at which alone you would have been desirous to receive the remittances in advance'.[1]

In 1826 deposits were again received. To a Capt. O. Ross of Calcutta or Bombay who in 1823 had sent $30,000 for deposit with Magniac & Co. the firm wrote: 'Since the employment of money in China has now become more practicable we have allowed you interest at 6% since 1825'.[2] The Macao firm 'The Widow Payva and Sons' deposited $128,000 with Magniac & Co. in 1827, when loans to Hong merchants were partly resumed. Then 'the fund raised by subscription among the English gentlemen for the benefit of Mrs Anna Maria Steyn of Macao and her children, was placed at interest in the hands of Chemqua Hong merchant'.[3] Sometimes money was advanced to the Chinese opium dealers on the security of the opium. This last was unsatisfactory since it did not yield a regular and certain interest per month. But 'the risque attending loans to the Hong merchants is so very considerable as to require strong nerves on the side of the parties advancing the cash; and deprived of this mode of employing funds there is only that of advances on the drug (opium), or speculation left'.[4] 'Speculation' in opium was increasingly the outlet for funds seeking investment, as the credit of the Hong merchants became precarious. This in turn, because it promoted a heavy export of dollars and sycee from China, led in the '30s to an exceptional shortage of cash at Canton, which sent the current rate of interest back to the old level of 12% per annum, and higher; thus contributing to the financial stringency of the Canton money market which beset the Hong merchants in their last years.[5]

In addition to deposit banking, the Canton Agency Houses from the beginning undertook a variety of financial operations arising from the need to remit funds continuously from China to India and England to balance the trade. The importance of this question of remittance in the China trade has already been

[1] *I.L.B.* 1.4.1825.   [2] *Ibid.* 2.10.1826.   [3] *Ibid.* 26.5.1826.
[4] *Ibid.* 20.8.1828.   [5] *P.L.B.* W.J.

touched upon from several points of view. Since China goods were so rarely profitable in India and tea was still withheld from the private merchants, while so much of their Canton trade was on Indian account, financial methods of remittance had to be used. The basic method, that of paying the proceeds of the Country Trade into the East India Company's Canton Treasury in return for Company Bills in the Court of Directors or the India Presidencies, has already been examined.[1] While satisfactory from the standpoint of the Company, the method became inadequate to the needs of the private merchants in proportion as their Country Trade outdistanced the fairly static requirements of the Company's investment. Even in the early years of the 19th century, the Select Committee generally accepted only about half the money tendered by the private merchants. Thus in 1804 Beale & Magniac tendered 9 lacs of dollars, but were allotted Bills for only 40% of this sum, this being the portion of the local tenders actually accepted by the Select Committee. Secondly, the Company's Canton Treasury was only open to receive tenders of money for a few months each season. There were times when there was no point in the private merchants making a sale, because no Company's Bills would be available for remittance until the following season.[2] Thirdly, the terms on which the Company's Bills were issued were often disadvantageous in point of 'sight' and rate of exchange. Thus in 1810 the Bills on London were at 15 months sight, in 1821 at 730 days sight—both far too long for the convenience of the private merchant. Only necessity made them accept these 'miserable terms'; in 1826, the Company's Bills were for a short time actually at a discount of 1%.[3] The private merchants were therefore driven to seek other means of effecting remittance.

[1] In Chapter I, above.

[2] *L.B.* 5.2.1801.

[3] This dependence of the private merchant on the Company's financial policy was one of the issues in the free traders' campaign of 1833 against the renewal of the Company's charter. See Chapter VII below.

One early method was that of 'respondentia bonds'. Loans were granted to shippers in Canton to help them purchase an export cargo and charter a vessel; the money to be repaid in India, within a fixed number of days after the landing of the cargo which was security for the loan. Since the interest charged was heavy, this was a popular field of short-term lending. This was no doubt the reason why the space in front of the European Factories at Canton was called 'Respondentia Walk'! But as a method of remittance it was unsatisfactory, both because it depended on the shipping being available and because it frequently led to disputes over the conditions of the loan and the real value of the cargo. Another way of remitting was to purchase 'Company certificates for certain sums which their commanders have the privilege of paying to the Select Committee, on condition of receiving the same in London at an exchange to be fixed by the Court of Directors'. The private merchants were often prepared to buy these certificates at a premium; but the amount available was limited and the 'sight' unsatisfactory. A captain's certificates were limited to $12,000, an officer's to $6,000; in both cases half was payable at 12 months and half at 6 months. Again, odd Bills might be picked up at Canton, drawn by the Dutch or Swedish or Danish companies. But these were irregular and drawn in quantity only on particular occasions—as when in 1823 the Java Government raised money to suppress a native rebellion by selling its Bills on the Netherland Government to the Canton agents. To supplement these uncertain methods of remittance, and their inadequate export of China goods, the 'private English' had to ship treasure, both bullion and specie.

One source of treasure was Manila, whence for many years it was shipped in extensive quantities to the Canton merchants to be reshipped to India as remittance. Thus, in the season 1819-20 fully 2 lacs of dollars worth of Spanish coin and quicksilver was sent by Robert Stevenson & Co. of Manila to Magniac & Co., in return for short Bills at 90 days sight. But this inflow was checked when in 1821 the Spanish Government placed a heavy duty on the export of specie from the Philippines. Peruvian silver, however, and *Plata Pina* from South America continued to come to Canton. Likewise, much of the annual supply of specie brought by the Americans to finance their Canton purchases found its way, via the Hong merchants and the shopmen, into the stone treasuries which the private British merchants had built in their Factories, to await remittance to India by the first available ships. There were indeed occasions when the dollars went straight from the American ships in 'unopened packages' into the holds of the Country vessels without ever entering into circulation in China; for which boon, of course, the British agents had to pay a suitable premium.

But the greatest stand-by of the remittance seekers was Chinese sycee, the uncoined shoe-shaped ingots of pure silver. The export of all metals from China was of course illegal; that of sycee was specifically prohibited several times.[1] It could, however, by bribing the local Mandarin, generally be smuggled out via Macao or Lintin; there was a gentleman's agreement with the Hong merchants that none should be shipped from Canton or Whampoa.[2] Sycee was often directly exchanged for opium from junks in the lower estuary. Sycee made a profitable remittance, since at the Calcutta mint it was found 15% purer than silver dollars, while in China it could often be obtained at a discount—in 1815 as high as 7%—compared with coined dollars, on certain types of which the Chinese set a more than intrinsic value.[3] But gradually, as the

---

[1] An edict of 1809, prohibiting the export of sycee, is reprinted in *Chronicles*, III, 128. See also *ibid.* 140, 187, 321. Vol. IV, 259.   [2] R.T. and J.M. 5.12.1821.

[3] The foreign merchants were at times also able to extract profit from the Chinese prejudices in favour of certain kinds of silver dollars which elsewhere were of equal value. This is not the place to add to the notoriously complicated subject of Chinese Imperial currency, on which Morse has written with authority. It may be remarked, however, that in our period the British merchants were much irritated by the refusal of the Chinese to accept the new 'Independent' or 'Republican' dollars, or those Spanish dollars bearing the image of Ferdinand VII, at the same value as the Old 'Carolus' dollars.

imports of the Country merchants increased, sycee was in such great demand for remittance as to be obtainable only at a premium, and sometimes not at all.[1] On those occasions, the returning Country ships had to be filled with 'chopped' dollars, i.e. old dollars which had become defaced or 'broken' by frequent stamping of the shroffs and which were bought by the weight. These, however, did not answer well at the Calcutta mint.

There were seasons when the supply of treasure available for remittance was insufficient for the voracious demand. The years 1826-8 were especially difficult, for a number of reasons. The increase in European trade via Singapore adversely affected the rates of exchange, especially as the East India Company's policy was now to limit its drafts on London; as a result, from 1825 few private or Company Bills on London could be obtained at a more favourable exchange than 4s. 3d. to the dollar. In June 1828 the rate actually dropped to 3s. 10d. In 1829 Jardine wrote: 'The China exchange in England is so low that it is scarcely worth the while of the Bombay shippers to use it as a medium of remittance'.[2] Secondly, the commercial crisis in the U.S.A., which led to several bankruptcies among the tea merchants, severely curtailed the customary American import of new Spanish dollars to Canton.[3] When two U.S. ships brought a supply of dollars in the middle of October 1826, they demanded 2% premium 'for Cowshings even', i.e. new dollars. This was the season when Magniac reported that no new dollars or South American bullion was procurable. Sycee was at a premium of 6-7% and very 'hazardous' to smuggle, owing to the exceptional vigilance of the Mandarins. There were few good private Bills available, and those drawn by Magniac & Co. and Dent on their local agent at 6 months sight were eagerly negotiated by the Parsees; while the 'wants of the Select Committee were soon satisfied and the

---

[1] E.g., R.T. and J.M. 27.12.1820. 'Sycee is not to be had.'
[2] *I.L.B.* 6.12.1824; 30.6.1828; 25.6.1829.
[3] *Ibid.* 7.10.1826. See Appendix for table of American imports of specie.

Company's treasury closed suddenly'.[1] 'We are using all our influence among our friends in the Company's service to get the refusal of their certificates and bills for the profits of their (privilege) cotton, which they are allowed to pay into the treasury at Canton. These certificate bills are not negotiable at Bombay, having to be accepted on the pleasure of the Court of Directors'.[2] These commanders' certificates were supplemented as remittance by a very large shipment of metals to India, which happened fortunately to be in great demand there. Even the Company's stock of British iron and lead intended for the China market were bought up by the private merchants and sent to India.[3]

But these were merely stopgap devices. The great expansion of the Country Trade created a problem of remittance which had to be solved in a new way. The solution was to draw in more closely to the China trade that between England and America, and to link London, New York and Canton in a triangular system of interlacing credits.[4]

The American traders, having no Indian Empire, had always been obliged to bring large quantities of specie to Canton, with which to purchase their return cargoes of teas and silks. The season 1810-1 was the first in which they brought drafts on London mercantile houses to any considerable amount. The vigilant Select Committee of the East India Company shrewdly remarked that 'If the Americans were annually provided with an extensive credit on Houses of respectability in England, we are not aware of any circumstances to deter the Indian Capitalist from remitting the proceeds of his speculations in the China market by means of the bills which might be purchased in Canton in preference to returning his property to Calcutta, and from thence returning it

[1] *I.L.B.* 28.2.1827; 29.4.1828.
[2] *Ibid.* 17.10.1827.
[3] *Ibid.* 27.8.1827; 20.10.1827.
[4] L. H. Jenks, *Migration of British Capital*, Chapter III. See also N. S. Buck, *Organisation of Anglo-American Trade*, 1800-50.

through the Company's treasury to England'.[1] But the intervention of the Anglo-American War had the effect of checking for
some years the use of London credits by the Americans in
substitution for the import of specie.[2]

The private British merchants at Canton did occasionally make
use of the American trade to remit funds. Magniac & Co. would
remit to India drafts on their London agents, to meet which they
would place funds in London by advancing to the Canton agents
of certain American firms (Perkins of Boston, Perit & Cabot, or
Thomson of Philadelphia) for the purchase of teas and silks (on
the security of the bills of lading), the advances to be repaid by
the shipment of American cotton, etc., to London.[3] This was,
however, a cumbersome and tedious method. It was only in the
course of the remittance crisis of 1825-7 that the British merchant
at Canton really saw the possibility of using American Bills on
London. Magniac & Co. wrote in June 1826 that since there was
no other recourse 'we have taken up a considerable amount of the
Bank of U.S. Bills on Baring Bros. & Co. London'.[4] In the
following year they arranged with 'a gentleman here who has
authority from a highly respectable House in America to draw on
T. Wilson & Co., London, to take his bills to the extent of his
credit or to such an amount as he may have occasion to draw
when he has completed his investment'.[5] To the Americans this
negotiation of their Bills at Canton was a great boon. They therefore began to rely increasingly on Bills instead of specie for their
Canton investment. By 1830 fully half of the value carried by U.S.
vessels to China consisted in Bills on London. In 1831, perhaps
an exceptional year, they brought $4,770,000 worth of Bills and
only $680,000 in specie.

At first the British merchants were cautious in handling this
innovation. As late as November 1829, Magniac & Co. refused to
take the Bills offered by an American Supercargo drawing on

---

[1] *Chronicles*, III, 179.   [2] Cf. *I.L.B.* 11.11.1824.   [3] *I.L.B.* 5.6.1826.
[4] *Ibid.* 17.10.1827.   [5] Jenks, *op. cit.* and see Appendix.

T. Wilson & Co. under a credit from a house in New York, 'having no certain information as to the stability of the American House and consider broken coins as affording an equally advantageous result with infinitely greater security'.[1] On the other hand, the Bills of J.J. Astor and Stephen Girard of Philadelphia, or those drawn under letter of credit from Baring Bros. and half-a-dozen other London houses, were always negotiable in Canton. But it was the great Calcutta credit crisis of 1829-34 which finally converted the Canton houses to an extensive and regular use of American Bills.

In 1832 James Matheson wrote an expository letter on the Canton firm's financial policy to his nephew Hugh, partner in Lyall Matheson & Co., Calcutta: 'We shall not trouble you with many London bills till credit resumes a healthier aspect in Calcutta. We seldom remit bills bearing our endorsement, except when called for by our constituents, demand for them being lately very great especially in Bombay . . . It is likely that three-quarters of all the exchange business of Canton have passed through our hands this season. Bills drawn by ourselves are sought after by the Parsees agents here at 1d. or ½d. lower than those we endorse; but this we attribute to their finance, or to the nature of their orders from Bombay . . . they have the security of the drawers in addition to ours but all security in commerce is only relative. Hazards are incident to all human affairs, and only minimised by distributing the risk among a number of good houses whose bills we purchase rather than by relying on a single House however strong.

'Of the bills that we endorse, thereon Baring Bros. & Co. are always under credits either from themselves or their attorney in New York, Mr F. W. Ward . . . Other bills are either drawn under

[1] *I.L.B.* 18.11.1829. In the season 1829-30, of the £175,000 remitted by Magniac & Co. to their London agents, Fairlie & Co., only £68,000 worth was sent in Bills, £50,000 being remitted in treasure and the rest in goods, mainly raw silk. 7.4.1830. *P.L.B.* W.J. Sycee continued to be shipped extensively, since it was found in London to contain a small admixture of gold.

credits from a known capitalist, John Jacob Astor of New York, who owns land almost equal to a principality in the U.S. Bills on Gledstone, Drysdale & Co. are in turn drawn under credits from them, or in the security of bills of lading for goods. They are a House of known property. Mr T. Weeding on whom we draw is a merchant possessed of at least a "lack" of pound sterling. T. Wyatt is a still greater capitalist, though only an oilman (?). Then there are Messrs Spode and Copeland, chinaware men of solid wealth. On the whole we feel that we are committing ourselves to people of greater solidity than those whose bills are bandied forth in Calcutta. If any disappointment should occur to us, divided as our risk is among various parties it must but prove comparatively insignificant'.[1]

Some other houses on whom American Bills were drawn were Timothy Wiggin & Co., Gillespie Moffat, Finlay & Co., Small Colquhoun & Co., London, Brown & Co., Liverpool. But Barings were the chief guarantors of American Bills, and Jardine Matheson & Co. therefore asked their confidential agent MacVicar to keep him especially informed of whispers about the credit of Barings.

The advent of a regular supply of American Bills on London completely altered the remittance situation. A circular letter of 1831 to Bombay firms from Jardine Matheson & Co. declared that 'It is generally in our power to remit funds to England on more advantageous terms than can be effected in Bombay'. The result was that the Bombay merchants annually sent vast amounts, usually in the shape of Malwa opium, to Canton for the sake of a favourable remittance to England. Thus, Jamsetjee Jeejeebhoy and Sons, the largest trade constituent of Jardine Matheson, with whom in the 1830s they were annually transacting more than £1 million worth of business, remitted to London through China about £150,000 each year.[2] Other constituents, of course, wanted

---

[1] *I.L.B.* 25.4.1832.

[2] *P.L.B.* J.M. 27.7.1828. The J.M. papers throw much light on this great Bombay firm, 'the best-managed business this side of the Cape', as Matheson

less sums remitted. With this aggregate, the Canton agents were able to cope principally through the instrument of the American drafts in London. The system was convenient and profitable to all parties concerned in the China trade. Moreover it gave to the 'private British' at Canton a measure of financial independence from the Company which was one of the pre-requisites of their victory of 1834. It also gave them strength to weather the great Calcutta credit crisis.

Between 1829 and 1834 all the great Agency Houses in Calcutta failed, bringing down with them some of the London East India Houses. The list of debts, not allowing for some recoverable assets, was, in order of failure:

Palmer & Co., Calcutta	= £5,000,000
Alexander & Co., „	= £3,500,000
Mackintosh & Co., „	= £2,500,000
Colvin & Co., „	= £1,000,000
Fairlie & Co., London & Calcutta	= £1,800,000
Richard Mackintosh & Co., London	= £950,000

One Bombay firm, Shotton Malcolm & Co., went down for £250,000.

The total liability was about £15,000,000—'an amount of debt which a century ago would have shaken the Government of this country with fear of bankruptcy'.[1] The writer in *The Times*, in examining the causes of the catastrophe, 'the great sums lost and extent of the misery', criticised the mode of business of the Agency Houses. 'It is a matter of notoriety that from each of these large Indian establishments, the partner has every two or three years advertised out, and gone home to England with overflown fortunes, being succeeded by another who in his turn again advertised out and went home very rich and this arrived by from

admiringly wrote. Jardine began dealing with them in 1822, and the two firms were still associated in business at the end of the 19th century. Biographical details of Jamsetjee Jeejeebhoy, who from the humblest beginnings accumulated an enormous fortune, are given in *The First Parsee Baronet* by G. S. Nazir.

[1] Extract from *The Times* in *Canton Register*, 13.5.1834.

no other causes than the profits of their now bankrupt houses, whose affairs, if justly examined, have been for years in a state of irretrievable ruin.' He admitted, however, that there had been other reasons than the 'rage for speculation and inordinate gains on the part of the directors'. First, the establishment of a bank of issue and deposit by the India Government reduced the profits of the Agency Houses, who continued to pay the same interest 6-8% to depositors, to outdo the Government rate of 4%.

Secondly, 'after 1813 Indian commerce was opened to more active competition of private adventurers'. The great number of new houses started in Calcutta competed with those founded half a century before, forcing the latter to further exertions, especially to making heavy advances to the indigo planters. James Matheson believed that it was the avid speculation in 'that most treacherous of articles', indigo, which was the prime cause of the crash. Phipps points out that, until superseded by opium, indigo was 'the principle article for investment of capital as the medium of remittance to England'. In 1800, 40,000 maunds of indigo were exported from Calcutta to England; in 1815 its export suddenly shot up to 120,000 maunds, in 1826-30 it averaged 118,111. In 1810, according to Milburn, the Calcutta price was 130 rupees per maund; in 1824 it was over 330 rupees. The demand for indigo in England was strictly limited. As early as 1812 the Calcutta agents had declared that cultivation ought to be restricted and a Bengal Indigo Fund was set up to buy the surplus production from the Factories. But the influx of new firms into Calcutta stimulated production to even greater heights. The collapse was finally ensured by the report in 1829 that Prussian blue had been successfully used in Liverpool as a substitute dye much cheaper than indigo.[1] The average London price, which in 1825 had been 10s. a lb., dropped to 3s. 7d. Palmer & Co. advertised their indigo concerns for sale at one quarter their price of a few seasons ago. There were few buyers; and the failure of Palmers, the largest of

[1] J. Phipps, *Indigo*.

the old Agency Houses, created a universal shock—from which not even Fairlie & Co., who floundered on until November 1833, was able to extricate itself. Some of the London firms, however, managed to survive; the partners of others were able to secure their discharge from bankruptcy and make a fresh start. Thus the partners of Mackintosh & Co. set up in 1833 a new firm, Calder & Co. 'entirely of Agency—monied or commercial, confining ourselves in the latter branch to orders or consignments requiring no advance of money and no risk of loss. Having no transactions on our own account, we do not require the use of any funds'.[1]

The Calcutta failures naturally affected the Canton agent. Dents in particular suffered, being unprepared for the failure of Palmers in 1830.[2] Jardines, forewarned by the fate of the others, were able to divide their risks by resorting to the system of American Bills on London. When, in November 1833, Fairlie & Co. finally suspended payment, Jardines got off lightly, with the loss of a mere £22,000. Partly owing to the influence of Hollingworth Magniac, who emerged from his rural retirement to support his old firm in the City, its Bills were 'instantly protected by that powerful capitalist Mr Timothy Wiggin; our friends inform us that our character on 'change is not only unimpaired, but stands higher than ever'.[3] Nevertheless, the old East India House was shaken. In 1834 when, on the expiration of the Company's charter, Jardines were about to enter the tea trade, they were without a London agent. The London money market was indeed essential to the China trade; but for some time they preferred to deal with a number of Acceptance Houses specialising in American Bills.[4]

[1] Calcutta 'Correspondence In', 9.2.1833. *P.L.B.* 10.3.1832.
[2] According to James Matheson, the origin of the bitter feud between Dents and Jardines lay in the dispute as to the latter's withholding of the correspondence brought from Calcutta in a Jardine clipper which bore the news of the failure of Palmers.   [3] *P.L.B.* J.M. 26.5.1834.
[4] *Ibid* 24.11.1832. 'The considerable amount of bills drawn or endorsed by us circulating in the home money market, is the inevitable consequence of the

However, in 1835 Hollingworth Magniac provided them with a new London Agency House, forming, with John Abel Smith, M.P., and Oswald Smith of the famous banking family, Magniac Smith & Co. of 3 Lombard Street. William Jardine, 'fully aware of the wealth, respectability and high character of the parties', agreed to make them their London agents, with the reservation that 'at no time shall it be expedient that we should give up the option of carrying on transactions with other London Houses to a certain extent, always, however, giving a preponderatory share of business to whatever House may act as our principal agents'. 'The principal advantage we look to from our home connection is the certainty of our Bills being protected to whatever extent we may have occasion to draw in the course of any one season, without reference to immediately available assets to meet them.'[1] Magniac Smith & Co. were a great source of strength to the Canton firm in their greatly increased business after 1834. Their 'powerful support' enabled Jardines to weather the collapse of the American Bill system in 1837, the 'crisis of the three W's', so-called because the three chief failures were Messrs Wiggin, Wilson and Wildes.

The ease of that system, the complaisance with which the London 'American Houses' accepted 'open credits'—i.e. Bills of Exchange unsecured by invoices or bills of lading—produced a speculative boom in the American trade, with its inevitable reaction.[2] In August 1837 news reached Canton of the failure of some dozen American firms in New Orleans, Philadelphia and New York, and the consequent alarm over the London 'American Houses', even the situation of Barings being queried. In September

extent of our business. We find the amount for bills greater than we can supply. From a wish to avoid possible inconvenience to our agents from too large an amount of acceptances we have lately gone on the plan of limiting our own bills as far as possible, by negotiating those of others with our endorsement, when satisfied of their security. It is by no means inadvisable to persevere on our system of employing more than one agent, though I know the London Houses dislike it.'

[1] *P.L.B.* W.J. 9.2.1835; J.M. 3.12.1826.   [2] Jenks, *loc. cit.*

Matheson wrote to his Manila agent: 'Baring's House seems to be out of reach, supported by the means furnished by their former partner, now Lord Ashburton, with assistance from the Bank [of England]. Morrison & Co., whose obligations were not so extensive, seem to have secured themselves by a loan from the Royal Bank of Scotland. Geo. Wildes & Co. have all their existing engagements secured by the Bank of England, on condition of the winding up of their affairs. But by a reasoning which we cannot understand, they do not appear to consider as engagements, bills not previously accepted, drawn under letters of credit. T. Wilson & Co., and T. Wiggin & Co. were still struggling with their difficulties, after more than once receiving assistance from the Bank. Some confusion and inconvenience would be experienced from their refusing to honour bills (under credits) which are yet to appear, but this would be nothing compared with the confusion likely to ensue from their entire stoppage ... Our widespread business will probably involve us in some loss. I should think our London friends, Magniac Smith & Co. must under any circumstances stand A.1.'[1] In October came the news that 'the Bank of England in consequence of the Bank of U.S. rejecting certain proposals which they had made', were under necessity of refusing further assistance to the American Houses who were in difficulties, and between 1-5 June the following Houses consequently stopped payment: 'G. Wildes & Co., T. Wiggin and T. Wilson, Gowan and Marx, Bell & Grant and others not named'.[2] Jardine Matheson & Co. thereby lost over £110,000; but, as they wrote to Capt. Grant, the retired Commodore of their opium fleet, 'to you who know our affairs so well, I need hardly observe that this will fall lightly upon us. M.S. & Co. have kindly protected our signatures'.[3]

Henceforth they modified their system of remittance. In a letter explaining the 'motives of our embarking so largely in American paper', Matheson argued that since the firm were

[1] *P.L.B.* J.M. 18.8.1837; 9.9.1837.   [2] *Ibid.* 12.10.1837.   [3] *Ibid.* 20.10.1837.

compelled by the nature of their Indian business to become either large holders or endorsers of Bills on London, they had decided, at the period when Fairlie's credit was being questioned, to divide the risk among several leading houses, such as Barings and Wiggins. 'Thus grew up a system which would not have been necessary, could we have always reposed the same unbounded confidence in our agents, as we are now enabled to do. But once established it was impossible to make a sudden change in it on the formation of our connection with M.S. & Co. The convulsion which has occurred will, however, enable us to set on foot a plan for conducting our business generally on greatly improved principles of security'[1]—whereby all credits had to be supported by shipping documents passing through the hands of Magniac Smith & Co.

When William Jardine went home from China in 1839, he became a partner in the Lombard Street firm, which became Magniac Jardine & Co. in 1841, when he bought out the Smith family. In 1848, following upon the financial crisis, the firm was reorganised by James Matheson, who had gone home in 1842, as Matheson & Co., one of the most powerful firms in the City. Thus, Jardine Matheson & Co. were enabled to develop a banking business, which on the withdrawal of the East India Company's Finance Committee from Canton in 1839[2] handled the lion's share of the lucrative exchange transactions arising from the China trade. Wherefore, it naturally, though unsuccessfully, opposed the formation of the Hongkong and Shanghai Banking Corporation in 1865, which was to revolutionise the whole of British Exchange banking in the East.[3]

C. *Insurance and Shipping*

In addition to banking, there were two other major aspects of Agency business which sprang directly from the China trade,

[1] *P.L.B.* J.M. 9.12.1837.   [2] See following Chapter.
[3] Cf. article by A. J. Baster in Supplement to *Economic Journal*, 'Economic History', Vol. III, No. 9, p. 140.

marine insurance and shipping. Insurance was indispensable in a trade of rich cargoes—opium and treasure, and great risks— pirates, treacherous seas and periodic warfare. In 1801 there was no public insurance office of any kind at Canton, but several individuals would combine in temporary associations to under- write a ship and its cargo up to a maximum of $12,000.[1] As the Country Trade grew, a number of Calcutta insurance offices appointed Canton agents. But the great convenience of having losses payable in China led, in 1805, to the founding of the Canton Insurance Society.

This institution, which lasted for thirty years, was remarkable for the fact that, by an ancient custom, it was managed alternately by the Davidson-Dent house and that of the Beale-Magniac- Jardine firm, the society being wound up every five years and a new one established. The concern consisted of a number of shares, usually 60, which were held each quinquennium by the managing agents in Canton and their 'friends' in Calcutta and Bombay. These shares were much sought after by 'the first class of mer- chants in India and China presenting an almost undeniable solidity of security', since there was no limit to the responsibility of each shareholder. No cash deposit was exacted, and the profits generally yielded a dividend of from $3,000-4,000 per share. But the main inducement to become a shareholder was the prestige and indication of being considered among the most 'respectable' houses which it conferred. Wherefore in 1832 Jardine Matheson & Co., as Managers of the 10th Canton Insurance Company, bestowed the Calcutta agency on their protegé, Lyall Matheson & Co.[2] The shares were distributed by the local agents partly to those who had a hereditary connection with the concern,

[1] *L.B.* 4.5.1801.
[2] On this occasion James Matheson wrote an avuncular letter to Hugh: 'On your judicious management will depend much of the hitherto well-maintained high character of the concern as well as the justification for going out of our way to secure you the Agency. Bear in mind for whom it is you are acting'. *P.L.B.* 10.12.1832.

and partly with a view to 'influencing risks to it'. Writing to
Motichund Amichund, one of the largest Malwa shippers of
Bombay, who wanted a greater number of shares, Magniac & Co.
replied: 'In the distribution of shares we have naturally turned
our attention to those of our constituents and friends who as from
the magnitude of their transactions with ourselves or the benefit
they are likely to confer to the office by contributing "risks" are
entitled to a preference'.[1]

The reason for this strong competition in 'risks' was that each
of the principal Agency Houses in Calcutta and Bombay had an
insurance office of its own, likewise a co-partnership of commercial
'friends' and their connections in the other centres. Thus Fairlie
& Co. were managers of the Calcutta Insurance Society, with
Magniac & Co. as its Canton agent; Palmers ran the rival
Calcutta Insurance Company, with Dents as its Canton agents.
Likewise Forbes controlled the Bombay Insurance Company,
Remingtons the Bombay Insurance Society. James Matheson
brought with him to Canton in 1819 the agency for Mackintosh's
'Hope Insurance Company', and Dent's 'Phoenix'—which he
took with him on entering the firms of Yrissari & Magniac. In
fact, these various Insurance Companies were but aspects of the
differing Agency Houses. They generally derived a substantial
income from these Insurance Companies, not only as dividends
on their shares, of the surplus of premiums over losses, but also
from the regular commission of $\frac{1}{2}$% for every insurance effected.
A list printed in *The Canton Register* of February 1829 shows
Magniac & Co. as agents of no less than six Insurance Companies
including the 8th Canton, and Dent & Co. as agents of four.[2] In
1829 Jardine started a private underwriting account 'J.M. and

[1] *I.L.B.* 24.12.1832.
[2] M. & Co. agents of: 8th Canton Insurance Society; Bengal Insurance Society;
Bombay Insurance Society; Calcutta Insurance Society; Equitable Insurance
Company; Phoenix Insurance Company.
    Dent & Co. agents of: Bombay Insurance Company; Calcutta Insurance
Company; Globe Insurance Office; India Insurance Office.

friends', his firm holding 20 out of the 36 shares. The concern wound up each year, dividing about $1,000 per share. In 1836 it made a surplus of £20,000. With the increase in the volume of the China trade, the revenue from insurance increased proportionately. One result was that in 1835, on the 10th Canton office coming to a close, Dents decided to end the 'ancient custom' of alternate management, the revenues of which were relinquished every five years period, and set up their own 'China Insurance Company'; the 'Canton' remaining permanently in the hands of Jardine Matheson & Co.[1]

Equally successful was the undertaking of shipping activities by the Canton Agency Houses. In the early days they acted merely as resident agents or Supercargoes for Country ships owned in India, receiving from the owners a commission—5% for obtaining outward cargo, 1% for handling inward freight, some higher percentage for chartering or selling a ship at Canton. Particular agents came to be the regular consignees, year after year, of the same ships, e.g. Leckie & Co. of Bombay sent their good ship *Ann* to the consignment of Magniac & Co. every season for a quarter of a century and J. Jeejeebhoy his *Good Success* for almost as long a period. These 'Country Wallahs', heavy and slow, of 500-800 tons with an occasional 1,200-tonner built in India of solid teak, shaped like 'galleons with curved galleries', only able to run up the China Sea before the south-west monsoon and return with the north-eastern, provided for the staple elements of the Old China Trade a kind of private version of the stately 'Indiamen' of the Company. In the case of the smaller barques and brigs which ventured forth on speculations to the islands, the Canton agent's part was more important. Upon his instructions to the captain as to the details of the proposed voyage and the proper line of action in any eventuality depended the out-turn of the adventure.

It was the development of the opium trade which forced on

[1] *I.L.B.* 12.1.1835.

the Canton agent the more active rôle of shipowner. It became necessary to have a special fleet of clippers, receiving-ships, coastal vessels, tenders. These ships would often be the joint property of the Canton agent and his principal India constituent who supplied the opium. Jardine and Matheson made a point of giving their captains an interest in their clippers, and of allowing their 'active' correspondents a reduction of demurrage charges on their 'receiving' vessels.

In this way, around the larger Canton Agency Houses and their connections there grew up a shipping interest. Jardine Matheson & Co. in particular were able out of the accumulation of profits from the opium trade to build up a considerable private fleet, the beginnings of its dominant position in the carrying trade of the China seas.[1]

The Agency House was thus a many-sided edifice. It was a structure well able to adapt itself to every line of growth, every avenue of remuneration which the China trade offered; and yet capable of bearing the stress of that extreme tension which the 'opening' of China was to involve.

---

[1] A list of J.M. ships in 1838 is given in the Appendix.

Chapter VII

THE VICTORY OF THE FREE TRADERS

A. *The End of the Company's Charter*

'The extinction of the Company's monopoly and the simultaneous opening of the China trade to the enterprise and industry of British manufacture and shipping, marks a new and memorable era in the commercial annals of our Nation'. With these words of explanation, Phipps offered his *Treatise on the China Trade* to an eager public. A private letter of December 1833 from a British merchant established in China for the previous fifteen years agreed that 'the opening of the home trade in April, 1834, will form a grand epoch in the Annals of Canton'; but it proceeded to express uncertainty as to the outcome of the change.[1] If it is realised that more than half of British trade with China was already in private hands before 1834, it will help to put that 'memorable' year in its true perspective. (Thus, in the season 1825-6, $15.7 million out of £21.2 million of British imports into China, and $12.6 million out of $21.1 of exports, were on private account.) The change was not, therefore, primarily a matter of taking over the Company's trade.

It will be recalled that by the 1820s the 'private English' had succeeded in obtaining an established footing at Canton within the framework of the Company's monopoly, and that these two groups of British merchants in China were able to exist together for a time because their respective trades moved in 'different spheres'. But the rapid growth of the Country Trade upset the balance and produced a divergence of interest. Moreover, the use of Singapore to effect direct shipments to and from England and

[1] *P.L.B.* J.M. 29.12.1833.

the equally important development of their own credit structure based on the American Bills on London gave the private merchants of Canton a considerable measure of independence from the Company. Whereas old W. S. Davidson, who had come out to China in 1807 and left in 1824, when speaking of the early days of the Country Trade, though he complained that it was 'merely a trade on sufferance', yet admitted deriving advantage from the existence of the Company's China Factory; young James Matheson, who came out in 1819 and left in 1841, in one of his first letters denounced 'that destructive monopoly which has so long existed'.[1] William Jardine repeatedly attacked the Company for its 'vacillating' opium policy, and its 'unbusinesslike' financial methods, which at one point caused Company Bills to be bandied about at a discount.[2] This divergence of views over financial policy was most marked in the struggle over the rate of exchange for remittances to London. The India agents made it the main ground of their attack on the Company's monopoly that private traders were penalised by having to depend on a rate of exchange determined by the needs of the Company.[3]

Above all, the new spirit of the private merchants expressed itself in opposition to the Company's passive policy towards the Canton Commercial System. *The Canton Register* put the issue squarely.[4] 'The Company's last monopoly, since its homeward investments are confined to tea, may not find much material injury though their cotton cargoes turn out dreadfully deficient compared with former values. But the commerce of the Company in China, when taken in view of the whole trade of the port, does not bear such a mighty comparison. The American and Country trade is very extensive and deeply affected by every mal-arrangement. It seems impossible from the fettered state of all mercantile operations here, that intercourse can be increased substantially'.

---

[1] R.T. and J.M., 2.6.1821. Davidson's evidence before *S.C.H. of C.*
[2] *I.L.B.* 22.6.1825; 18.3.1826; 10.6.1826, etc.
[3] Cf. evidence of Rickards, *S.C.H. of C.* 1830, 5238.   [4] *C. Reg.*, 2.8.1828.

The issue was forced in 1829 by the action of the merchants of Bombay and Bengal, who had suffered great losses in their cotton shipments to China for several years. In May of that year 44 Parsees of Bombay, 'nearly all the native wealth and commercial influence of that side of India', petitioned the Governor-General to bring pressure to bear on the Canton Select Committee 'to avert a severe calamity' by exerting itself to secure improved conditions of trade with China. In amplifying these demands to the Select Committee the Canton agents argued that the Country Trade at Canton had outgrown the regulations intended to control it. To their surprise and delight 'the Select' decided to act. 'The object we have in view, is not so much the removal of petty grievances as the establishment of commercial intercourse on a more extended basis. The change which it will be our endeavour to effect in the trade to China involves a fundamental reformation of the whole system.'[1]

But the President of the Select Committee was opposed to such a change of policy, and went home to London, to rouse the Court of Directors, who promptly dismissed the Canton Committee. Jardine wrote bitterly to Thomas Weeding: 'The good people in England think of nothing connected with China but tea and the revenue derived from it, and to obtain these quietly will submit to any degradation . . . The old Committee were the first that took the British trade of the port under their protection or afforded protection to the property and interests of individuals. I wish you could persuade your friends of the Directorate of the propriety of a more decided line of conduct being adopted under sanction from home, or if from His Majesty so much the better . . . the general opinion in Canton is in favour of many valuable concessions being procurable from the Chinese if properly asked for'.[2] In another letter Jardine declared that he found it impossible to place confidence in the Company's new Select Committee.

[1] C. Reg., 26.8.1829; 3.10.1829.
[2] I.L.B. 11.12.1830. P.L.B. W.J. 27.12.1830.

In December 1830[1] a remarkable petition to the House of Commons was drawn up and signed by 47 private British subjects in China, including ships' captains. It argued that the China trade had increased in defiance of Chinese restrictions 'to a point of such magnitude as will raise the anxiety of your Honourable House to place it upon a permanent and honourable basis; that the total failure of both Embassies to Pekin [i.e. the Macartney and Amherst Missions] will forcibly suggest to your Honourable House how little is to be gained in China by any refinements of diplomacy'; that the Cohong was 'a limited medium of intercourse not even in an efficient state'. 'Your petitioners', it continued, 'would anticipate the most beneficial results from the permanent residence at Pekin of a representative of His Majesty, instructed to act with becoming spirit in protecting the interests of his countrymen'. Without this direct intervention of H.M. Government (the petition argued) it was to be feared that no material extension of commerce with China could be expected. At the least, it was hoped that the British Government 'would adopt a resolution worthy of the nation and by the acquisition of an insular possession near the coast of China, place British commerce in this remote quarter of the globe beyond the reach of future despotism and oppression'. Hongkong was not yet thought of as the best 'insular possession'. Matheson favoured one of the Lintin group, Jardine Formosa. To the news of a formidable insurrection in Formosa in 1832 Jardine's reaction was 'What an opportunity for us to lend them a little hand and gain a footing on the island'.[2]

The private merchants were demanding stronger political support than the East India Company would or could give. This was perhaps the main reason why they desired the abolition of the Company's charter. On the other hand they were doubtful

---

[1] There survives a MS. draft of the petition in James Matheson's handwriting, dated 24.11.1830. The date given in *The Canton Register* is 24.12.1830.

[2] *P.L.B.* 3.1.1833.

about the immediate commercial consequences of such a step. Enjoying a quasi-monopoly under the Company's régime, as far as the Country Trade went, they were afraid of an influx of new 'free merchants' who would flood the China market with British goods and bring unbridled competition to Canton. 'We would prefer working on our comparatively quiet routine, but in the event of the Company's monopoly being abolished, the trade from England will become so mixed up with that between India and China, that it will be impossible for us to avoid participating in it and at the same time maintain our present situation'.[1] In November 1833 Matheson wrote to a Leith correspondent: 'Such is my impression of the extent to which the trade in British manufactures will be overdone here by the resistless impulse of steam that I cannot consider it desirable for a general merchant to engage in it in competition with the lowest scale of remuneration that will enable them to work their machinery without loss'.[2]

Moreover,. the Canton 'free' merchants were convinced that the abolition of the Company's monopoly would not of itself unlock the gates of the Chinese market. 'Great Britain can never derive any important advantage from the opening of the trade to China while the present mode of levying duties and extorting money from the Hong merchants exists. We must have a commercial code with these *celestial barbarians* before we can extend advantageously our commercial operations. We have the right to demand an equitable commercial treaty. So say we residents. But I am afraid our friends at home differ from us'.[3]

B. *Manchester and Canton*

The decisive pressure against the East India Company's monopoly came not from Canton but from Manchester. Right down to the end of the 18th century, the Company had been attacked by English textile merchants for *importing* fine Indian cloths with which they could not yet compete. The grounds of opposition

[1] *P.L.B.* W.J. 16.1.1831. [2] *P.L.B.* J.M. 15.11.1833. [3] *P.L.B.* W.J. 29.2.1832.

had shifted as the technical supremacy of British manufacture began to dominate the industrial situation. The Company's monopoly was now regarded as an obstacle to that continuous development of new export markets which was held to be essential for the expansion of machine-powered industry.

In 1813, when the Company's charter had come up for renewal, petitions from Manchester, Blackburn, Glasgow and other textile centres had demanded 'freedom of commerce as the birthright of all Britons'.[1] The throwing open of the India trade (with certain restrictions) in 1813 had been followed by a rapid increase in the export of cotton goods, much greater·than that of other articles.[2] But the Company still retained the monopoly of the China trade, which withheld from the Manchester merchants not only a potential market but also a means of remittance from India. 'The difficulty of making profitable returns is a great obstruction to the future expansion of our India trade.'[3]

In February 1827 the Manchester Chamber of Commerce decided to set up a committee to enquire into 'the state of our trade with the East Indies'. In March the Committee presented a significant report to the Directors of the Chamber.[4] After expressing its gratification at the vast increases in the export of cotton now amounting to two-thirds of the whole export trade of the Kingdom 'independently of forming a principle article of home trade', and giving employment to numerous hands, the report proceeded: 'But other countries are straining equally with ourselves to promote it (i.e. cotton manufacture), aided by cheapness of living and freedom from restrictions on their foreign

[1] A. Redford, *Manchester Merchants and Foreign Trade.*
[2] The figures, cited in the *Proc. M. Ch.* II, 9.3.1827, are:

Total British exports to East India	Cotton goods
1818 = £2·5 million	190,000 pieces
1821 = £3 „	511,000 „
1822 = £3·7 „	710,000 „

[3] *Ibid.* Vol. I.   [4] *Ibid.* Vol. II, 9.3.1827.

commerce. Thus many of the countries of Europe and the U.S.A. are rapidly becoming manufacturers themselves, and we are now beginning to find out great capital and means of production of goods cramped for want of more extensive markets. The vast fields for commercial enterprise which the East Indies offer to us . . . would assuredly make up for the falling away from all our former customers and give full employment to our redundant capital and dense population'. The substance of this report was then embodied in a petition to the House of Commons which stressed that greater facilities in other markets, especially in the East, were necessary to maintain the actual extent of cotton manufacture, let alone promote its expansion.[1]

In 1829 the campaign against the Company's monopoly was begun in earnest. On April 27th a public meeting was called at the Manchester Town Hall by the Borough-reeve and Constables on the requisition of the Directors of the Chamber of Commerce. 'A numerous and most respectable meeting of merchants, manufacturers and others interested in the trade and commerce of Manchester' passed several resolutions demanding the ending of the tea monopoly and full freedom of trade to China 'which still remains subject to the Company's interdict'. It was decided to set up a permanent 'East India Trade Committee' to promote the object of the meeting.[2]

At the first meeting of this Committee it was resolved to advertise the proceedings of the public meeting in the Manchester and London newspapers, and to print five hundred copies of the resolutions for postal distribution 'to the chief officers of the principal towns and others interested'. Secondly, signatures were to be collected for another petition to Parliament. Thirdly, other towns were to be urged to hold similar public meetings, and the Committee was to collaborate with the Liverpool East India and China Trade Association in a joint campaign.[3] The Liverpool Association had written to its M.P., William Huskisson, President

---

[1] *Proc. M. Ch.* II, 25.4.1827.   [2] *Ibid.* 27.4.1829.   [3] *Ibid.* Vol. I, 29.4.1829.

of the Board of Trade, to arrange for an audience of His Majesty's Ministers. Huskisson's reply urged the necessity of the widest propaganda. 'They are not the interests alone of the commerce and industry of the country but those of the whole community which are involved in the considerations connected with the Charter of the East India Company, and it is therefore material that all classes should be made sensible that they have an interest in obtaining their relaxations which are more immediately called for by the commercial and manufacturing towns'. It was decided to invite the co-operation of other provincial centres. On 15 May, 1829, deputies from Manchester, Liverpool, Glasgow, Bristol, Birmingham, Leeds and Calcutta met at Fenton's Hotel, St James's Street, to lobby Parliament and send a united deputation to the Government. In their annual report the Directors of the Manchester Chamber of Commerce were able to record that, as a result of the exertions of the various provincial committees, His Majesty's Government had agreed that full enquiry should be made into the Eastern trade, and that Sir Robert Peel was presenting a motion for a Select Committee to consider the matter.[1] These proposals were gratefully acknowledged at another public meeting held in Manchester Town Hall on the 21 January 1830, which resolved to petition Parliament once again for free trade with China. A vigorous resolution was passed that the monopoly of the trade with China vested in the East India Company 'is unnecessary for its security, prejudicial to the public interest, and galling to the feelings of the people, exposing it to the humiliation of witnessing a valuable commerce extensively carried on by the free adventurers of other states, whilst our own merchants are prohibited from engaging in it, under the disparaging pretext of a want of ability to conduct it with safety and advantage'.[2]

As the time for the Parliamentary enquiry approached, the free traders intensified their propaganda. Hundreds of copies were

[1] *Proc. M. Ch.* II, 8.2.1830.   [2] *Ibid.* 21.1.1830.

printed of a brief statement of the free traders' case and sent to the chief merchants and newspapers of the various towns which had sent deputies to London in the previous year, and also to Dublin, Macclesfield, Hull and Newcastle. A new edition of Mr Crawfurd's pamphlet on *Free Trade* was brought out.[1] Letters were sent to the public authorities of 270 towns urging the propriety of writing to each member of both Houses of Parliament. Leaflets were even sent somewhat maliciously to the Directors of the East India Company and the proprietors of East India Stock. The Manchester East India Committee circulated the chief inhabitants of neighbouring towns in Lancashire and Cheshire urging co-operation in the campaign. While the local East India Committees in the seven principal towns continued to be active, it was decided to maintain permanently a united delegation in London, appoint a secretary at a salary of £300 a year and rent a committee room in the King's Arms, Palace Yard.[2] 'The deputies of the commercial and manufacturing towns opposing the Company's monopoly held their first meeting on 24 February 1830. It decided to raise a 'fighting' fund of £1,000 from mercantile and manufacturing houses in the various cities.'

The delegation proceeded 'to excite public attention to the subject (of a free China trade), to obtain and spread information regarding it', and to interview M.P.s. It issued a circular 'which had been generally sent throughout the Kingdom'. Above all, it prepared evidence to be laid before the Select Committee of the House of Commons. Against the arguments of the Company's representations, the free traders stressed several points: (1) The commercial disposition of the Chinese and the extraordinary facilities of the port of Canton. (2) The great opening in China for the sale of British manufactures. (3) The certainty of a lowering of the price of tea to the English consumer

---

[1] Mr John Crawfurd was the Parliamentary agent and London publicity manager of the Calcutta merchants at a salary of £1,500.

[2] *Proc. M. Ch.* II, 11.2.1830; 27.2.1830; 3.3.1830.

upon the cessation of the monopoly. (4) The benefit which would accrue to shipping and commercial interests 'which otherwise must continue paralysed', since the China monopoly 'impedes even those lines of trade with which it appears at first sight to have the least connection'.[1]

The struggle lasted throughout 1831 and 1832. There was no relaxation of effort by the free traders. Petitions continued to pour in from the various commercial and industrial towns, the larger towns using their influence to secure support from the smaller. It was decided to print and circulate as a pamphlet an article in *The Edinburgh Review* written by McCullogh from facts supplied by Crawfurd. A suggestion was considered, though thought impolitic, that at the General Election of that year candidates be asked to declare in favour of freeing the China trade. A standing committee of representatives from the provinces remained in London throughout the enquiry, extra delegates coming up for a day or two on occasion of interviews with ministers. It is notable that when a deputation from the merchants of Calcutta, Manchester, Liverpool and Birmingham saw the Prime Minister, Earl Grey, they argued that the opening of the China trade would be of much greater benefit to the commercial world than the opening of the India trade had been.[2] The outcome of the struggle was in little doubt. The future belonged to the new men and interests of the North and Midlands. In the England of the Reform Bill, Edmund Burke's equation of the Company and the Country was no longer valid.

C. *The Economic Consequences of 1834*

The fruits of the hard-won victory were not easy to pick. The doubts of the Canton agents were based on a closer understanding

[1] *Proc. M. Ch.* II, 28.5.1830. See the evidence before *S.C.H. of C.* 1830; especially that of J. Crawfurd, J. Maxwell, W. Brown, and T. Rickards of Rickards Mackintosh & Co., the London correspondents of Dents, and of Hollingworth Magniac and J. Crawfurd before the *S.C.H. of L.*
[2] *Proc. M. Ch.* 5.2.1831.

of the China trade than the hopes of the Manchester merchants. It is difficult, however, to appraise the effect of the ending of the Company's monopoly on the trends of the trade after 1834, because that event cannot easily be isolated from other influences. It is probable that the American R. B. Forbes, partner in the Canton firm Russell & Co. during the '30s, was right in arguing that the real commercial effect of 1834 on the Canton commerce was limited, since less than half of it remained by then to be divided up among the new army of free merchants.[1] Certainly, within the inelastic framework of the Canton Commercial System, the influx of new firms to China (the British community increased from 66 in 1833 to 156 in 1837) naturally produced a general rise in the price of exports and a fall in those of imports. Quite apart from other incentives to over-trading, this was sufficient to dislocate the market and bring about the speedy demise of a number of the new firms. The old houses, continuing to rely mainly on agency business and rarely shipping on their own account except in opium, were able to avoid the speculator's losses arising from disadvantageous prices while swelling their own commission accounts with the increased volume of business. Jardine Matheson & Co., especially, emerged with increased strength, as 'the general focus or medium' for the Canton trade, transacting a large share—fully a third—of 'the business of the Port'.[2]

Most disappointing to the free traders was the irregular import curve of British cotton piece goods. The Americans whose carrying of British cottons to China had been one of the strongest arguments against the Company's rule, after a last-minute fling in Manchester goods which ruined the market for Manchester, began to export American cotton manufactures from Lowell, U.S.A., in even larger quantities. The Americans brought to

[1] *Remarks on China and the China Trade*, 1844.
[2] *P.L.B.* J.M. 15.10.1834. In one season, no less than 75 ships were sent to the consignment of J.M. & Co. Cf. G. Nye, *Reminiscences*.

Canton 62,000 pieces of British cotton cloth in 1831-2, 143,000 pieces in 1833-4, and only 1,600 pieces in 1837-8. But by 1842 they were importing 500,000 pieces of American cotton![1]

Nevertheless 'Mr MacVicar and his Lancashire gentlemen', from Clitheroe, Preston and the like, persisted in extending their shipments. Yarn sold fairly well—it was 'now in general use in all the manufacturing districts and much liked by the workmen'.[2] But piece goods, partly because of the incidence of the Canton duties, had to be smuggled from Canton and off the coast to avoid loss. Then suddenly, much to the gratification of Mr MacVicar and other members of the Manchester Chamber of Commerce, the Hong merchants began to take up a greater quantity of piece goods. Horrocks' celebrated cambrics were especially favoured.[3] Only in 1837 did the crisis among the Hong merchants, which we are about to examine, reveal that they had been making a sacrifice of 5%-7% on their purchases of piece goods for the sake of ready cash from the dealers. As a result of this 'system of raising cash carried to a ruinous extent' by the most of the Hongs, 'piece-goods have borne a fictitious value, which must now cease'.[4] The piece-goods business had for some years been a 'forced trade'.

A similar course, with variations, is to be observed in the article of tea, the richest jewel in the East India Company's commercial crown. There was a 'sad scramble' for 'free tea', and 'disgraceful exhibitions' marked its introduction to the London market. Forty per cent more teas were shipped to England in the first season after the abolition of the Company's monopoly than in the previous one. As Forbes remarked, every merchant and ship-owner who had ever seen a chest of tea immediately turned his attention to China.[5] But the men on the spot had a natural advantage. On 22 March 1834 Jardine despatched the first 'free ship'. the *Sarah*, from Canton to London, though her cargo contained

[1] Forbes, *op. cit.*   [2] *P.L.B.* W.J. 3.11.1835.
[3] *Ibid.* 16.11.1833, etc.   [4] *Ibid.* 4.4.1837.
[5] Forbes, *op. cit.*, p. 45.

no teas, *pace* Hunter,[1] because he was 'still in the dark' as to the exact date when they could legally be shipped. But on April 24, Jardine Matheson & Co. despatched four ships crammed with teas to Glasgow, Liverpool, Hull[2] and Falmouth, the first to be sent to the provincial 'outports'. The firm became the largest buyers of tea in Canton[3] mainly on account of 'friends' both Chinese and English, but also at first on their own account. They ceased to 'speculate', however, when the Canton price rose rapidly in response to the demand,[4] and were thus able to save themselves from many of the losses which the speculators from England sustained when the home price fell in the following season.

For several seasons the tea trade continued to be in difficulties. These were accentuated by three attendant circumstances. First, the East India Company did not completely retire from the field, but maintained a Financial Committee at Canton, on the plea that it was still necessary to remit the home charges from India via the China trade. This Committee advertised that it was empowered to advance up to £600,000 in return for Bills on England to individuals intending to ship merchandise from China to London. This policy provoked violent opposition from the private Canton merchants. Jardine wrote angrily to Weeding:[5] 'We are all very much surprised here at the quiet way in which you merchants and agents at home submit to the Company's Finance Committee at Canton. We consider it in direct opposition to the Act of Parliament [ending the charter], and what is worse, it is likely to turn out a vile job. The merchants in the outports [i.e. provinces] have

[1] *Fan-Kwai*, p. 33.

[2] The *Camden, Princess Charlotte, Georgiana,* and *Pyramus. P.L.B.* W.J. 17.7.1834.

[3] They found it worth while to bring out a tea-taster from London and employ him at a salary of £500 plus board and lodging.

[4] Thus in December 1834 the first quality of tea, which the Company used to procure at 28 taels, was being bought at 35·5 taels, with a corresponding increase in the price of the three inferior qualities. *P.L.B.* J.M. 7.12.1834.

[5] *P.L.B.* W.J. 21.8.1834.

reason to complain as they are not permitted to share in the advances made here. The manufacturers have still more reason to be dissatisfied, as the (Hong) merchants will not barter their teas for unsaleable piece goods, when they can get two-thirds the value of their teas advanced in cash, and the chance of the English market and the Honourable Company for their agency. These advances may do harm in another way by enabling the tea dealers and Hong merchants to keep up the price of any particular description of tea by shipping and taking advances on it. But what is worse than all, the Company, by advancing enough cash, may run off with all the agency for China. Added to all this it enables needy adventurers to use public money to carry on a ruinous competition with the fair traders'.

The 'free traders' were now 'fair traders', objecting to a 'ruinous competition'.[1] But in spite of petitions to Parliament and intrigue in the City and at Westminster, through the instrumentality of Jardine's agent, John Abel Smith, M.P., the private merchants were unable to force the removal of the Company's Finance Committee, which continued to control the Canton exchange and foster the 'rage for speculation' in the China trade, until it voluntarily withdrew at the outbreak of the Opium War.

The second adverse circumstance was the attempt, sustained over several seasons, of the London Tea Brokers to secure control of the market. Their method was to force down the price to be paid to the shippers by assigning to the teas inferior gradings of quality. Thereupon the shippers would complain to the Canton agents for selecting poor 'chops'. At first Jardine Matheson attributed this deprecation to capriciousness of taste—'really it

---

[1] Any apparent inconsistency of principle would have been explained away by the argument, which Matheson actually used in another context, that competition was unfair with a rival who was a sovereign, as the East India Company was in India. In the present case, it was strongly objected that Messrs Daniels & Astell, who managed the operations of the Company's Canton Finance Committee, also formed a firm of their own which used funds provided by the India revenue to finance shipments of tea to London. cf. *P.L.B.* J.M. 23.12.1832.

seems quite a lottery what estimation the most carefully selected teas may meet with in the English Market'. But when different valuations were set on the same 'chop' of tea to an extent of 40% they began to suspect some knavery. 'It appears to us that powerful and wealthy interests are combined in keeping up the mystery and uncertainty of the trade to which the Brokers seem to lend themselves with a too ready acquiescence'. John Abel Smith was, therefore, instructed to do all in his power to prevent their teas from being 'sacrificed by the over-fastidiousness and caprice of the Brokers who, when the market is overstocked, scruple not to attribute to inferiority of quality what is really the effect of flat and forced sales'.[1] An arrangement was then arrived at with two firms of Tea Brokers, T. and R. Moffat, and Watkins Smith and Hope, which effectively spoilt the game; though tea remained a precarious object of speculation.

Parallel with the action of the London Tea Brokers was a Chinese attempt to force up the price made by 'a combination of the Black-Tea men'. These 'slippery and saucy fellows', as Jardine called them, were the middlemen from whom the Hong merchants bought their 'black' tea—the chief type exported to England.[2] After 1834 these tea merchants—there were over a hundred of them—demanded higher prices from the Hong merchants, who were now without the support of the Company, whose demand had always dominated the market. In 1836 the tea-men made even higher demands and refused to deliver teas, though contracted for under advances, without previously receiving cash or security from the Hong merchants.[3] Jardine explained the position to a London tea dealer. 'We have been endeavouring of late to induce the Hong merchants to act with more unanimity and resist the unreasonable demands of the tea merchants, who have for the

---

[1] *P.L.B.* J.M. 9.12.1837; 6.1.1838; 1.8.1838.

[2] The American taste, on the other hand, favoured 'green' teas. The adjectives implied a non-existent difference in colour; the actual difference lay in the preparing of the leaves. See R. Fortune, *Three Years' Wandering in China*, 1847.

[3] *P.L.B.* J.M. 21.12.1836.

last two years been reaping large profits while the Hong merchants have not made enough out of teas to pay for the expense of their Hong establishment. This must appear to you almost impossible, when you look at the relative position of the parties . . . the tea merchants cannot ship off a single chest unless through one of the ten Hong merchants.'

This 'refractory conduct' of the tea-men had the important[1] effect of seriously undermining the credit of the Hong merchants. Jardine and the other European buyers, seeing that the tea-men were too strong for the Hongists, 'who cannot trust each other in any combination they may enter for the common good',[2] entered into direct relations with the tea-men themselves. This, indeed, ensured the usual supply of tea for England, but made the position of the Hong merchants even more serious.

It was at this point that the Hengtai Hong, already weakened by other losses,[3] stopped payment, owing its creditors $2,261,000; and Kingqua followed suit for the smaller sum of $100,000. This was not all: every one of the Hongs, except two, was placed in a precarious position by the action of the tea-men. There was no Select Committee now to help them out. 'I am convinced', wrote Jardine, 'that not one of the recently made Hongs are free from debt, and except Howqua and Puankequa there is now not one Hong with $20,000. If we break one, we may break the whole; and if we do break the whole, the *Hoppo* will quickly make six or eight more, charging them 40,000 taels each for the privilege. These would of course be men of no property and little character who would in a few years break in their turn. This is a gloomy picture but it is a true one.'[4] Jardine, who was hoping to retire from China, found it 'unthinkable' to go until some arrangements were made for settling the debts of the Hongs and 'placing the trade of the port on a more solid and safe basis than it is'.[5]

[1] *P.L.B.* W.J. 16.4.1836.   [2] *Ibid.* 16.4.1836.
[3] See Chapter III above.   [4] *P.L.B.* W.J. 4.2.1837.
[5] *Ibid.* 16.1.1837.

Abolition of the Company's charter was thus followed by a period of acute difficulty in the China trade, quite apart from the question of opium. 'The truth is', wrote Jardine in 1837, 'the China trade has been too much run on: the Company's advances have afforded too much facility for wild speculations.'[1] Matheson wrote to an American correspondent: 'We are sighing almost for a return of the Company's monopoly in preference to the trouble and endless turmoil of free trade'.[2] But this comment was made in a rare mood of defeatism. His general attitude and that of the other Canton merchants was still that of 1830: that the fruits of free trade could not be gathered until the whole of foreign commerce in China had been put on a new footing. The logic of free trade required the abolition of the Cohong.

D. *Political Consequences of 1834*

Paradoxically, the most immediate result of the victory of the free traders was to bring the power of the British state to bear directly on the China trade. After 1834 the Foreign Office replaced the Court of Directors, and the 'Superintendents of British Trade in China' superseded the Select Committee of Supercargoes. To the diplomatic historian this change is so fundamental as to constitute a starting point in China's 'international relations'. Whence follows the familiar argument that conflict was 'inevitable', because the Chinese persisted in regarding as a mere *taepan*, or chief merchant, the direct representative of British Government.[3] The significant thing from our point of view is that in fact Lord Napier, the direct representative of the British Government, *was* superintendent of British trade in China. His instructions were to assist the British subjects in their mercantile pursuits and to explore the possibilities of extending trade

---

[1] *P.L.B.* W.J. 3.1.1837.   [2] *P.L.B.* J.M. 8.3.1837.

[3] Costin, for example, writes of Napier: 'as the bearer of a royal commission, a Scottish peer of ancient lineage and a Foreign Office Servant, he was something more than a mere Superintendent of Trade'. *Britain and China, 1833-60*, p. 21.

to other parts of China. Throughout his brief but stormy period in Canton and Macao, Napier was in constant touch with the British merchants; he was especially intimate with William Jardine, in whose house he lived and who acted as his go-between with the Chinese, when negotiations were broken off.[1] The appointment of Lord Napier as First Superintendent of Trade had 'created a sensation' among the British merchants in China, who had feared that Sir George Staunton or some other former member of the Company's Factory would be appointed. On receiving the news, Jardine wrote to Thomas Weeding in London: 'I hope you did your best to impress upon his mind the necessity of a dignified, firm and independent conduct in his dealings with the Chinese. He has a very difficult game to play'.[2] When Napier's tactics led to the Chinese stopping British trade, Jardine wrote optimistic letters to his anxious constituents in support of Napier's policy. After Napier's failure and death in October 1834, Jardine wrote further letters in his defence, revealing incidentally that Napier had 'always intended to leave Canton rather than allow trade to be suspended beyond the month of October'—the beginning of the trading season.[3] Matheson's considered opinion was that though Napier had obtained no concrete benefits for the merchants, on the whole 'his proceedings have done good . . . the Chinese have had a lesson they will not forget'.[4]

When Napier's successors, Robinson and Davis, decided to pursue the famous 'policy of quiescence' the response of the British merchants in China was to intensify their demands for a 'forward policy'. They had, on Lord Napier's recommendation, organised themselves into a Chamber of Commerce[5] 'for the

---

[1] *P.L.B.* W.J. 10.7.1836. [2] *Ibid.* 10.6.1834.
[3] *Ibid.* 23.10.1834. [4] *P.L.B.* J.M. 25.9.1834; 10.10.1834.
[5] *Ibid.*, and J. Phipps, *op. cit.*, Appendix. The Parsees were not admitted to membership of the Canton Chamber because 'in case of negotiation with the Chinese requiring *more* on the part of the merchant (and it is in such cases that the Chamber is likely to be useful) the natives of India are sure to fail'. When Napier's action had resulted in the Chinese stopping the trade, the Parsees had

purpose of giving form and efficiency to the British mercantile community'. They now proceeded to conduct a campaign in India and England against the two pressing evils of the Canton Commercial System and the East India Company's Finance Committee. In December 1834 they drew up a petition[1] to be presented to the King-in-Council, asking for the appointment of a plenipotentiary supported by three warships to demand: (1) redress for the trade stoppage, (2) the opening of the Northern ports to foreign commerce, and (3) the ending of the Cohong monopoly. These measures were necessary to maintain 'the advantages which a safe and uninterrupted commerce with China is calculated to yield to the revenues of Great Britain and to the important classes interested in its arts and manufactures'. James Matheson believed that 'the point of direct communication with the [Council] Government without the corrupt interventions of the Hong merchants is of *such vital importance to the well-being of the trade that the British Government cannot rest until it is obtained'*.[2] Elected the first President of the Canton Chamber of Commerce, he decided to accompany Lady Napier back to England, both to commission a marble memorial for Lord Napier and to persuade the British Government to stronger action in China. By the time Matheson reached London, the Grey Ministry had fallen, and he had audience, not with Palmerston but the Duke of Wellington. The latter was far from sympathetic to the aspirations of the *parvenu* commercial and industrial classes; and it is not surprising that Matheson found the hero of Waterloo 'a cold-blooded fellow . . . a strenuous advocate of submissiveness and servility'.

Rebuffed by the Government, Matheson turned to the country. Through the correspondents of his firm, he was able to get in touch with the mercantile communities of Manchester, Liverpool and Glasgow. Already many years previously Matheson had

appealed to Napier to abandon his stand, since otherwise 'ruin appears certain to thousands of our countrymen dependent on the China trade'.
[1] Printed in J. Phipps, *op. cit.*   [2] *P.L.B.* J.M. 25.9.1834 (my italics).

appreciated the importance of enlisting the support of the manufacturing interest for a stronger policy in China. In 1832 he had
written to Mr MacVicar, the firm's Manchester agent: 'I hope you
will have the leisure to take some interest in the British subjects'
grievances in China, and endeavour to stir up a fellow feeling
in your manufacturing friends'.[1] MacVicar, a Director and Vice-
President of the Manchester Chamber of Commerce, acted as a
link between the Canton merchants and the home manufacturers
and shippers interested in the China market. It may have been he
who in 1835, on instructions from Jardine, had drawn up a
memorandum on the evil effects of the Company's Finance Committee at Canton, which was then presented, on behalf of the
Manchester Chamber of Commerce, to the Board of Trade.[2] And
it was through his initiative that the Manchester Chamber of
Commerce drew up in February 1836 the all-important memorial
to the Foreign Secretary, on 'the unprotected state of our Trade
with China'.

This memorial,[3] which was followed by similar documents
from Liverpool and Glasgow, began by drawing attention to
the great importance of the China trade to the mercantile,
manufacturing and shipping interests of Great Britain, and
the unprotected situation of the British merchants resident in
China, through whose medium the trade was conducted. It then
pointed out that the China trade not only provided employment
to 100,000 tons of British shipping and a market for British
manufactures, but also afforded an outlet for the products of
India to the extent of over £3 million per annum, 'which enables
our Indian subjects to consume *our* manufacturers on a largely
increased scale'. Secondly, it argued, the China trade was capable
of great extension, since its products were suited to English wants

---

[1] The letter continues 'How did you excape examination by the Committee
of the House of Commons? I should like to have seen you brought before them'.
P.L.B. J.M. 14.11.1832.

[2] *Proc. M. Ch.* II, 18.3.1835.   [3] Cf. *Proc. M. Ch.* II, 10.2.1836.

and vice versa: 'We cannot contemplate without the most serious alarm the uncertain and unprotected state in which this most important trade is placed particularly since the failure of Lord Napier's "Mission".' Without adequate protection, it argued, the trade was liable to be stopped at the caprice of the Hong merchants or Mandarins. British property was in daily jeopardy, our industry liable to be paralysed, our revenue exposed to the loss of £5 million a year. This accumulation of evils called for the protecting influence of the British Government. Therefore the memorialists prayed for the Government's serious consideration of the state of our political relations with China.

In other words, by 1836 the weight of the 'home' manufacturing interests of Britain was thrown behind a 'forward policy' in China. This was perhaps the most important consequence of 1834. The abolition of the Company's charter had brought together the Country traders and the Manchester merchants. William Jardine had now become a celebrated figure in *English* commercial circles.[1] James Matheson, in his vigorously written pamphlet of 1836,[2] makes the climax of his argument for a 'forward' policy in China the fact that it has been demanded by the commercial communities of Manchester, Liverpool and Glasgow. The elimination of the Honourable Company from the China trade had brought up a new and powerful phalanx against the ramparts of Canton.

---

[1] In 1836 'one of the finest vessels belonging to Liverpool' was named after him. *P.L.B.* W.J. to Sir John Tobin, who was responsible for the compliment.

[2] J. Matheson, *Present Position and Future Prospects of Trade in China*, London, 1836.

Chapter VIII

LEDGER AND SWORD

A. *The Opium War*

The victory of the free traders over the East India Company, so far from resolving the contradictions of the China trade, had accentuated them. The more the trade increased, the more obvious became the inadequacy of the Cohong to cope with it. The more desirable China appeared as a potential market for British manufactures, the more restrictive and intolerable seemed the Canton Commercial System. The greater the recourse to illicit trading from the receiving-ships at Lintin and along the coast, the greater the danger of the Chinese Government stopping the trade. Lastly, the more extensive the opium trade became, and with it the outflow of treasure, the nearer came the day when the Chinese authorities would have to take action. Wherefore, in the years after 1834 there flowed a constant stream of propaganda in pamphlets, newspapers and letters, drawing attention to the 'precarious and defenceless position' of the British merchants in China, and calling for the British Government's 'prompt interference and vigorous superintendence in reconstructing the system of our commercial relations with China' to place the trade 'upon a safe, advantageous, honourable and permanent footing'.[1]

Already in 1830 the private merchants at Canton had envisaged the use of, at least the show of, force to attain their demands. On the occasion of a visit to China of a naval squadron from India in

---

[1] These phrases are from J. Matheson's pamphlet of 1836, but similar expressions are to be found in almost every issue of *The Canton Register* and *The Canton Press*. Cf. Sir J. B. Urmston's pamphlet, the *Treatise* of Phipps, the *Remarks* of G. Staunton, and H. Lindsay's *Letter to Palmerston*, all published in these years. For Parliamentary propaganda, cf. *P.L.B. J.M.* 5.1.1838.

1831, Jardine had written to Weeding[1]: 'I am at a loss from what authority the Admiral can receive instructions that would warrant the commencement of a system of warfare against China, unless he could provoke the war junks to fire upon him, which is unlikely. Time must determine, but I cannot bring myself to contemplate seriously an open rupture'. In the following year he thought a rupture possible: 'nothing can now be done unless the British Government interfere'. Jardine's anger at the cautious attitude of the home Government burst out periodically in his letters to Matheson. Thus his comment on the news that the Chinese had seized a British naval officer and put him in irons was: 'I wish most sincerely H.M. Ministers were in irons with him.' But he still maintained that an 'equitable commercial treaty' might be obtained without bloodshed.[2] After Lord Napier's unsuccessful attempt to force a change, Jardine observed that the Chinese seemed more determined than ever to maintain the existing system, and were incurring heavy expenses in repairing and building forts all along the coast and river banks.[3] It was now realised even in London that no change was possible without a show of force, which might lead to war.

Matheson's letters from England in 1835 reported that the British Government was not prepared to take such a step so long as the revenues which derived from the China trade continued to be provided. It was, therefore, the breakdown in the trade itself which brought matters to a political head. The struggle between the Black Tea-men and the Cohong threatened not merely the supply of tea but the whole future of the foreign trade at Canton. 'On the issue of this struggle the existence of the Hong merchants as a public body depends'.[4] Jardine had hardly penned this judgment when the failure of Hengtai's Hong proclaimed the

[1] *P.L.B.* W.J. 25.4.1831.
[2] *Ibid.* 16.3.1832.
[3] *Ibid.* 11.11.1835.
[4] *Ibid.* 22.11.1836.

collapse of that body.[1] But the final paralysis of the Old China Trade was brought about by the stopping of its heart, the trade in opium.

We know from Chinese sources[2] that by November 1836 the Imperial Government, after debating the rival policies of legalising the opium trade or enforcing its prohibition, had finally decided on the latter. The foreign merchants were not unduly alarmed. There had been edicts against the opium trade before; it had been 'persecuted' frequently. In 1834 it had for some months been impossible to obtain sycee in payment for opium owing to the exceptional vigilance of the local authorities. In the summer of 1836 the Hong merchants had conveyed to the foreign traders the gist of the debate at Pekin.[3] Some excitement had indeed been caused by the rumour that the Viceroy of Canton had reported to the Emperor in favour of the legal admission of opium through the Hong merchants, but in strict barter and not for sycee.[4] Little alarm was felt at the news that certain 'censors' had urged death as the penalty for opium smugglers, including foreigners.[5] Jardine was 'annoyed' at the uncertainty caused by the debate at Pekin,[6] and its immediate effect on the market. Legalisation of the drug would be followed by heavy speculation and rising prices in India; an attempt at prohibition would, if serious, complicate the remittance problem for some time. Already the opium brokers in Canton had absconded 'and the smug boats are all laid up'. Nevertheless Jardine believed that this affair would end as opium edicts had previously ended. 'In the interim', he wrote to Bombay,[7] 'it should reduce prices with you. Therefore please

---

[1] See Chapters III and VII. In March 1838 the creditors of the bankrupt Hongs petitioned Palmerston to intervene at Pekin on their behalf. *Corresp.*, pp. 260-2. The debts were not recovered until after the Treaty of Nanking.

[2] Kuo, *op. cit.*, Chapter VI.   [3] *Ibid.*

[4] *P.L.B.* W.J. 7.6.1836.   [5] *Ibid* 5.11.1836.

[6] 'We must now await the result of the contention of the parties, which is annoying'. *Loc. cit.*

[7] *Loc. cit.*

invest all our funds in Malwa'! When, in November 1836, the reluctant Hong merchants were commanded to expel from Canton the leading foreign opium importers, Jardine resisted, pleading that he had over twenty ships loading. 'I cannot let Hong merchants sell and buy for me. Such a proceeding would be contrary to reason.'[1] Right until his departure from China in January 1839, Jardine was convinced that the storm would blow over.[2]

He was equally convinced that 'sooner or later this article will be admitted, and when admitted the consumption will be increased, and the order from the Government respecting the export of sycee silver disobeyed: but unless the Europeans are careful not to give credit to the Hong merchants, heavy debts will be contracted and many Hongs ruined. The order of the Government prohibiting the payment of cash for opium will never answer in practice . . . *Without sycee or gold as remittance to India we should never be able to get on;* and I am of the opinion that the opium will never be brought in if the regulations laid down are strictly enforced.'[3] As to direct prohibition, Jardine was not alarmed. This was partly due to his being misinformed by Mowqua that legalisation of the opium trade was likely. Had he been on better terms with Howqua, the head of the Cohong, he might have been undeceived, as were Howqua's confidants, Russell & Co.[4]

In 1837 the effects of the Chinese campaign began to be felt. 'The drug here [Canton] is completely at a stand; but the article has become so high [in retail price] in the City, that the temptation to smuggle at all hazard is very great. Prices are kept up by the holders, though deliveries from the the Lintin vessels are but trifling, owing to total absence of demand.'[5] This was in January; in June, Jardine was reporting that the Canton drug market was

---

[1] *P.L.B.* W.J. 27.11.1836.   [2] Cf. *P.L.B.* 5.12.1838.
[3] *P.L.B.* W.J. 4.2.1837.   [4] *Ibid.* 28.2.1839.
[5] *Ibid.* 27.1.1837.

entirely closed down and no smug boats allowed to run. 'We are doing everything in our power to work the article off on the coast and among the islands in European boats.'[1] But even on the coast the Mandarin junks were vigilant. In one 'severe battle'. in which an opium junk was attacked by the Viceroy's boats, a number of men were killed and a hundred chests destroyed. Several ships of the coastal fleet were obliged to return to their Lintin base without delivering a single chest.[2] In November 1837 Jardine wrote: 'The drug market is getting worse every day owing to the extreme vigilance of the authorities.' The only thing to do was to send more armed European ships along the coast and try out new markets such as Formosa.[3] 'But the number of vessels along the coast must sooner or later attract the notice of the Pekin authorities and *force them to adopt a new system.*'[4]

In the Canton river the Viceroy had succeeded in breaking the ring of smugglers and destroying the native 'fast crabs'. Whereupon several merchants, led by the fiery Innes, and attracted by the high prices which Canton addicts were willing to pay, began to convey the drug right up the river in specially armed European cutters under the British flag. The new Superintendent of British Trade in China, Captain Elliot, much alarmed by this 'great and hazardous change in the mode of the opium trade', wrote off an urgent dispatch to London warning Palmerston that *the whole China trade was threatened thereby.*[5] But the change arose from necessity. 'Our drug market', wrote Matheson,[6] 'has undergone a complete revolution in the last twelve-months. There is no such thing now in operation as a smug boat . . . The limited deliveries now effected here are made entirely in decked European sailing boats, which convey the drug to various points on the coast and as high up the River even as Canton, to the great alarm of the Hong merchants. It is even said that some Parsees retail it from

[1] *P.L.B.* W.J. 3.9.1837, etc. [2] *Ibid.*
[3] *Ibid.* 13.6.1837; 19.7.1837. [4] *Ibid.* 13.10.1837.
[5] 18.11.1837. *Corresp.* [6] *P.L.B.* J.M. 9.1.1838.

their Factories. All this is tolerated only on account of the Viceroy being afraid to interfere with the property of foreigners. It is evident that such a system cannot endure for any length of time. A change must take place, but of what nature it is impossible to say.'

This use of European smuggling boats helped bring about an illusory boom in the summer of 1838. Only the big houses could afford to operate several armed vessels. Jardines and Dents were able to corner the supply of opium and force up the price of Patna from $390 to $580 per chest, within a fortnight in May. Matheson wrote happily[1] that the opium season had opened splendidly, and as for 'the pretended opposition in the shape of edicts, these were scarcely more regarded than if they were so much waste paper.' But in September panic seized the Chinese dealers as the anti-opium campaign was intensified. In Canton province, the Viceroy sent his officers on house-to-house searches by night. Soon over 2,000 Chinese were in prison for smoking or smuggling the forbidden drug. By the end of the year Jardine reported: 'Not an opium pipe to be seen, not a retail vendor of the drug . . . not a single enquiry after the drug and the persecution becoming more general every day.'[2] Along the coast matters were equally bad, the Foochow Mandarins being particularly vigilant. Smokers and sellers were being seized all over the Empire. Finally, the Hong merchants had become 'so harassed with threats' that they had stopped business altogether.[3]

In this situation it is somewhat astonishing to find that both Jardine and Matheson placed their hopes of a change on the possibility of popular discontent against the Government's policy breaking out into rebellion. 'We cannot look for any improvement unless popular discontent should be manifested in much

---

[1] To the Governor of Ceylon, the Right Hon. J. Stewart Mackenzie, the largest landed proprietor in Ross-shire and a family friend of Matheson, who frequently wrote him information which he desired to reach official ears. They had an interesting correspondence on the possibilities of sending out Chinese coolies to Ceylon.

[2] *P.L.B.* W.J. 16.12.1838; 11.1.1839.   [3] *Ibid.* 5.12.1838.

stronger terms than hitherto.[1] An insurrection is the only chance we see of any great relaxation.' In Canton, many inhabitants, annoyed that the Viceroy's officers were searching their houses without warrants, had posted abusive placards on the gates. Jardine wrote to Captain Rees up the coast, 'I should think such severity in your quarter would produce an open rebellion. They are timid fellows here and stand a great deal from their oppressive rulers.'[2]

Less wishful were the opinions Jardine set forth in a private letter[3] written on New Year's Day 1839 'after much thought'. After admitting that he was uncertain as to the outcome of the crisis, he pointed out that the present 'persecution' of opium dealers was not much more severe than on some previous occasions; but that it had now spread to every province of the Empire, 'a circumstance never before known to have occurred.' If the same rigid campaign were to continue another twelve months, the consumption of opium was likely to decline by two-thirds; but he believed that this would 'excite the spirit of discontent . . . in the more turbulent provinces'. His next point was that, *pace* Captain Elliot, the *inside* trade up the river was not the cause of 'the late severe proceedings'; and therefore Elliot's desire to distinguish between the 'inside' and 'outside' opium trade was 'idle discussion', and would bring no relaxation of the campaign. He therefore instructed his Bombay agents not to purchase opium, since 'in the present stage of affairs the drug is better in the hands of the Company than of mercantile Houses or individuals.' The Company was, of course, the Government of India!

The Chinese anti-opium campaign, as the reports[4] from Jardine's captains along the coast prove, had achieved considerable success before the appointment of Lin Tse-hsu as Special

---

[1] *P.L.B.* J.M. 21.1.1839; W.J. 11.1.1839.   [2] W.J. 16.12.1838.
[3] *Ibid.* 1.1.1839 to J. Jeejeebhoy.
[4] *C.L.B.* 1839, passim. Cf. *P.L.B.* J.M. 21.1.1839.

Imperial Commissioner. 'Every part of the coast has been visited by vessels with opium but without any success worth mentioning.' The appointment of Lin, however, raised both the level and the tempo of the campaign. Matheson pointed out that Lin's office of *Kinchae* was one of extraordinary authority, equal to that of the Emperor himself, and conferred only four times before since the accession of the Ching dynasty (in the 17th century).[1] What Lin did which was new was to go at once to the root of the opium problem, the foreign importer. In March 1839 he ordered the immediate surrender of all opium brought to China, and demanded that in future the heads of foreign firms sign a bond assuming full responsibility before Chinese law for all ships consigned to their charge. On the European merchants prevaricating, he suspended all trade and confined them to their Factories at Canton until all the opium had been surrendered and the bond signed. In 'this most disastrous crisis' something had to be done.

It was not only that £2,400,000 worth of British property (the estimated value of the 20,283 chests of opium at current prices) was about to be destroyed; not merely that the whole China trade had been brought to a standstill; but, as Matheson declared,[2] even if the 'smug' boats were to start running again, Lin's action had *destroyed all confidence at Canton 'for ever'*. The old system could not continue.

In this 'disastrous' situation, a way out was offered by Captain Elliot's order to the British merchants to surrender the opium on the pledge of the British Government to remit its full value. Though Elliot was loudly denounced by the merchants for 'weakness', his offer was accepted with gratitude. They were enabled thereby to get rid of half the annual crop of Indian opium at a fair price guaranteed by the British Government and thus relieved from the embarrassment of having a whole season's stock unsold on their hands. Then there was the prospect of the rest being sold at higher prices than before because of the quantity

[1] *P.L.B.* 1.5.1839.   [2] *Loc. cit.*

destroyed. And above all, the British Government were now directly drawn in. In the important letters[1] which Matheson wrote in May 1839 to Jardine and John Abel Smith in London, he argues that Elliot's order was 'a large and statesmanlike measure, more especially as the Chinese have fallen into the snare of rendering themselves directly liable to the Crown. Had they declined receiving [the drug] and left us burdened with so heavy a stock under the new law punishing with death any foreigner dealing in the drug, the consequences would have been most disastrous.' Matheson also reveals that before Elliot's arrival at the Factories, several merchants had transferred orders for their opium to the Deputy Superintendent 'by way of shielding it from the grasp of the Chinese.'[2] He also states that 'All consignees of opium newly arriving are glad to include them in Captain Elliot's surrender'. Matheson himself had almost decided to remove the opium ships beyond reach at the first appearance of danger; but fortunately that was not done, as it would have 'placed the property beyond the pale of the protection of the British Government'.[3]

The British Government had been urged to intervene to save the whole China trade, with its vast ramifications, from collapse. Already in 1837, Captain Elliot had asked for a naval force to be sent to China 'for the relief of the whole trade from the embarrassment into which it is thrown by the restrictive spirit of the local government'.[4] Following the surrender of the opium, Elliot had written urgently to the Foreign Office, the Governments of Bombay and Bengal, begging them to announce that all claims on opium would be paid in full; 'the object being', writes Matheson, 'to improve general confidence and prevent a shock to commercial credit with all its disastrous consequences . . . the excitement of a general panick would prove disastrous to every branch of commerce as happened in regard to the American

[1] *Loc. cit.* and 3.5.1839.   [2] *Ibid.*
[3] *Ibid.* 3.4.1839.   [4] *Corresp.*, 189.

Houses in 1837.' At long last the British Government had taken up the interests of the merchants at Canton. 'I suppose war with China will be the next step',[1] wrote Matheson in April 1839, while still confined in the Factory. The seizure of British property and the detention of British subjects provided a *casus belli*.

Not that the detainees were badly treated. The horrors of the so-called siege of the Factories have been ludicrously exaggerated. Forbes[2] wrote of the imprisoned British merchants: 'They suffered more from absence of exercise and from overfeeding than from any actual want of the necessities of life.' True, their servants were taken away, but 'having no business to attend to, they cheerfully turned their attention to the various domestic departments, and there was never a *merrier* community than that of the foreign merchants of Canton, during their imprisonment within the limits of their own houses.'

In May 1839 an edict was issued commanding the foreigners to leave China unless they agreed to sign the opium bond. The Americans and later the captains of the British ships the *Thomas Coutts* and *Royal Saxon* were prepared to sign, and were thus allowed to trade. The form of bond they signed contained no unacceptable clause making offenders liable to capital punishment. The theory, based on the papers laid before Parliament, that such a clause was the real cause of the Anglo-Chinese quarrel and not opium has enabled our historians to pursue 'patriotic fictions', as Sir John Pratt puts it. In face of signature of the bond by the Americans and the two British captains, the British merchants stood firm, not sending their ships up to Whampoa. Matheson's attitude was: 'The above edict may be considered tantamount to closing this port against foreign trade.'[3] *To have surrendered to Lin would have meant trading in China on China's terms.* Against these the British merchants had been consciously fighting for a decade.

[1] *P.L.B.* J.M. *loc. cit.*   [2] Forbes, *op. cit.*
[3] *P.L.B.* J.M. 11.5.1839.

In June 1839 Matheson and the other British merchants were expelled from Canton for refusing to obey the orders of the Chinese Government. They continued to reside at Macao without further molestation. Meanwhile events were being set in train in London.

In August 1839, H.M.S. *Volage* arrived in Chinese waters, and on the same evening fired on three Mandarin junks, smashing them to bits. When, in November, Lin ordered the destruction of all the opium receiving-ships 'loitering' off Hongkong, the junks were met with destructive fire from the British frigates. However, it was not until the following spring that the glad news was brought of the troops being sent from India. On their arrival in June 1840, a blockade of the Canton estuary was established and the Opium War had formally begun.

B. *Trade during the War*
Commissioner Lin had, in November 1839, declared British trade to be excluded from China for ever. Captain Elliot had previously, in September, announced a British blockade of the Canton river; though soon cancelled, it was again imposed in June 1840. Yet the indefatigable merchants contrived to carry on business throughout the war. Driven from Canton, after a brief stay at Macao, they took to their ships, hovering off Hongkong and the other islands. James Matheson established himself and his firm's office aboard the *Hercules*. 'Whatever happens, our firm will endeavour to maintain a floating position in this vicinity.'[1] Only the bigger concerns possessing considerable fleets were able to acquire the necessary mobility and continue their 'business as usual'. But if the risks were great, their reward was equally so; especially in the forbidden drug.

On the news of the opium troubles in China, panic had followed in India. The clippers turned back or waited idly at Singapore; at Bombay the new Malwa crop could be bought for

[1] *P.L.B.* J.M. 24.8.1839,

a mere $200 a chest. But James Matheson saw 'no cause for alarm in the present circumstance' and shipped $100,000 to Singapore to be invested in the new opium on the firm's own account, sending at the same time a further order to Calcutta for a like sum.[1] The pledge never again to import opium which he had given to the Chinese during the 'siege of the Factories' Matheson considered well advised as being given under durance.[2] But it meant that *for the first time* it was necessary to conduct the opium trade in secret. Accordingly letters were written unsigned and in code; all reference to the traffic was omitted in the weekly trade circulars and in the 'Prices Current'. Many of the firm's papers and books are missing for this period. It is therefore impossible to give a detailed account of trade during the war; but the salient features can be indicated.

A new method of operating the drug trade was necessary. Matheson had hardly been released from the Canton Factories five days, when he wrote privately to Calcutta that Andrew Jardine was being sent to Manila to co-operate with Otadui & Co. in managing the business.[3] Only the close 'friends' among his India constituents were let into the secret. To them Matheson wrote that since they had so much opium on hand in India without any means of realising it owing to its being excluded from the China market, 'it occurred to me as a sort of duty to extend a branch of our firm at Manila for drug business only until times mend.'[4] There was no local demand at Manila whatever, and sales were made there either for junks or clippers to take up the China coast. The Manila Government obligingly halved its import duty on opium which was to be re-exported, and even agreed to provide warehouses. It was now that John Shillaber went to London to see John Abel Smith about the possibility of

[1] *I.L.B.* 25.6.1839; *P.L.B.* J.M. 24.8.1839.
[2] *P.L.B.* J.M. 24.8.1839.
[3] *Ibid.* 29.5.1839.
[4] *Ibid.* 25.6.1839. In fact Manila became an entrepôt for other India goods, especially cotton.

floating a loan for the Philippine Government. Matheson was sceptical about the finances of that Government and the project fell through.

On his release from Canton Matheson had written to Jardine in London that his friends the captains of the coastal fleet were at their old work again—'we shall adhere to your old routine'.[1] The volume of sales was relatively small, but profits were fantastically high, since chests which had been bought for $200 were sold at $800 and more.[2] Most of this was 'speculation', but some was on account of the few favoured constituents. For their commission business a new plan was adopted of crediting the proprietors at the period of the drug's despatch (from Manila) with an estimate of the proceeds, after deducting the charges of 'our numerous flotilla' and a 'reasonable allowance for the heavy risks run by ourselves and our commanders'.[3]

For about nine months Jardine Matheson & Co. had practically a monopoly of this opium trade via Manila. But increasing competition and the consequent rise of Calcutta prices by almost 50% forced the firm back into the open. Andrew Jardine was recalled from Manila, and by April 1840 'the golden days of the trade were over'.[4] To keep control of the market Matheson ordered his captains on the coast to sell at no matter what prices.[5] But the Chinese authorities were still determined to stop the traffic and the clippers and tenders were soon involved in fighting. The *Hellas*, cruising off Namoa, was attacked by junks, and for four hours there was a hand-to-hand struggle. Captain Jauncey and the crew were wounded and the ship set on fire. Captain Rees, the Commodore of the coastal fleet, resigned rather than carry on a trade attended with loss of life.[6] The danger ceased on the

---

[1] *P.L.B.* 27.5.1839.

[2] Morse, Owen and others state that the price of opium jumped to over $1,500 per chest, quoting Hunter and the *Chinese Repository* as authority; but the J.M. papers show that this was not so, the highest price quoted being $1,000 and that only for a very small parcel.   [3] *P.L.B.* 24.11.1839.

[4] *Ibid.* 26.4.1840.   [5] *Ibid.* 16.5.1840.   [6] *Ibid.* 10.12.1839.

arrival of the Expeditionary Force from India. With military defeat the Chinese Government lost prestige and its edicts were once more flouted. 'Smug' boats began to run again, and deliver opium from the foreign receiving-ships in daylight. Opium prices were again published in *The Canton Register*. The trade was back to the old position.

During the rest of the war, the opium ships followed the flag. As soon as Canton surrendered, receiving-ships went up to Whampoa; when British troops occupied points to the north, opium ships were sent in their wake, to Amoy, Chusan and Woosung (near Shanghai). Victory attracted a mass of small speculators; in 1842 prices fell to $400 and below. Jardine Matheson & Co. fought the newcomers in the old way—by confining themselves largely to agency, and working for bulk sales at low rates. To maintain their superiority faster clippers were built. The *Mor* and *Anonyma* carried on the work of the old *Sylph* and *Red Rover*.

Opium was not the sole business carried on by the expelled foreign traders during the war. In defiance of both Lin and Elliot, trade on British account continued at Canton, by means of neutral shipping, to and from which goods were transferred at Hongkong. The old device of foreign colours was once more pressed into service. Jardine Matheson & Co. had the names and flags of several vessels changed,[1] mainly to Danish nationality —James Matheson was still Danish Consul! Swedish and Prussian colours were also used, and on one occasion a Hamburg ship was chartered. There was one additional resource, the employment of American agents at Canton.

The Americans, as neutrals in the war, remained at their Canton Factories, eager to profit from the enforced absence of the British merchants by arranging their business on commission. Jardine Mathesons employed for a while the services of the American, C. W. King, the partner of Olyphant & Co., handing

[1] *P.L.B.* 12.7.1839; 19.8.1839; 4.11.1840.

over their Indian cotton in exchange for American Bills on London. King charged no commission for this service, looking for his profit to the advantageous exchange of the Bills. But Jardines found that it paid better to appoint their own American agents at Canton, who would buy teas and silks and sell cotton on their behalf at a fixed commission of $1\frac{1}{2}\%$-2%; such was the flexibility of the agency system that it was possible to have any number of agents and sub-agents at a distance from one another according to circumstances. In the summer of 1839 they appointed as Canton agents two Americans, James Ryan and Joseph Coolidge, who had recently left Russell & Co.[1] Every few days detailed instructions would be sent from the floating office of the British firm up to the Americans at Canton, giving orders for purchases or advice as to how the different Hong merchants were to be handled so as to avoid their getting heavily into debt. These two Americans stayed on at Canton, at considerable personal risk, throughout the war. Their correspondence provides our only source of information as to what was happening in Canton while the British were elsewhere.

There were also attempts to sell British cotton goods along the coast where possible. When in 1840 Chusan was captured, David Jardine and Donald Matheson went there to exploit the new market, but met only with the hostility of the natives. This field of trade was not perservered with during the war, because, apart from opium, the merchants concentrated on the tea trade.

The London price of tea depended very much on the reports received from the Canton exporters as to the quantities expected to be shipped. In the summer of 1839 there was an attempt by Dents and certain other agents of London houses interested in keeping up the price of tea to get all British trade in the river

---

[1] These two later joined with Augustine Heard of New York to found the firm of A. Heard & Co., which was absorbed by Jardine Matheson & Co. in 1875. Its records survive, and are now deposited in Harvard University.

stopped.[1] 'Strange as it may seem', wrote James Matheson in September, 'a small part of our merchants, looking to nothing but the support of the tea market in England, are still doing all they can to prevent business from being carried on'. Matheson himself went on loading two ships flying American colours with teas, confident that in spite of the blockade they would somehow be got out. But as the month passed and the ships were not allowed to move, he became anxious. In a remarkable letter to John Abel Smith, he wrote: 'It is worthy of consideration, whether, as *tea is such a necessity of life in England*, the British Government will not in the event of hostilities with China, prefer to connive at the export of teas through foreigners, rather than by establishing a blockade, cut off the supplies to the distress of our turbulent home population, not to mention the defalcation of the revenue. You can easily ascertain the views of the Government on this head and regulate your proceedings accordingly.'[2] In a similar letter to Jardine he even suggests that the non-arrival of tea to England would 'excite distress and discontent among the people at home endangering the Government's popularity'. Captain Elliot informed Matheson privately that he would allow neutral ships with British property aboard to pass through. Whereupon Matheson was able to get his teas to London, to the great profit of his 'friends', who shared in the speculation, and the angry protests of his neighbours, who lost considerably thereby.[3] These disgruntled merchants at once launched a fierce attack on Elliot, presenting a petition to the House of Commons on the subject of the tea-ships. Matheson felt it his duty to engage a lawyer to defend Elliot in the newspapers. Even in later accounts, Captain Elliot remained a controversial figure.

With the capture of the Bogue forts in March 1841 it was

---

[1] There is not sufficient evidence in the J.M. papers to decide whether Elliot's decision to order a blockade was influenced by his then intimacy with Dents.

[2] *P.L.B.* J.M. 29.2.1840.

[3] *P.L.B.* 23.1.1841.

H

thought that the American agents at Canton could now be dispensed with, and Andrew Jardine went up to take over. But the hostility of the Cantonese forced the British merchants to leave their Factories once again, only a few Americans remaining.[1] Their trade continued until the end of the war. When the Treaty of Nanking was signed in August 1842, a number of British merchants, without waiting for its ratification, returned to Canton.

In December 1842 'a most terrible riot' broke out in Canton. The foreign Factories and their valuable property, including much treasure, were set on fire and destroyed. The demolition of the Factories by the Cantonese was a fitting sequel to the destruction of the old Canton Commercial System by the foreigners.

C. *Trade and the Flag*

To the Chinese the war was fought over the opium question; but for the British merchants the issues were wider. 'The grand cardinal point of the expedition' was to Matheson 'the future mode of conducting the foreign trade in China'.[2] He was therefore sceptical of Elliot's attempts to secure an early truce. Peace, he believed, was impossible until 'the greatest of all questions as to how and where the trade of British subjects is henceforth to be conducted in China' was settled.[3] In May 1839, before the war had begun, he had written from Canton[4]: 'War seems inevitable, the result of which it is hoped will be our obtaining a settlement of our own, on which to establish ourselves under the British flag, besides safe and unrestricted liberty of trade at the principal marts of the Empire.' The war aims of the British merchants were thus clear.

There was still some doubt as to what would be the most suitable independent settlement. Matheson still favoured Formosa, but Jardine wrote[5] from London that the island was too large to

---

[1] *P.L.B.* 28.3.1841.
[3] *Ibid.* 26.12.1840.
[5] 'Correspondence In'. 16.9.1839.
[2] *Ibid.* 4.1.1841.
[4] *Ibid.* 5.5.1839.

control unless the inhabitants were well disposed towards us, which was doubtful. Jardine and John Abel Smith preferred the island of Chusan (off Ningpo) and persuaded Palmerston to instruct Elliot to occupy it. But the latter on his own initiative accepted the offer of the barren, mountainous island of Hongkong made by the Chinese minister Kishan. Matheson's comment was that the advantage of Hongkong would be that the more the Chinese obstructed the trade of Canton, the more they would drive trade to the new English settlement.[1] Moreover, Hongkong was admittedly one of the finest harbours in the world. When in January 1841 the British flag was hoisted over the island, Matheson built a large stone *godown* and moved the firm's headquarters there. On Elliot's recall Matheson was afraid that 'Elliot's unpopularity would in some measure descend on his pet child [Hongkong]'. He therefore urged Jardine and John Abel Smith to use their influence if 'not for its retention at least for the retention of some place near this river, where alone the British people are known and multitudes of natives are ready to become our subjects and trade with us, in place of being scared away as at Chusan and elsewhere . . . Many prefer Kowloon, but we ought to have both.'[2] Twenty years later both had been obtained.

On every point demanded by the British merchants in China vigorous propaganda was carried on by their agents in England. As soon as Jardine reached London in the autumn of 1839 he arranged with Abel Smith to interview Lord Palmerston. 'Parties connected with India and China are becoming very impatient and threatening to go to Windsor [where Palmerston was attending the Queen]. Some talk of calling a meeting to draw up an address . . . We prefer doing things as quietly as possible, though the delay is provoking.'[3] One danger was anti-opium feeling in England. Steps were therefore taken to meet 'the vituperation of the High Church party' and the 'Saints' with counter-propaganda.

[1] *P.L.B.* 22.1.1841. [2] *P.L.B.* 25.8.1841. Kowloon was annexed in 1860.
[3] 'Correspondence In'. 18.9.1839.

For a long time Matheson was afraid of Elliot's 'recorded prejudice against the drug'. But as the war proceeded, he was able to write: 'As the drug sales here form the only source from which they can obtain money for the war in China, it is some consolation to us that they cannot do without it.'[1] The replacement of Elliot by Sir Henry Pottinger, whom Jardine was able to see before he left England, removed all danger on this head. 'I have had two or three conversations with him [Pottinger] of a very satisfactory nature.'[2]

On 29 August 1842 the Chinese, 'choosing between danger and safety, not between right and wrong',[3] signed the Treaty of Nanking. The terms of the Treaty represented, in substance, the aspirations of the British merchants. The Cohong was abolished, four new ports to the north were opened to foreign trade, duties were limited to 5% (except on tea), British Consuls were to be admitted to the new ports, Hongkong was to become a British colony, and the opium trade was not to be mentioned. A year later, Alexander Matheson, who became head of the firm on James' going home, wrote happily: 'The new tariff and port regulations are really very moderate and favourable, and if strictly adhered to by the Chinese, our trade with England is sure to increase very much. The drug trade continues to prosper.'[4]

It was twelve years after the petition of 1830 demanding a 'new commercial code' that the Treaty of Nanking was obtained. When Palmerston heard that the Treaty had been concluded, he wrote to John Abel Smith: 'To the assistance and information which you and Mr Jardine so handsomely afforded us it was mainly owing that we were able to give to our affairs naval, military and diplomatic, in China those detailed instructions which have led to these satisfactory results . . . There is no doubt that this event,

---

[1] *P.L.B.* 7.8.1840.
[2] 'Correspondence In'. W.J. to J.M. 31.5.1841. Jardine was now M.P. for Ashburton, in which seat he was succeeded by Sir James Matheson, Bart., and afterwards by Sir Alexander Matheson.
[3] Kuo, *op. cit.* 'Memorial of Kuying', Document 50.   [4] *P.L.B.* A.M. 31.7.1843.

which will form an epoch in the progress of the civilization of the human races, must be attended with the most important advantages to the commercial interests of England.'[1]

* * * *

In 1782 John Henry Cox had come out to Canton to sell his stock of 'singsongs'. Sixty years later there was neither Company nor Cohong in China, and the British merchants were ensconced at the mouth of the Yangtse as well as in possession of an island base.

The rise of the 'private English' had taken place on the basis of three fundamental changes in the Old China Trade. First, the expansion of the Country commerce had reversed the balance of trade and the flow of silver. Secondly, the development of smuggling via Lintin and along the coast had undermined the Canton Commercial System. Thirdly, the abolition of the Company's monopoly had brought to China the irresistible power of the new manufacturing interests of Britain. Against those who came equipped with steam-power and Adam Smith the discipline of Confucius was of little avail.

The Canton Register confidently wrote in 1833: 'As in all parts of the world, trade will find its level and a people's wants be satisfied: maugre the opposition of a government even far stronger than the inefficient weakness by which this Empire is ruled. What the Milan and Berlin Decrees failed to do for the Continent and the exclusive possession of Spain for South America, the wretched burlesque of military and naval power in this country can scarcely hope to effect.'

A century earlier, by both Voltaire and the Jesuit missionaries, China had been praised as the most civilized and well-governed country in the world. Now the Mandarin Empire seemed but a 'wretched burlesque', incapable of resisting the new 'princes' of Europe, the spearheads of an industrial West.

[1] 28.4.1842. Quoted by H. Easton, *History of a Banking House* (Smith, Payne, Smith).

APPENDIX I. TABLES

A. COMPANY AND PRIVATE TRADE AT CANTON, 1817-33[1]

Unfortunately for the student seeking statistical clarity the trade between India and China was never quite co-extensive with that of the private merchants. Not only did the Company continue to import to Canton some Indian goods on its own account, but the private merchants hired tonnage on the Company's ships as well as using the private 'Country' ships; while the early J.M. papers reveal occasions, admittedly rare, where the Company availed itself of space in the private ships. In some years, indeed, to encourage the Country trade the Company granted free tonnage on *its* ships to private merchants; thus in 1788, out of 61,632 piculs of Indian raw cotton taken to China on Company ships, only 3,300 piculs were on Company account. This was, however, an exceptional year in which the Company's servants admitted 'we were utterly incapable of supplying the deficiency from our own resources'. Furthermore, after 1821 Country ships often made several unrecorded journeys a year to illicit 'outer' anchorages (see Chapter III). These considerations affect the interpretation of the statistics of the Old Canton Trade; because the familiar lists compiled by Morse and other of 'Company' ships and 'Country' ships at Canton do not provide that precise picture of British and India trade with China which is intended. To add to the confusion, the 'privilege' trade of the Company's marine officers, mainly in all kinds of minor articles with which the Company did not wish to trouble itself, is called by most writers 'Private trade'. In the present study, the 'privilege' trade is called only by that name, and the term 'Country trade' is used to note that part of the India-China commerce carried on by the private merchants.

[1] Based on data in *Chronicles*, Vols. III, IV passim. The figures for the earlier years are not precise.

Estimated value in dollars ('ooo omitted)
not including shipments of treasure

Season	Imports			Exports		
	Company	Private	Total	Company	Private	Total
1817	5045	8650	13645	6127	3642	9769
1818	4334	8714	13048	5946	4126	10072
1819	4212	4408	8620	8036	3671	11707
1820	4856	10128	14984	8335	5081	13616
1821	4877	9123	14000	7998	5689	13667
1822	3663	13268	16931	8548	4163	12711
1823	5180	10954	16134	8674	4047	12721
1824	5158	10896	16054	7986	4056	12042
1825	5157	15701	21218	8213	5264	13477
1826	5871	15710	21581	9370	4293	13663
1827	4519	15846	20365	8479	3562	12041
1828	4940	15373	21313	7676	6255	13931
1829	4484	18412	22896	7531	6265	13796
1830	4154	17393	21907	7757	5293	13050
1831	3688	16832	20520	7763	5176	12939
1832	4039	18258	22297	8018	4646	12664
1833	4358	19099	23451	7668	5778	13446

B. SILVER EXPORTED FROM CANTON BY THE PRIVATE BRITISH MERCHANTS, 1817-34

(from the data in *Chronicles*, Vol. III, IV passim.)

Season	($ 'ooo omitted)	Season	($ 'ooo omitted)
1817	3920	1826	4083
1818	2689	1827	6095
1819	861	1828	4703
1820	495	1829	6656
1821	481	1830	4684[1]
1822	234	1831	2845[1]
1823	2619	1832	3835[1]
1824	1743	1833	6577
1825	4341		

[1] In these years, the East India Company also exported larger quantities of silver on the orders of its Court of Directors. This additional drain amounted to $1,911,000 in 1830, $1,174,000 in 1831, and $1,356,000 in 1832.

C. IMPORTS OF SPECIE AND BILLS INTO CANTON BY THE AMERICANS, 1805-33

(from K. S. Latourette's Article in
Transactions of the Connecticut Academy, Vol. 22, 1917)

Season	Specie	Season	Specie	Bills on London
	Dollars		*Dollars*	*Dollars*
1805	2,902,000	1819	7,414,000	200,000
1806	4,176,000	1820	6,297,000	—
1807	2,895,000	1821	2,995,000	—
1808	3,032,000	1822	5,125,000	—
1809	70,000	1823	6,292,840	—
1810	4,723,000	1824	4,096,000	—
1811	2,330,000	1825	6,524,500	—
1812	1,875,000	1826	5,725,200	—
1813	616,000	1827	1,841,168	400,000
1814[1]	—	1828	2,640,300	300,000
1815[1]	—	1829	740,900	657,000
1816	1,922,000	1830	1,123,644	423,656
1817	4,545,000	1831	183,655	1,168,500
1818	5,601,000	1832	2,480,871	667,252
		1833	682,519	4,772,516

[1] These were the years of the Anglo-American War.

D. OPIUM TABLES

No absolutely reliable figures are possible because the trade was, after all, a smuggling trade. Such statistical statements as exist differ from one another because they are derived from a variety of sources. The first of the two tables given below refers to the annual *consumption* of the drug in China and the money received from its sale. It is based on the lists compiled by Magniac and Co., and printed in their *Canton Register and Price Current*, 1828-32, passim. The second table refers to *imports* and is less accurate, being drawn up from Morse's *International Relations*, Vol. I, and based on a variety of contemporary lists which cannot always be reconciled.

(1) CONSUMPTION AND VALUE OF INDIAN OPIUM IN CHINA, 1821-31.

Season	Bengal (Patna & Benares)		Malwa		Total	
	Chests	Value $	Chests	Value $	Chests	Value $
1821-22	2,910	6,038,250	1,718	2,276,350	4,628	8,314,600
1822-23	1,822	2,828,930	4,000	5,160,000	5,822	7,988,930
1823-24	2,910	4,656,000	4,172	3,559,100	7,082	8,515,100
1824-25	2,655	3,119,625	6,000	4,500,000	8,655	7,619,625
1825-26	3,442	3,141,755	6,179	4,466,450	9,621	7,608,205
1826-27	3,661	3,667,565	6,308	5,941,520	9,969	9,610,085
1827-28	5,114	5,105,081	4,361	5,277,000	9,475	10,382,141
1828-29	5,960	5,604,235	7,171	6,928,880	13,132	12,533,115
1829-30	7,143	6,149,577	6,857	5,907,580	14,000	12,057,157
1830-31	6,660	5,789,794	12,100	7,110,237	18,760	12,900,031

(2) OPIUM SHIPMENTS TO CHINA 1800-39

SEASON	BENGAL (Patna & Benares)	MALWA	TURKEY	TOTAL
	Chests	Chests	Chests	
1800-01	3,224	1,346	—	4,570
1801-02	1,744	2,203	—	3,447
1802-03	2,033	1,259	—	3,292
1803-04	2,116	724	—	2,840
1804-05	2,322	837	—	3,159
1805-06	2,131	1,705	102	3,938
1806-07	2,607	1,519	180	4,306
1807-08	3,084	1,124	150	4,358
1808-09	3,233	985	—	4,208
1809-10	3,074	1,487	32	4,593
1810-11	3,592	1,376	—	4,968
1811-12	2,788	2,103	200	5,091
1812-13	3,328	1,638	100	5,066
1813-14	3,213	1,556	—	4,769
1814-15	2,999	674	—	3,673
1815-16	2,723	1,507	80	4,321
1816-17	3,376	1,242	488	5,106
1817-18	2,911	781	448	4,140
1818-19	2,575	977	807	4,359
1819-20	1,741	2,265	180	4,186
1820-21	2,591	1,653	—	4,244
1821-22	3,298	2,278	383	5,459
1822-23	3,181	3,855	—	7,773
1823-24	3,360	5,535	140	9,035
1824-25	5,960	6,663	411	12,434
1825-26	3,810	5,563	—	9,373
1826-27	6,570	5,605	56	12,231
1827-28	6,650	5,504	—	12,434
1828-29	4,903	7,709	1,256	13,868
1829-30	7,443	8,099	715	16,257
1830-31	5,672	12,856	1,428	18,956
1831-32	6,815	9,333	402	16,550
1832-33	7,598	14,007	380	21,985
1833-34	7,808	11,715	963	20,486
1834-35	10,207	11,678	?	21,885
1835-36	14,851	15,351	?	30,202
1836-37	12,606	21,427	243	34,776
1837-38	19,600	14,773	?	34,373
1838-39	18,212	21,988	?	40,200

APPENDIX II. JARDINE MATHESON & CO.

A. *The Firm and its Partners*

	Firm	*Partners*
1782	*Cox and Reid*	J. H. Cox, Daniel Beale (& John Reid)
1787	*Cox and Beale*	Daniel and Thomas Beale
1799	*Hamilton and Reid and Beale*	Robert Hamilton, David Reid, Thomas Beale, Alexander Shank
1800	*Reid and Beale*	Reid, Beale and Shank (Hamilton has died)
1801	*Reid Beale & Co.*	Reid goes home, Charles Magniac comes out to China
1803	*Beale and Magniac*	Beale, Shank and Magniac
1811	*Beale & Co.*	Hollingworth Magniac arrives
1817	*Shank and Magniac*	Beale leaves the firm on account of his personal insolvency
1819	*Charles Magniac & Co.*	Shank has died; partners are now Charles and Hollingworth Magniac. In 1823 Daniel Magniac becomes a partner

	Firm	*Partners*

| 1824 | *Magniac & Co.* | Charles Magniac goes home. 1825 William Jardine joins the firm. 1827 Hollingworth Magniac goes home but remains a sleeping partner. 1827 James Matheson joins the firm. 1828 Daniel Magniac leave the firm |
| 1832 | *Jardine Matheson & Co.* | William Jardine and James Matheson |

1819		James Matheson joins Robert Taylor, who died 1820
1821-7	*Yrissari & Co.*	F. X. de Yrissari and J. Matheson
1827	*Matheson & Co.*	James and Alexander Matheson, who then join Magniac & Co., James as partner

---

| 1819-23 | | William Jardine is loosely associated in business with T. Weeding, London, and Framjee Cowasjee, Bombay, but remains a free agent, in which capacity he begins to do opium business for Magniac & Co. |
| 1825 | | W. Jardine joins Magniac & Co. |

B. THE FIRM'S SHIPS AND OFFICERS AT THE OUTBREAK OF THE OPIUM WAR

SHIP	COMMANDER
Hercules	E. Parry
Austin	J. Rees
Col. Young	H. P. Baylis
Lady Hayes	A. Paterson
Red Rover	H. Wright
Governor Findlay	F. Jauncey
Hellas	A. Scanlon
Omega	W. Strachan
Jardine	F. Denham
Harriet	J. Hall
Venus	W. Erskine
Coral	?

APPENDIX III.   THE HONG MERCHANTS

The following list, drawn from C. de Montigny, *Manuel du négociant français en Chine*, 1846, gives the full names of the Hongs in existence at the ratification of the Treaty of Nanking, 1843. It is doubtful whether the family names were correct.

Name as known to Europeans	Family name	Name of Hong
Howqua	Wu-han, kwang	Ewo-hong
Mowqua	Lu-man, „	Kwangli hong
Puankequa	Puan-ching wee	Teng-ling „
Goqua	Sie-ngo, kwang	Tung-ling „
Kingqua	Kiang-King „	Tien-pan „
Mingqua	Puan-ming „	Ching-ho „
Saoqua	Mu-sao „	Shintai „
Punhoyqua	Puan-hai „	Jinho „
Samqua	Wu-Shwang „	Tong shin „
Kwanshing	Yih-Kwang „	Futai „

BIBLIOGRAPHY

This list does not claim to be a complete bibliography of the subject, but is intended to indicate the sources of information or opinion which have influenced the writing of the text.

A. MANUSCRIPTS

I. *The Jardine Matheson Archives.*
This is deposited in the Cambridge University Library. The papers used for this study cover the years 1799-1843.
(*a*) *Letter Books.* Copies of letters sent out from Canton (folio).
I.L.B. 1800-42, 33 volumes.
E.L.B. (series not intact), 4 volumes.
P.L.B. 1830-42, 15 volumes.
C.L.B. 1833-41, 4 volumes.
Y. & Co. 1821-27, 5 volumes.
R.T. & J.M. 1819-21, 3 volumes.
C.I.C. 1836-38, 2 volumes.
(*b*) *'Correspondence In.'* Loose originals of letters coming into Canton packed in over 40 large boxes. These have been used only in connection with the outgoing letters which reply to them.
(*c*) *Account Books.* The *Ledgers* from 1800 have been consulted. But many of them are defaced, or eaten away by termites, or missing. The *Accounts Sales* from 1819, *Accounts Current* from 1812, *Journals* and *Invoice Books* from 1811 have been looked at but not consistently. They are of little value, as most of their data was transferred to the *Ledgers*. Lists of *Prices Current* are found from 1823, loosely attached to various volumes.
II. *Proceedings of the Manchester Chamber of Commerce.*
1821-42, 5 volumes.

III. *The East India Company's China Factory Records.*
These are preserved in the India Office. As they have been fully summarised by Morse in the *Chronicles*, I have consulted them only on specific points relating to the private merchants.

B. PUBLISHED CONTEMPORARY SOURCES

I. *Blue Books.*

1810 Fourth Report of the Select Committee on the affairs of the East India Company, China, etc.

1821 Second and Third Reports of the Select Committee on Foreign Trades.

1829-31 Correspondence of East India Company on Opium.

1830 First and Second Report from the Select Committee of House of Commons on the affairs of the East India Company.

1830 Report from the Select Committee of House of Lords on the affairs of the East India Company.

1831 Report on the affairs of the East India Company.

1831-32 Papers on China.

1833 Report of Manufacturers.

1840 Correspondence relating to China, 1834-9.

1840 Memorials addressed to His Majesty's Government by British Merchants interested in China (re Opium).

1840 Report from the Select Committee on the grievances of the British merchant interested in trade with China.

1842 Communication of Capt. Elliot explaining transactions with the Chinese.

1843-45 Correspondence rel. to the value of the opium delivered up to the Chinese.

1844 Statement of Foreign Trade with China.

1843-44 Treaty of Nanking and supplementary treaty.

II. *Newspapers and Periodicals.*
The Canton Press, 1835-44.
The Canton Register and Price Current, 1827-43.
The Chinese Courier, 1831-33.

The Chinese Repository, 1832-51.
East India Register, 1800.
The Edinburgh Review, 1837.
The Quarterly Review, 1840.

III. *Pamphlets, Treatises, etc.*

AUBER, P. China, 1834.

BACKHOUSE, E. and BLAND, J. O. P. Annals and Memoirs of the Court of Pekin (from the 16th century), 1914.

BRUCE, J. Annals of the East India Company, 1810.

BLANCARD, P. Manuel du Commerce des Indes Orientales et de la Chine, 1806.

COX, J. Descriptive Inventory of Jewellery, etc., 1773.

CRAWFURD, J. China Monopoly examined, 1830.

DAVIS, J. F. Scenes in China, 1820.

—— The Chinese, 2 volumes, 1836.

—— Sketches of China, 1841.

DOWNING, C. TOOFORD. The Fan-Qui in China in 1836-37, 3 volumes, 1838.

FORBES, R. B. Remarks on China—the China Trade, 1844.

GUTZLAFF, C. China Opened, 2 volumes, 1838.

HARDY, C. A Register of ships employed in the East India Company, 1810.

HERTSLET, G. Treaties between Great Britain and China, 1877.

HUNTER, W. C. The Fan-Kwai at Canton before Treaty Days, 1825-44.

KELLY, P. Oriental Metrology, 1832.

LINDSAY, H. Bits of Old China, 1882.

—— Letter to Palmerston, 1840.

MACPHERSON. Annals of Commerce, 4 volumes, 1805.

—— History of European Commerce with India, 1812.

MATHESON, J. Present position and prospects of British Trade with China, 1836.

MEARES, J. Voyages made in 1788-89, from China to North West Coast of America.

MEDHURST, W. H. China, 1838.

MILBURN, W. Oriental Commerce, 2 volumes, 1813.

MONTIGNY, C. de. Manuel du négociant français en Chine, 1846.

MORRISON, J. R. A Chinese Commercial Guide, 1834.
MORSE, H. B. Chronicles of the East India Company Trading to China, 1635-1834, 5 volumes, 1926-9.
PHIPPS, J. Guide to Commerce of Bengal, 1823.
—— A Practical Treatise on the China and Eastern Trade, 1836.
—— Treatise on the principal products of Bengal, Volume I, Indigo, 1832.
SAINTE CROIX, F. Voyage commercial aux Indes, 1800.
SHAW, S. Journals, 1841.
SLADE, J. Notice of British Trade to Canton, 1830.
STAUNTON, G. T. Miscellaneous Notices rel. to China, 1825-50.
URMSTON, J. B. Observations on the China Trade, 1834.
WARREN, S. Opium, 1839.
WILLIAMS, S. W. Chinese Commercial Guide, 1844.
WISSETT, —— Compendium of East Indian Affairs, 1802.

C. SOME SELECT BOOKS AND ARTICLES

ANSTEY, V. The Trade of the Indian Ocean, 1929.
BANERJEA, P. Indian Finance in the days of the Company, 1928.
BASTER, A. 'Origin of British Exchange Banking in China', in Supplement to 'Economic Journal', January, 1934.
BERESFORD, Lord C. The Break-up of China, 1899.
BOEKE, J. H. 'Recoil of Westernisation in the East', in 'Pacific Affairs', September, 1939.
BUCK, N. S. Anglo-American Trade (1800-50), 1925.
CAREY, W. H. The Good Old Days of Honourable John Company, 1906-7.
CHI, CHAO-TING. Key Economic Areas in Chinese History, 1936.
CLARK, A. H. The Clipper Era, 1911.
COATES, W. H. The Old Country Trade, 1911.
CORDIER, H. Historie Générale de la Chine et de ses rélations avec les puissances étrangères, 4 volumes, 1920-21.
— Les Marchands Hanistes de Canton, in 'T'oung Pao' II, Volume III, Leiden, 1902.
COSTIN, W. C. Great Britain and China (1833-1860), 1937.

COULING, S. Encyclopaedia Sinica, 1917.
DENNETT, T. Americans in Eastern Asia, 1922.
DULLES, F. R. Old China Trade, 1930.
DUTT, R. Economic History of India, (1757-1837), 1902.
EAMES, J. B. The English in China (1600-1843), 1909.
EASTON, H. J. History of a Banking House (Smith, Payne, Smith), 1903.
EITEL, E. I. Europe in China, being a History of Hongkong, 1895.
FAIRBANK, J. F. The Legalisation of the Opium Trade, in 'Chinese Economic and Political Science Review', Volume XVII.
FORTUNE, R. Wanderings in China, 1847.
FOSTER, Sir W. England's Quest for Eastern Trade, 1933.
GILES, H. A. China and the Manchus, 1912.
GRAS, N. S. B. Business History, in 'Economic History Review', IV, 4.
HART, Sir R. These from the Land of Sinim, 1901.
HOLZMAN, J. M. The Nabobs in England, 1926.
HOWER, R. Business History, in 'U.S. Journal of Economic and Business History', Volume III.
HSIEH, P. Ç. The Government of China (1644-1911), 1928.
HUBBARD, G. E. Eastern Industrialization and its effect on the West, 1935.
HUDSON, G. F. Europe and China to 1800, 1931.
HUGHES, E. The Invasion of China by the Western World, 1938.
JENKS, L. H. Migration of British Capital to 1875, 1917.
JERMIGAN, T. R. China in Law and Commerce, 1905.
KEETON, G. W. The Development of Extraterritoriality in China, 2 volumes, 1928.
KRISHNA, BAL. Commercial Relations between India and England (1601-1757), 1924.
KUO, P. C. A Critical Study of the First Anglo-Chinese War, 1935.
LATOURETTE, K. S. Early Relations between the United States and China (1784-1844) in 'Transactions of the Connecticut Academy', Volume XXII.
LATTIMORE, O. Inner Asian Frontiers of China, 1940.
LINDSAY, W. S. History of British Shipping, 1876.
LUBBOCK, B. Opium Clippers, 1933.
McCULLOCH, J. R. History of Commerce, volume I, 1847.

MACKENZIE, A. A History and Genealogy of the Mathesons, 1886.
MICHIE, A. The Englishman in China, 2 volumes, 1900.
MORRISON, S. E. Maritime History of Massachusetts, 1932.
MORSE, H. B. Trade and Administration of China, 1921.
—— International Relations of the Chinese Empire, 1910-18.
—— Chronicles of the East India Company Trading to China, 1635-1834, 5 volumes, 1926-9.
—— The Gilds of China, 1909.
—— The Provision of Funds for the E.I.C.'s Trade at Canton during the 18th Century, in 'Journal of the Royal Asiatic Society', April 1922.
—— Currency in China, in 'Journal of the Royal Asiatic Society', 1908.
NAZIR, C. S. The First Parsee Baronet, 1866.
NYE, G. Morning of my Life in China, 1873.
OVERLACH, T. W. Foreign Financial Control in China, 1919.
OWEN, D. E. British Opium Policy in China and India, 1928.
PARKER, E. H. Chinese Account of the Opium War, 1881.
PARKINSON, C. N. Trade in the Eastern Seas, 1937.
PORTER, K. W. J. J. Astor, 2 volumes, 1931.
PRINSEP, G. A. Steam Vessels in India, 1830.
PRITCHARD, E. H. Anglo-Chinese Relations (1750-1800), in 'Research Studies of College of Washington', 1929.
REDFORD, A. Manchester Merchants and Foreign Trade (1794-1858), 1934.
REICHWEIN, A. China and Europe in the 18th Century, 1925.
REMER, C. F. Foreign Trade of China, 1928.
ROBINSON, F. P. Trade of the East India Company (1700-1813), 1912.
SARGENT, A. J. Anglo-Chinese Commerce and Diplomacy, 1907.
SEE, CHONG-SU. Foreign Trade of China, 1919.
SMITH, A. H. Village Life in China, 1895.
SOOTHILL, W. E. China and England, 1928.
SPALDING, W. F. Eastern Exchange and Finance, 1917.
TAWNEY, R. H. Land and Labour in China, 1932.
T'IEN, TSE CHANG. Sino-Portuguese Trade, 1933.
TSIANG, T. F. Chinese and European Civilisation, in 'Politica', II, 1936.

VINACKE, H. M. Problems of Industrial Development in China, 1926.
WARE, E. E. Business and Politics in the Far East, 1932.
WILLIAMS, S. WELLS. The Middle Kingdom, 2 volumes, 1883.
WILLOUGHBY, W. Foreign Rights and Interests in China, 1927.
WITTVOGEL, K. Wirtschaft und Gesellschaft Chinas, 1931.

INDEX

Lightning Source UK Ltd.
Milton Keynes UK
09 March 2010

151126UK00001B/21/P